D1153917

They All Sang My Songs

Frank

Ella

Bing

Rosie

Nat

Dinah

Tony

Sarah

Billie

They All Sang My Songs

Jack Lawrence

FOREWORD BY
MICHAEL FEINSTEIN

BARRICADE
BOOKS

Fort Lee, New Jersey

Published by Barricade Books Inc.
185 Bridge Plaza North
Suite 308-A
Fort Lee, NJ 07024

www.barricadebooks.com

Library of Congress Cataloging-in-Publication Data

Lawrence, Jack, 1912-
    They all sang my songs / Jack Lawrence ; foreword by Michael
Feinstein.
        p. cm.
    Includes index.
    ISBN 1-56980-279-3
    1. Lawrence, Jack, 1912- 2. Lyricists--United States--Biography. 3.
Composers--United States--Biography.

ML423.L265A3 2004
782.42164'092--dc22
[B]
                                                        2004054957

First Printing
Manufactured in Canada

FOR RICHARD
who helped me through the night

To Kathleen —

Loved your singing —

Jack Lemmon

11/2004

Contents

FOREWORD 9

Introduction THE VERSE BEFORE THE CHORUS 17

Chapter 1 THE FIRST TIME I WENT TO
CARNEGIE HALL 21

Chapter 2 FROM RUSSIA WITH LOVE 29

Chapter 3 NEPHEW—OR IN-LAW? 42

Chapter 4 SYLVIA, DANNY—AND ME 55

Chapter 5 WHAT WILL I TELL MY HEART? 64

Chapter 6 JACK OF ALL TRADES 73

Chapter 7 THE DOORS BEGIN TO OPEN 80

Chapter 8 PUBLISHED AT LAST 90

Chapter 9 —AND SUED! 96

Chapter 10 HOW I GOT TO HOLLYWOOD 106

Chapter 11 MAINE'S FAVORITE SON, RUDY VALLEE 115

Chapter 12 A SONG A DAY 120

Chapter 13 HOLLYWOOD AGAIN . . . BUT WITH A
CONTRACT 126

Chapter 14 WELCOME TO TIN PAN ALLEY 139

Chapter 15 BYE-BYE BROOKLYN 154

Chapter 16 HOW I REWROTE COLE PORTER AND MADE A
STAR OF DINAH SHORE 162

Chapter 17   LOSSES   177

Chapter 18   HOW I FOUGHT WORLD WAR II AND SAVED
NELSON RIDDLE   180

Chapter 19   I DO—AND I DIDN'T   191

Chapter 20   WHAT COMES FIRST—THE CHICKEN OR
THE EGG?   201

Chapter 21   SIN-SATIONALLY, MAE WEST   210

Chapter 22   MORE COLLABORATORS   217

Chapter 23   REMEMBERING ROSIE   224

Chapter 24   THE REAL THING   231

Chapter 25   IT'S A CRAPSHOOT BUSINESS   245

Chapter 26   BEYOND THE FRENCH   257

Chapter 27   LIFE WITH WALTER   265

Chapter 28   EDITH HALPERT AND THE DOWNTOWN
GALLERY   273

Chapter 29   ARTISTS AND ARTIFACTS   284

Chapter 30   TWO GREAT LADIES—
BELLA AND TALLULAH   292

Chapter 31   THE LAST GOOD-BYE   299

Chapter 32   I HAVE A SON   310

Chapter 33   THERE'S NO BIZ LIKE SHOW BIZ   320

Chapter 34   SHOW BIZ IS NO BIZ FOR ME   328

Chapter 35   CALL ME COUNTRY SQUIRE   348

INDEX   359

Foreword
by
Michael Feinstein

Imagine being able to do exactly what you've always wanted to do and make millions of people happy doing it. This is what my extraordinary songwriting friend, Jack Lawrence, has done for most of his ninety-plus years. I happily count myself among the lucky masses who have benefited from his understated musical genius. I am perhaps doubly lucky because as a minstrel, I get to sing his songs for a living and thereby benefit by osmosis from Jack's warm wit and clever turn of phrase. I can best put Jack's accomplishments into perspective by recounting an event that occurred recently in New York.

A few years ago, I enjoyed the thrill of paying tribute to Jack at Weill Recital Hall in the Carnegie Hall complex. I began my introduction by saying, "Before I present our guest this evening, I would like to quote from a newly released book titled *Reading Lyrics* by Gottlieb and Kimball." This book is a comprehensive anthology of all the great songwriters of the last century and some of their better-known songs. I then proceeded to read, "Born in Brooklyn and educated at Long Island University, Jack Lawrence has had a long and varied career as a lyricist, composer, theater owner, on- and- off-Broadway producer, and art collector. His first published song, 'Play, Fiddle, Play,' was an international hit in 1934, 'Sleepy Lagoon,' was number one for Harry James ten years later, and 'Ciribiribin' became Harry's theme song. Jack gave their first hits to Frank Sinatra: 'All or Nothing at All'; Dinah Shore: 'Yes, My Darling Daughter'; the Inkspots: 'If I Didn't Care'; Rosemary Clooney's 'Tenderly,' which went on to become a true standard; and Bobby Darin with 'Beyond the Sea.' In 1946, five different recordings of 'Symphony' reached the top ten. At least one of his assaults on Broadway had a superior score: *I Had a Ball*; and his songs graced many movies, from *Dinner at Eight, Torch Song, Apollo 13*, and *Shawshank Redemption* to many Woody Allen films."

Then I continued, "Following this introduction, their book included seven of Jack's wonderful lyrics. I should also tell you that last year, PRS, Public Radio Service, held a nationwide poll to pick the hundred best songs and compositions of the past century, including such classics as 'Rhapsody in Blue.' And Jack's 'All or Nothing at All' came in close to the top."

Then, more than slightly nervous with the author present, I played and sang three of Jack's standards, "Beyond the Sea," "Symphony," and "All or Nothing at All." A friend who attended that evening, Ed Shanaphy, wrote about the rest of it in his trade paper, *Sheet Music Magazine*.

Feinstein then asked Jack if he would sing his song *Linda* and tell how it came to be written. Jack rendered a toe-tapping version and in conclusion told that it had been written for the three-year-old daughter of his attorney at the time, Lee Eastman, whose little Linda grew up to marry Paul McCartney. "So you see what a song can do!" Jack quipped.

When Michael asked if Jack would like to do another song, Jack replied that he would prefer to do a new song—to show that he was still an active writer of words and music. Taking center stage Jack then sang a lovely, touching ballad titled: *In Praise of Older Women*. When he concluded, the entire audience rose to their feet, (many of them wiping their eyes) as they applauded. Here is Jack's lyric and with his permission in the future we will print his lovely melody:

IN PRAISE OF OLDER WOMEN
Verse:
The poet who wrote it was telling the truth.
The sweet gift of youth is wasted on the young,
I'm filled to the brim with a glorious hymn
In praise of older women—
The praise of older women must be sung:

Chorus:

Her hair—bright with frost in it
Some white winter tossed in it,
The glow in her wise woman eyes,
The dream on her face that no years can erase,
Her laugh with a half-note of sighs;
Her kiss—sweet maturity,
Her arms—deep security,
She smiles and my heart overflows;
A young girl is Spring, a green, tender thing,
A bud blossoming as it grows,
But then in the autumn sun,
How grand the phenomenon
When time puts the bloom on the rose.

(after a 16-bar interlude the vocal resumes)

Ah yes! I know authors who
Agree with my point of view,
They praise older women—in prose,
But my eyes embrace that heart-warming face,
Serene, filled with grace in repose;
It's then I grow lyrical, beholding that miracle
When time puts the bloom on the rose.

Yes, Jack has done it all, yet retains an enthusiasm and love for the music business that belies his years. He has seen countless fancies pass, but can remain secure in his repertoire's survival. Aside from writing his own music to many songs, he has collaborated with a veritable Who's Who of composers including legends like Hoagy Carmichael, Sammy Fain, Victor Young, Harry James, and Raymond Scott. And if Mozart, Debussy, and Tchaikovsky were still corporeally extant, they would have been mighty pleased with the rebirth of their classics in his modern lyrical guise.

Jack also became known as the guy who could take a foreign song and make it an American hit when dressed up in his particular vernacular, as he did with "La Mer," "Le Pauvre Jean de Paris," "Vous qui passez sans me voir," and "Symphonie." Jack said that whenever he was asked to do such a job, he never did a literal translation. "If that's what they want, they can use a French-English Dictionary!" He added that what he preferred to do was to play the original melody over and over until it echoed in his mind and heart. Only then would he start to create the words that he felt complemented the melody.

Here's an example of how he worked. "La Mer" (literal translation "The Sea"), by Charles Trenet, speaks in its French lyric of the sea and how its various changes and moods affect the singer. Jack decided to create a story rather than a tone poem. The one word, "beyond," that he added to the original title suddenly invests it with distance and mystery. Then look at how he created an entire story by playing with that one word, "beyond."

Somewhere—BEYOND THE SEA	(way out there)
Somewhere—waiting for me,	(so there are two people!)
My lover stands on golden sands	(a lover is waiting)
And watches the ships that go sailing,	(obviously waiting for a sailor)
It's far beyond a star	(a vast distance separates them)
It's near beyond the moon	(vast and yet within view)
I know beyond a doubt—	
My heart will lead me there soon,	(that love is strong!)
We'll meet beyond the shore	
We'll kiss just as before	
Happy we'll be beyond the sea	
And never again I'll go sailing	(and the story has a happy ending)

I would like to add one more brief example of how Jack, through the use of simple words—but the right word in its proper place—fashions his poetry. Look at his opening lyric for "Tenderly."

The evening breeze caressed the trees . . . tenderly,
The trembling trees embraced the breeze . . . tenderly,
(Immediately he's created a scene of passion. Later in the lyric comes the culmination of this passion.)
Your arms opened wide and closed me inside,

You took my lips, you took my love,
So tenderly.

(That's lyrical creativity!)

Jack is a living time capsule. He has seen much change in the world this past century. His work reflects the plethora of experiences he has collected, yet they only tell a small part of his life story. His is a varied and vastly interesting tale, and I am glad that he has decided to tell it. Characteristically, Jack is not one to moralize or tell others how to live life, but he recognizes that by telling his story, it may "help someone out there to focus on their own dream."

Thanks for sharing your dream with us, Jack. The world is a much better place because of it!

Michael Feinstein
June 2004

The Verse
Before the Chorus

A writer of songs usually follows a long-established formula. First comes the verse, which is the introductory setup of the main story that will be told in the body of the song, the chorus. So, dear reader, you may consider these few words the verse to what I hope will prove to be my lengthy chorus.

Memory can be a fascinating companion and an ephemeral stranger as one grows older. In my ninth decade, I find myself recalling long-forgotten incidents of my early life with utter clarity—a direct contradiction to my occasional inability to remember exactly what happened last week. I, who prided myself on the skillful recitation of friends' telephone numbers and addresses, now find myself groping for the name of a recently introduced stranger.

Therefore, when I started to write this recollection of my long life, I discovered that the mind works like a kaleidoscope. The colors, patterns, and remembrances of past and present swirl before one's eyes. Events do not flow sequentially, but flash like subliminal images. A particular incident tends to trigger a memory of some unrelated occurrence in your early childhood, and you can't help but wonder why such completely disparate events are playing out on your mind's screen.

Inevitably, at some point, you stop to think—why are you dredging up all this minutiae? This life of yours, which you may consider so unusual, in retrospect has truly not been so different from thousands of other lives. The births, the deaths, the successes and failures, the loves, and the losses—hasn't everyone experienced the same in a greater or lesser degree? Why this presumption that your life is worth a book?

Truth be told, every life is worth the telling. How else would one learn if not from the experiences and mistakes of others? In that spirit, I hope that this American and very personal adventure I have lived will in some small way guide and ease the path for all those who also harbor a dream. This is probably the appropriate place and time to remember and thank all those generous souls who helped and encouraged me in this endeavor. I am fortunate to have had dear and close friends who gave me enthusiastic support throughout. Ed Shanaphy, the owner and editor of a truly unusual publication: *Sheet Music Magazine*, gave me a rare opportunity to test my literary skills by inviting me to contribute articles about the music business and my career in his publication. My success in this endeavor was what convinced me to undertake this larger work. Further encouragement came from Douglas Rae who had a long career as a literary agent in London and now resides in the States with his lovely wife, Sally Ann Howes. They were also instrumental in introducing me to my agent, Eric Myers, who went beyond the call of duty, making many corrections and additions to my manuscript.

Bill Giles, another warm friend and advertising mogul, collaborating with my son Richard, came up with an eye-catching cover presentation which sparked the present brilliant dust jacket. Lyle and Carole Stuart who run Barricade Books, have been constantly supportive, along with their entire staff. Sandra Lee Stuart, my editor, with her sharp eye and blue pencil, caught many an error. Jeff Nordstedt and Kay Shuckhart are responsible for the elegant overall look of the book. Two more people I thank profusely for their efforts, suggestions and research are Diane Ventura and Fred Romang. Bella Linden, my attorney and close friend for over half a century, not only supplied a few reminiscences, but made certain that what I wrote was legally irreproachable.

Last, but definitely of equal and unqualified support of my efforts, there has always been my beloved son Richard, bolstering and encouraging me with his love and patience throughout this difficult and cathartic journey.

To one and all, and to anyone I have inadvertantly overlooked, I hearby deliver my love, gratitude, and thanks.

—Jack Lawrence
June 2004

CHAPTER ONE

The First Time
I Went to Carnegie Hall

t was a Friday summer evening in our five-room Brooklyn apartment. Uncles, aunts, and cousins were seated around the dining-room table sipping tea and munching poppy-seed kuchen baked that day by grandma, Mama's mother, who was fondly called "Bobbeh." Next to an overflowing fruit bowl, in the center of the table, stood the brass samovar glowing under an embossed, glass-leaded, gas chandelier. Mama had lovingly polished the samovar that day, and Papa had stoked the chimney with glowing charcoal embers to heat the water and steep the tea leaves. The proper tea-drinking procedure was to put a sugar cube in your mouth, pick up the thick glass, and sip the hot, lemon-flavored tea. No, we didn't have teacups . . . just a collection of *yahrzeit* glasses whose memorial candles had been consumed.

Our dining room served many purposes. It was a combination dining-living-family room that metamorphosed into a bedroom where I slept on the couch while my two older brothers shared a double folding bed. Also occupying this already crowded room was a battered upright piano, abandoned in a recently vacated flat across the hall, which my pleas and tears had persuaded Mama to salvage. She was convinced that I had latent musical talent because I was constantly pretending to play piano on her iron-legged Singer sewing machine while I kept rhythm on the grilled treadle below.

I had just finished my usual Friday night performance for all the relatives, playing and singing my latest creative efforts, when my *Tante* Eydis, she of the solitary tooth and high-pitched voice, spoke up to berate my mother. "It's a *shande*! A boy with such talent! Do with him something."

"What's to do?" said Mama. "Piano lessons he's already stopped. He says he's too old . . . that ten-year-old pisher! Believe me, Yankele [my Yiddish name], you'll be sorry someday you gave up the teacher."

When I first got my hands on that old upright, I started picking out popular songs of the day with one finger, gradually adding a thumping bass for rhythm, and Mama felt she had been justified in taking that old piano. From the day I first picked out "If her eyes are blue as skies . . . that's *Peggy O'Neill*," it was impossible to keep me away from the keyboard. So Mama found me a piano teacher. Where and how she found him, I don't know.

There were no other budding musicians in our tenement and few pianos on our block. For twenty-five cents a lesson, my teacher came by trolley from some distant world and brought me status, the rudiments of reading music, and an unwashed odor that hovered miasmatically over his underfed body and seedy clothes.

Twenty-five cents a week plus the cost of beginner's folios came to a lot of money that depression year, and Papa began to decry the expenditure when I quickly lost interest in practicing. Mama took me to task, but I argued that I already knew all the notes and was bored banging out "The Happy Farmer." Papa and I won the argument, and my teacher disappeared along with his strange smell. But Mama constantly chastised me.

"Yes, someday, Yankele . . . you'll be sorry!"

"What kind piano lessons," cut in my Tante Eydis. "Lessons he don't need. He's already a genius. Listen to the songs he writes. Take him someplace somebody should hear his songs. The whole world will be singing them."

Mama, "Go take him? Where?"

Tante Eydis was our one relative with "kultur." She had graduated from gymnasia in Kiev. "Where you should take him? Go to Carnegie Hall in New York City. Plenty people there will recognize such a talent. Oy! He should only be my son." Poor Tante Eydis, like Sholom Aleichem's Tevye, had four daughters to marry off and no sons.

A week or so later, my mother, in her best cotton dress and fruit-brimmed hat, and I in my knee pants and long, black-ribbed stockings, clutching my precious notebook of songs, made our weary trek by subway and elevated train to the Third Avenue-Fifty-seventh Street station. It was my first trip into Manhattan, and I looked about with awe at the people and sights so completely different from the simple neighborhood in which I lived.

This was 1922. Horses and wagons, trolley cars, and elevated trains—with a fairly recent sprinkling of automotive vehicles—were the means of travel. World War I had been over for four years, and Woodrow Wilson's dream of a League of Nations had vanished. Now Warren Gamaliel Harding, a handsome, white-haired, dull Republican, was our twenty-ninth president and on the verge of an explosive scandal that would rock the country: Teapot Dome. Oil fields were transferred for the benefit of Harding's cronies, and the ensuing boondoggle put many in jail and almost led to the president's impeachment. He escaped punishment by dying.

During the first years of the decade, the women's vote had been ratified, dial telephones were being talked of, Sacco and Vanzetti were on trial in Massachusetts for anarchy, the Holland Tunnel was being dug under the Hudson River, the first Miss America contest had taken place on the boardwalk in Atlantic City, and our country was in the second year of a postwar depression. Families flocked to the movies to cry over Charlie Chaplin and Jackie Coogan in *The Kid*, to sigh over Rudolph Valentino in *The Sheik*, and to laugh at Harold Lloyd, dream with the Gish sisters, and thrill at acrobatic Douglas Fairbanks's adventures as *The Thief of Bagdad*. Theatergoers wondered how *Abie's Irish Rose* could survive on Broadway despite devastating reviews (it would run for years) and were titillated at the sordid details revealed in Fatty Arbuckle's trial for murder. Skirts were inching higher and higher as modern girls danced and sang the latest songs: "April Showers," "Chicago," and the double-entendre "I Wish I Could Shimmy Like My Sister Kate." Comic Fanny Brice had popularized "Second Hand Rose," Al Jolson "Toot, Toot Tootsie"-d his way through George Gershiwn's "Swanee." And at the age of ten, I knew very little of all the exciting news events, but I did know the words and music of every popular song on the records and piano rolls my cousins always played.

So there Mama and I were, making our hesitant way up Fifty-seventh Street looking for Carnegie Hall. Suddenly we came to an impressive window showcasing a gorgeous ebony Steinway grand. I stopped to gaze wistfully, and Mama declared, "Is here the place!" and immediately swept in, dragging a reluctant Yankele along. An elegant gentleman in gray-striped trousers, washing his hands, greeted us. "Yes, madam, how can I help you?" We were surrounded by a sea of gleaming grands and up-rights in all sizes and colors.

"Help wouldn't hurt!" said Mama. "They told me to bring here mine boy with the songs he writes. Such songs you wouldn't believe from a ten-year-old." Pushing me forward to the nearest piano, "Go play and sing your songs!"

I was furious at having my age given away. I also had a suspicion that we were not in the right place for the display of my talents. But Mama had a forceful hand, so without further ado, I was seated on the bench at a grand with my notebook propped open. My stockinged legs dangled above the pedals below.

"Sing for him 'Manya.' You'll like this one, Mister." Of course, Mama was partial to "Manya." I had been inspired by folk songs my parents sang to write a minor melody that translated a Russian phrase that Mama and Bobbeh often spoke.

Ya ta bella blu—which means I love you.

After "Manya," I followed with my latest effort, a waltz.

> I spend all of my time in *Pretending*
> That I'm loved by lovely you,
> Soon the silv'ry moon will be descending
> And I'll dream my dreams of you . . .

That one was followed by my big mournful opus.

> When you went away
> I let a *Song of Sorrow* fill my heart,
> Now my days are gray,
> I sing this melody since we're apart,
> Every day is just a *Song of Sorrow*—
> Can't I borrow of tomorrow's joys?

And so on. Such *weltschmertz* and inner rhymes yet from a ten-year-old! Prodded by Mama, I delivered my complete repertoire. Other pairs of striped pants kept wandering by, stopping in bewilderment, smiling tentatively, and moving on, but not the gentleman Mama had trapped. Not only couldn't he escape, he had to agree with Mama's superlatives at the end of each rendition. "I didn't tell you right? Is this a talent? Nu, Mister?"

A big throat clearing from Mr. Striped Pants. "Umm—yes. Tell me, Madam, does the boy have a piano at home?"

"*Eppes* a piano! A piece junk! From this he makes such beautiful songs."

Striped Pants' face lit up. "Ah! What this clever boy needs—a boy with so much talent—he should have a Steinway piano. Now, if you can't afford any of these new models, you might consider a used one. They've all been reconditioned and carry the Steinway guarantee. If you'll just step right this way . . ." He was halfway toward the rear of the showroom.

"Mister, wait a minute! For a piano we didn't come. I was told to bring my boy . . . Oy! Is not here Carnegie Hall?"

"I'm sorry, madam. This is Steinway Hall, where we sell Steinway pianos. Carnegie Hall is farther up the street. Now, if you'd like to see . . ."

"So you should excuse. But anyway, you heard all his songs. Maybe you can help?"

"Madam, we don't publish songs. We sell pianos. Now if you're interested, I can show you . . ."

"Mister, I'll tell you. Help with his songs. He'll make lots of money so I'll buy from you a piano."

The birth of my musical career was not on the agenda that summer day. Not only did Striped Pants turn down Mama's generous proposal that he publish my songs, but when we finally found Carnegie Hall—it was closed.

CHAPTER TWO

From Russia
with Love

have often been labeled a romanticist, and I own up to that dubious distinction. However, if that's what I am, I come by it naturally through my genes. For the story of my parents is a shining example of romanticism, and it had its start long ago in the Ukraine.

First, my father. Papa was the third son and youngest of seven children who were born and grew up in a Georgian corner of Russia. His father and mother had moved from shtetl to shtetl as most Russian Jews did, trying to escape the Cossacks and their pogroms.

My grandfather was a blacksmith in this out-of-the-way shtetl where he and his wife had settled, Bilatzerkvah. It was nothing like the romantic village of *Fiddler on the Roof*. It consisted of one muddy road and a few hutlike houses with dirt floors and outdoor privies. This small Jewish enclave clung together, and since grandfather's blacksmith shop was the largest space in town, it also served as synagogue. Times were bad, it was a hard life, and the shtetl was surrounded by gentile families who were only slightly better off. But the Jewish families were far enough away from the rampant anti-Semitism in the large cities, and their gentile neighbors were friendly.

Some years before their move to this town, my father's oldest brother, Sam, had managed to leave Russia for America with his wife and three sons. Left behind were his parents and six remaining siblings, three already married. They were all finding life difficult and food scarce. My father was ten years old, that was as close as he could figure his years since the majority of Russian Jews, not being considered citizens, had no official records of their births or deaths. Whereas births, marriages, and deaths of the gentiles were duly noted by church and state, Jewish people were born, married, and died observing their own religious ceremonies without these events being recorded. My parents and their siblings never knew exactly how old they were and would try to date themselves by such remembered and talked-about events.

One harsh winter, my paternal grandfather passed away, and my father, aged ten and large for his age, became his mother's sole support. His weak and frail next-older brother was a *chusud*, a religious student of the Torah, and as such, did not work at any trade. My grandmother hired out her youngest son, Beryl (my father-to-be), who had learned the trade from his father, as an assistant blacksmith to a gentile family some kilometers out of town. My father lived with this family for about ten years, taking care of the stable of horses and livestock. Because he was hard working and industrious, he was treated as almost a member of that gentile family. His pittance of a salary went to his mother, and it was only possible for him to make rare visits home to his own family, at which time he would bring them gifts of produce and live chickens to be slaughtered in the Orthodox manner.

My father grew quickly into manhood, a sinewy and muscular six feet, three inches with a shock of black hair and a luxurious reddish mustache. When he was twenty years old, the Russian Cossack army came through looking for recruits. They seized one of the farmer's sons along with my father, who was afraid to admit that he was Jewish because he could have been shot indiscriminately. The parting from his mother who was losing her youngest child and the sole means of support was tearful. It was at this sad farewell that Beryl learned from his mother that she had a married sister living somewhere on the outskirts of Kiev, the city where he was to be stationed. Since these sisters had not seen each other or communicated for years, all my grandmother could tell her son was her sister's married name, Goldman. She urged him to find his unknown relatives.

It's interesting how Jewish family surnames were created. Unlike gentile surnames that were recorded and passed down through the years, Jewish surnames were usually based on the family's business or trade. Thus a *schneider*—the Yiddish word for tailor—would be known as Schneider until he immigrated to America, where the name was often transposed into Taylor. My paternal grandfather's name had been inherited from his father, who had also been a blacksmith. It was Chernovsky, literally translated as *der zun fin de schvartze*—the son of the blacksmith. When my father's oldest brother, Sam, and his family arrived at Ellis Island in New York, the non-Yiddish speaking immigration officers at Ellis Island heard the word *schvartze* in the translation and recorded his surname as Schwartz.

Young Beryl was conscripted into an elite group of Russian Cossacks who were handpicked horsemen, strong and more than six feet in height. He was given two beautiful horses, one white and one black, which he learned to ride in the Cossack manner— standing upright with one foot astride each horse's back. He had no clue as to how or where to search for the relatives his mother had told him about. Whenever he had time off, he would wander the streets of Kiev, asking Jewish tradesmen if they know any families named Goldman. His uniform and size alone frightened most Jews into silence, although this same appearance won him many a gentile girl.

Then fate opened the door to Beryl. One day as he was strolling through the large Kiev general market, a lovely young girl tending one of the stalls caught his eye. He stopped and pretended to inspect her wares, trinkets, and odds and ends. He tried to make conversation, but her manner was cold and her responses curt. Conversely, she became warm and enthusiastic with other potential customers, bantering with them and making quick sales. He bought a trinket he didn't really want and left. For the next few days, he tried his luck at her stall repeatedly, but she remained uncommunicative and distant.

One day he decided to talk with a gentile butcher at a nearby stall and asked, "Do you know who that girl is?"

"Sure!" said the butcher. "She comes from a nearby village. She's smart—got a good head on her—she can sell anything. She's worked a lot of different stalls."

"How come she's so rude? She won't even talk to me."

"Aha!" said the butcher. "You're a Cossack. She's Jewish!"

Finally, Beryl understood why he was getting such a deep freeze. He hung around the market all day and decided to follow her home. He had become so intrigued that he wanted to explain that he, too, was Jewish. He stayed far enough behind so that she was not aware that she was being followed. Night was fast descending as she walked the few kilometers from Kiev to her village of Slabodkah. Suddenly she disappeared into a store as Beryl watched from across the road. The sign over the store read GOLD BOUGHT AND SOLD, and in the window were rings, watches, earrings, and prayer shawls (called tallises) embossed with gold leaf. Had she entered to make a purchase, or was this where she lived? He didn't know, but after a while, he followed her in. He thought of a ready excuse. He would ask if the proprietor knew a family named Goldman.

And now fate combines with romance. The gnarled little old lady who stood behind the counter turned out to be Beryl's Aunt

Chanah—his mother's long unheard-from sister. And the girl he had admired and followed was his cousin, Shana Fruma (literal translation Beautiful Faith). She was eighteen years old, tall and slender, with sparkling brown eyes and an abundance of hair piled up in the fashion of the day. Her mother had been a widow for years, and the Goldman family consisted of four daughters and three sons. Four of the older siblings were married and had started families. Still living at home were a son and two sisters, Rivka and Fruma, the youngest of the family.

The discovery of this new nephew and cousin was a joyous occasion for an impromptu celebration. After all had been explained to everyone's satisfaction, Beryl and Fruma could not take their eyes from each other. Of course, Beryl made many subsequent visits in rapid succession to the Goldman family, but this was a ticklish situation. It was almost impossible for the two young people to be alone together. Not only were Rivka and Fruma two unmarried young girls, but as his first cousin, any intimacy was taboo. Lovers, however, will find a way.

Now, whenever he had free time, Beryl would call on Fruma at her market stall where they could carry on their budding romance in relative privacy. A faded photograph of Beryl in his Cossack uniform shows a tall, slim, handsome young man, his hair close cropped in the Prussian style, a strong face adorned with a well-groomed, luxurious mustache. His dark, well-fitted tunic is buttoned all the way up to his square chin, where it reveals the trace of a white collar. Across one broad shoulder and around his narrow waist are leather holster-straps, and his gray, fitted pants are neatly tucked into knee-length, gleaming, black-leather boots with spurs at the heel. He stands proudly and confidently, with one hand resting next to his visored cap on a round table.

These lines from a lyric I wrote to a song titled "Moonlight Masquerade" may best describe what I believe happened the first time they met as cousins.

> The moment they looked, they longed,
> The moment they longed, they sighed,
> The moment they sighed, they loved,
> And that's how two hearts were tied . . .

A year passed quickly as the lovers made their secret plans. Beryl would desert the Cossacks, they would marry and elope to America. He had already written to his brother, Sam, in Brooklyn, who had agreed to act as the sponsor when they arrived. So important a plan had to have at least one accomplice, and the only one who could be trusted was Fruma's three-years-older, unmarried sister, Rivka. I stress "unmarried" because that, in itself, presented another problem.

In the Orthodox Jewish religion, it is a *shanda*, a great embarrassment, if not a sin, for the younger daughter to marry before the older, and taboo for first cousins to wed. If one is to believe the superstitions surrounding such an incestuous union, the resulting progeny could turn out weak in body and mind. My three brothers and I belie that myth. My brothers not only had successful careers, but were considered smart businessmen. In my own case, I've been called many things by music publishers, but never crazy.

However, all that was in the unforeseeable future, and the lovers' immediate situation had to be dealt with. The intrigue, the planning, and the romanticism must have captured little Rivka's imagination for she entered into the plot wholeheartedly. It was she who appealed to the *rhuv*, the local high rabbi, for his special dispensation. Two dispensations: permission for the younger sister to marry before the older—and to marry a first cousin. I never learned what persuasive arguments Rivka used on the rabbi to persuade him. But she did! Then she helped organize all the details of their elopement and kept it a close secret from her mother and the rest of the family. In retrospect, I can understand why all their lives these two sisters remained close to each other. Unfortunately, poor Rivka suffered the consequences of her aid and unselfishness.

One moonless night in 1905, the newlywed cousins packed their few belongings. Beryl traded his uniform for an inconspicuous suit, and with their hoarded rubles, they left, blessed by tears and kisses from the one lone member of their large family, little Rivka.

Their first mode of transportation was a wagonload of produce a farmer was delivering across the border into Poland, with the new bride and groom well concealed. They made their crossing very late in the night, and the one guard was too sleepy to make an inspection. They paid the farmer for his trouble and continued to travel in various stages, sometimes by horse and cart, sometimes by train or by foot, hiding out, stealing across borders from country to country to avoid showing identification papers, which they lacked. They were not alone in this exodus. Other families and couples, young and old, had banded together to escape the pogroms and tyranny of the czar's regime.

From Kiev through Warsaw they traveled, through Poland, across the breadth of Germany to Bremerhaven, where, as steerage passengers, they boarded a small, crowded cattle boat that was to carry them over the winter ocean on a two-week trip to the land of gold and opportunity—always referred to as *der goldena medina*. What an incredible adventure for two uneducated youngsters who had never strayed far from the narrow world of their birth and the warmth of their families. How little thought we give to those millions of brave souls from all over Europe, the true pioneers who built this great country.

Back in Slabodkah, Fruma's mother, my maternal Bobbeh, had to be talked out of covering all the mirrors in her house and sitting *shiva*, the Jewish ritual for mourning the dead. That is another part of the story I never learned. It took years of prying and probing to put these bits and pieces together from parents and relatives. My Bobbeh refused ever to discuss it. Suffice it to say that in time she forgave the lovers, but Rivka bore the brunt of her wrath for concealing the elopement. The unmarried-daughter problem had to be rectified quickly, so with the aid of a *schotchen* (a matchmaker) and a hastily scraped-together dowry, a penniless neighbor's young Talmudic son was bought, and Rivka was married to a virtual stranger.

At Castle Garden, the Ellis Island adjunct for immigrants in New York harbor, my Uncle Sam met his brother and bride. It was months before he learned that his new sister-in-law was also his first cousin. Upon their arrival at Ellis Island, Fruma Goldman and Beryl Chernovsky became Americanized as Fanny and Barney Schwartz. I've always been intrigued by the immigration process whereby ethnic names were transliterated into English. Interpreters stood by to help these "poor, tired, and dispossessed."

I've already explained how Schneider became the very English Taylor. There's an apocryphal story about one Schneider whose surname was completely garbled. The recorder thought he heard the interpreter say "sailor" instead of "tailor" and asked, "Sailor, you mean like Lord Nelson?"

"*Da, da,* yes!" replied the interpreter, anxious to appear agreeable. That "Schneider" went through life with the surname Nelson. I have a cousin who wound up with a Scottish name. His grandfather had been a tea merchant. In Yiddish, to make tea is spoken as *mach tay*. From there it is a short step to his recorded surname, MacTay.

While on the subject of names, I should explain how I arrived at my own *nom de plume*. In the early thirties, my two older brothers and my Uncle Sam's five sons were involved in a flourishing fuel-oil business and were known as the Seven Schwartz Boys. Proud of their reputation, they were convinced that I, as Jacob Schwartz, embarking on a dubious show-business career, might sully the family name (that name that wasn't ours to start with). Piqued at their attitude, I announced that I, born Jacob Lawrence Schwartz, would henceforth become Jack Lawrence.

"Good!" said my brothers. "Then we won't have to apologize."

"Just wait until I'm famous," I replied.

In later years, my older brothers were constantly explaining my name to friends and my younger brother, Murray, seriously considered changing his surname to mine. An amusing sidelight: My older brother, Joe was an expert fantasizer. In plainer terms, we called him a bullshit artist. He had the gift of gab and could be most convincing when romancing a gal. He would swear her to secrecy and tell her that he was really Jack Lawrence and had written all those hit songs. Because of his business connections as an oil mogul, it would be undignified to be known as a songwriter, therefore he was allowing me to front for him. You wouldn't believe how often this tall story lured many a female into his bed.

A few last remarks about names. In later years, when I began collecting art and meeting many artists whose work I purchased, I had the pleasure of making friends with a marvelously talented black artist, Jacob Lawrence, and his charming wife. Jacob became famous for his depictions of Harlem life and the black experience. Another creative man I got to know who became a good friend was Jerome Lawrence, coauthor of many successful plays like *Inherit the Wind* and *Auntie Mame*. In conversation one day on the subject of surnames, Jerry made a confession that floored me. His birth certificate reads Jerome Lawrence Schwartz. I never did learn where Schwartz came from, but he told me he dropped that surname for the same reasons I did—so as not to embarrass his family.

In due time, Fanny and Barney Schwartz , the newlyweds, found themselves a cubbyhole flat in Brooklyn's Brownsville ghetto, with common toilet facilities in the hall, for the huge sum of seven dollars a month. Their small flat was considered an improvement on neighboring tenements that still had one backyard outhouse for the entire building.

Daily at six A.M., my father trudged almost two miles to his job in Uncle Sam's blacksmith shop, worked hard, long hours every day (including holidays) but the Sabbath, and brought home six dollars a week, which Mama hoarded and spent sparingly. In January 1906, they celebrated the birth of their first son, Yussel, followed in quick succession eighteen months later by a second son, Chaim. Both were respectively Americanized into Joseph and Harvey.

Far removed from the consolation and love of their families, it was a hard life for the young couple, made even more difficult by penny-pinching older brother Sam and his demanding wife, Lena. With two infants to feed and clothe, my parents decided to delay any further increase in the population and save their pennies. From my earliest childhood, I can recall a little tin box known as a *pishka*, which hung on the kitchen wall of every Jewish home. This *pishka* was labeled *Eritz Yisrael* (Holy Israel), and into its small slot, all spare coins disappeared. Eventually, a little old bearded man in a long, black, shiny caftan would stop in twice a year to empty the *pishka* and bless the family. These pennies, faithfully hoarded, went to build the Jewish homeland with the blessing: Next year in Jerusalem.

Mama proved to be a good manager. She had been well taught by her mother and knew how to scrape and save, sew and alter clothes, buy the house necessities, and budget our weekly existence. My Aunt Lena was a curmudgeon who had produced five sons and one daughter and lorded it over her young sister-in-law. Papa's job depended on good relations with his brother, Sam, and family, so Mama learned to hold her tongue. But inwardly she fumed and planned. Mama had the reputation of being a *balabusta*—a most efficient housewife and manager—and Papa was grateful for her ability. Her sole project was to better their lives.

CHAPTER THREE

Nephew—Or In-Law?

By 1912 my parents had managed to improve their lot. They moved from that Brownsville slum to East New York, a slightly more suburban area that was being developed. It was often referred to as "the ass end of Brooklyn," where goats still gamboled in empty lots. Mama, turning pennies into dollars, had been able to send for her mother, whom she sorely missed.

That was a significant year in the history of our country. New Mexico and Arizona were admitted to the Union and made us a nation of forty-eight states. Two important women's movements were founded: the Girl Scouts of America and the Hadassah. The second trial of the Triangle Shirtwaist fire in Greenwich Village was underway. Many women and child workers were trapped and burned to death because of crowded conditions and inadequate fire exits. That tragedy gave impetus to the burgeoning labor-union movement and its fight for laws against child labor.

To cap that year, the world was shocked by the sinking of the "unsinkable" *Titanic.*

Irving Berlin, who had started out as a singing waiter early in the century, was showing a remarkable talent for songwriting with such ethnic pleasers as "Marie from Sunny Italy" and "Sadie Salome, Go Home." But now Irving was coming into his own with tricky new rhythms: "Everybody's Doin' It" and that classic, "Alexander's Ragtime Band," songs that started a new style of dancing that was described as the Turkey Trot and had couples gliding closely across the floor together. Another result of this new style of dancing was the radical change in ladies' fashions. Awkward bustles went out of style. The new look was a slim silhouette and a long skirt, ankle length and just wide enough to allow the feet to take petite steps.

I have always believed that a fascinating documentary could be produced on how the changes in musical styles through the ages dictated the changes in dancing and resulted in those necessary, accommodating changes in men's and women's clothes. As an example, when Prohibition was foisted on America by the Eighteenth Amendment and gangsters and speakeasies came into vogue, musical styles changed. Jazz was king, dancing became more abandoned, men wore swinging bell-bottom trousers, and ladies exposed their legs in skimpy skirts above the knees that gave them the freedom to do the Charleston, with its kicks and gyrations. Did the change in music dictate the change in fashion or vice versa?

But in 1912, couples were swaying to "On Moonlight Bay," "Waitin' for the Robert E. Lee," and W. C. Handy's "Memphis Blues" and being sentimental with "Melancholy Baby." President William Howard Taft, a reactionary Republican who had succeeded the liberal Teddy Roosevelt, was on the verge of defeat by the former president of Princeton University, Woodrow Wilson, a great Democrat who swore to keep us out of war.

In the world of arts, Theodore Dreiser, Zane Grey, and Jack London were writing bestsellers; the New York Armory was preparing to open a revolutionary exhibition of "Modern Art" by such painters as Marcel Duchamp with his abstract *Nude Descending a Staircase*, and new words like cubism, fauvism, and expressionism were being bandied about. Leopold Stokowski was the new director of the Philadelphia Symphony, the Minskys brought naughty burlesque to the Winter Garden Theater. Sarah Bernhardt in France made a film record of her play, *Queen Elizabeth*, "for posterity," she announced. Mack Sennett's bathing beauties would soon become a film rage, and a new, young writer, Anita Loos, sold her story, "The New York Hat," to D. W. Griffith for fifteen dollars, which he made into a two-reeler with "Our Mary," Miss Pickford. Her costar was an ex-art student, Lionel Barrymore.

And while all these historic events were taking place, that April, another momentous event—at least to my family—was my birth. I was duly welcomed at my *bris* (circumcision) as Yacov Loeb in honor of my long-departed maternal grandfather, who had been a brilliant scholar. At least, that's what I was told years later.

From my earliest recollections, it seemed as though I had two mothers to account to, Bobbeh and Mama. Bobbeh was the more important since Mama had to answer to her, too. At the age of awareness, I recognized that a peculiar relationship existed between Bobbeh and my father: They never addressed a direct word to each other. It was years before I heard the history of my parents' elopement and learned that they were first cousins. Yet all that time those three people lived in close proximity, under the burden of that knowledge, never speaking of it.

In time, when I was older, Papa confirmed my analysis of that strange relationship. It was not that his *Tante* Chanah, my Bobbeh, hadn't forgiven him for stealing her youngest daughter, but rather the fact that they were both at a loss as to how to address each other. She would not call him nephew, son, or son-in-law, and he was unable to address her as aunt or mother-in-law. Consequently, they tacitly decided not to speak to each other at all. This created difficulties that were simple to solve as long as there was a third person present.

"Ask him"—never "your father" or "your husband"—"what would he like for lunch," Bobbeh would demand of whomever was available.

Likewise, his reply, never directed to "your grandmother" or "mother," invariably was "Tell her I'll have the herring and potatoes."

As a child, I was intrigued by this third-person exchange and often wondered what their behavior was like when they found themselves alone with no one to talk through. So I would hide in the apartment and eavesdrop. But I never caught my father and Bobbeh in conversation! Anticipating his entrance when there was no one else at home, she would set his lunch on the table in advance, whatever *she* decided it should be, and busy herself in other parts of the house. On occasion, when he arrived before his regular time and the table was bare, rather than confront him, she would immediately disappear from the kitchen. He would inspect the icebox, fix a snack, eat, and leave quickly. Then Bobbeh would return to the kitchen, wash up his dishes, muttering under her breath about how long he had kept the icebox door open, melting the daily block of ice.

And yet, underneath all this silence, they harbored a definite respect and fondness for each other. He appreciated the efficiency with which his home was run and the delicious meals she created, and she gave grudging admiration to the good provider and husband he had turned out to be. On the rare occasions when either took ill, the other expressed concern—Bobbeh through Mama, forcing all sorts of home remedies on him—Papa insisting on spending money to call a doctor for Bobbeh's slightest illness.

The one fault Bobbeh found with Papa was his inability to train his sons with the flat of his hand or a strap to the buttocks. But my father was a gentle man. He had to be literally browbeaten into whipping us, no matter how terrible the crime we had committed. This often resulted in loud arguments, between Mama and Bobbeh and then between Mama and Papa. He would either retreat to another room or leave the house for a walk. I recall only one instance when Papa was forced to strap-whip my ten-year-old brother, Harvey, for some infraction. I still can see the picture of Papa wielding the strap, Harvey howling, and tears running down Papa's face.

Matriarchal as our household sounds, I do not mean to imply that Papa sat passively watching Bobbeh inflict her will on his family or that Mama resignedly allowed her mother complete control. Mama had an iron will of her own and knew when to take a stand. Papa good-humoredly put up with a lot—what we wore, what we ate, which relatives were temporarily banned from visits (usually one or another of his sisters who might have offended Mama or Bobbeh). Such matters were unimportant to him. But in a crunch, when it came to making vital decisions about the household budget or how much to put aside to pay for the emigration from the Ukraine of Mama's remaining brothers and sisters, our needs came first. Papa had a quiet, but stubborn streak that made arguments one sided while he sat implacably on whatever decision he had made. On the other hand, Mama was her mother's daughter with all the inherent strength and determination required to have her own way.

In the end, they both won. Although we had few luxuries, we never lacked for necessities, and eventually, by 1926, Mama realized the happy day when her many brothers, sisters, and their progeny were settled around her in Brooklyn. In 1919, when my last brother, Murray, was born, we had moved up to a five-room flat on Van Siclen Avenue. It was in this new home that Papa, Mama, and Bobbeh sat up nights nursing little me through infantile paralysis—a poliomyelitis epidemic had swept through the country. I'm thankful to say that I was more fortunate than Franklin D. Roosevelt, who was also affected by that crippling disease a couple of years later.

We siblings had a happy and fairly disciplined childhood, which is evidenced by many of the old family snapshots. There I am with a Buster-Brown haircut, in a homemade tweedy coat large enough to grow into, my lips pursed and cheeks puffed out in an incipient tear-fest. Here are my two older brothers, standing with their arms around each other's shoulders, Joe in his blue-serge bar-mitzvah suit, Harvey with one leg of his knee pants falling down. More snapshots of a summer spent at Aunt Rivka's rented cottage in the country outside upstate Albany, when we were thirteen, twelve, and seven, respectively. And there's my tall, slim mother and her short, favorite sister, Rivka, standing together, soft, piled hair framing their young, beaming faces. That was the summer Joe and Harvey, overcome with longing for Papa, who had remained in the city working in his own blacksmith shop, ran away to find him. The police picked them up that night in nearby Albany and returned them the next morning to a tearful family.

East New York, where we grew up, was a true melting pot in

those years. Irish, Italians, Polish, Germans, Jews—the entire alphabet of immigration was there. Our schoolmates were practically all first-generation Americans. Oh, that horrendous first day of school at P.S. 62, a small building that went only to the fourth grade. I was five years old when Mama abandoned me to some strange lady, and I had not yet learned to raise my hand as a signal for going to the toilet. And that grim lady, sniffing suspiciously, soon discovered that I was the cause of children giggling and pointing at me. I was sent home with overflowing eyes and full pants.

But there are joyous times I remember vividly: accompanying my father, who now had his own wagon-building and repair shop, in his Stanley Steamer automobile on Sunday collection rounds. My brothers considered themselves too old for such expeditions, but I looked forward to them eagerly because many of my father's customers were Italian ice-cream vendors whose carts he had fixed or whose wooden wheels he had iron-banded. Inevitably, I returned home with sticky hands and face and a slight bellyache from all the gooey presents. Another favorite adventure with Papa was strolling on a summer evening around the corner to the Glenmore Avenue German Beer Garden, an enchanted, parklike spot with colored lanterns in the trees, a long, wooden outdoor bar, and burly, white-aproned German waiters carrying trays of huge, icy, beer-filled pitchers to the tables. I would shyly cling to Papa's leg as he chatted with his foreign friends and customers, each with his indigenous, accented

English, yet somehow managing to communicate. I would be lifted to the bar and plied with pretzels and syrupy sodas. Alas, at the outbreak of World War I—even in Brooklyn—all Germans became suspect, and that fairyland beer garden closed down forever.

Then there were the weekends at the movies, two-for-a-nickel matinee admissions. Kids racing around yelling, "I've got three cents, who's got two?" And that inevitable brown-paper bag filled with cookies, apples, bananas, and sometimes grapes (there were no concession stands) to allay any sudden hunger pangs that might attack us. After all, we put in a long day at the movies, hiding out in the toilet after each show when tickets were being collected and thus managing to see three full programs until suppertime. Oh, yes! Those unforgettable serials: *Neal of the Navy*, Elmo Lincoln as *Tarzan*, Pearl White in *The Perils of Pauline*, and those exciting Westerns with Hoot Gibson, Tom Mix, and William S. Hart. Then there were those silent dramas that Mama and Papa took me to so that I could act as interpreter since they couldn't read the English dialogue. Lots of shushing noises were aimed in our direction as I read first in English and then translated into Yiddish. Papa invariably fell asleep as the film ground on. I recall one night sitting with Mama at the Vermont Avenue outdoor movie, which was on the roof of that building, while elevated trains kept rumbling by. The noise didn't matter since it was a silent tearjerker, Alla Nazimova in *War Brides*. We sat through two showings while Mama cried hysterically and kept repeating, "She's a great Russian actress!" I wonder whether Mama would have understood what I discovered many years later—that this great Russian actress was a lesbian.

It wasn't long after that when President Wilson sent our boys abroad "to end war for all time." My parents were thankful that their sons were all too young to go. But our free boarder, cousin Julius, whose parents were still back in Russia, was drafted. That was part of the reason for Mama's hysterics at *War Brides*. She felt guilty and responsible for having brought Julius to America and urging him to become a citizen. Her relief when he returned from France, unharmed, was boundless.

Those war years when coal was rationed and food was scarce, I was seven years old and had already found my way to the local library a mile or so from home in a greenbelt area called Highland Park. Oh, what magic I discovered in those books. It seemed I couldn't read fast enough—and they would only let me take out two books at a time. But during summer vacation, we were allowed to have *twelve* books.

At P.S. 62, those students who had earned enough gold-star paper medals were awarded the privilege of having their own tiny garden plot in the park. Daily we would troop off to plant and tend our own two-by-four bed, toting cans of water from a hand-pumped well and marveling to see radishes, tomatoes, and lettuce flowering under our eyes. It was quite a revelation for city kids whose only contact with vegetables was seeing them on pushcarts in the market. To actually pick our own-grown produce and rush home to show it off! And then to see Mama take that crisp, fresh lettuce, which she dubbed "raw," and pickle it in a brine for two days until it was limp and soggy, but pronounced fit to eat by her criterion.

There were hard times, too, when Papa's shop was slow, and despite Mama's nagging, he refused to dun his Italian customers who were having an equally bad time.

Joe and Harvey quit high school to look for nonexistent jobs. Harvey, at age sixteen, finally found a job as a "gofer" in a Manhattan men's club and overnight became quite adult, smoking cigarettes surreptitiously.

Welfare, food stamps, and Social Security were not yet in existence, and there was no government-created employment. Yet, somehow, everyone managed. Relatives and neighbors shared with and helped one another. Mama gave old, worn-out clothes that were still usable to less fortunate families, neighbors brought a taste of kugel or sponge cake they had baked, Papa's Italian ice-cream vendors gave backyard-grown vegetables and fruit. We were all in the same boat, striving to stay afloat. I look back at that time and marvel at the many different ethnic hands that were outstretched in friendship.

Through it all, our families never missed celebrating the Jewish holidays, attending services in the small, wooden neighborhood *shul* where all the men sat downstairs wrapped in their woolen prayer robes while all the ladies sat upstairs in the close, hot balcony under the eaves. In due time, when my brothers and I respectively reached our thirteen-year majority, we were bar-mitz-vahed in this small synagogue whose walls were decorated with murals of lambs and lions while the ceiling was painted with clouds and stars. Bar mitzvah! Such an auspicious occasion, when we were inducted as men. We stood on the dais next to Papa and the rabbi and recited, first in Hebrew, then in English, what we had painfully rehearsed for many months. At the conclusion of this performance, we were pelted with raisins and almonds by the women in the balcony.

During the High Holy Days, we all dressed in our best outfits and walked to *shul* as a family. Of course, we all fasted on Yom Kippur and waited impatiently for sunset when a ram's horn, the *shofar*, was blown, announcing the end of the holiday and the time to break our long day's fast. What a feast we would fall upon! And I recall so vividly Fridays before the Sabbath, when not only was the house being scrubbed and polished, but Mama rushed about helping Bobbeh mix and knead those wonderful, sweet-smelling *challahs*, plaited egg bread, plus gefilte fish, chicken, and health-giving soup. And in my mind's eye, I still see all those newspapers spread carefully over the newly washed kitchen floor.

And those Passover times, which corresponded to the Easter holidays. The house had to be scrubbed top to bottom. The corners of every room were carefully brushed to remove the slightest crumb—a process called *chometz*—then all the daily meat and dairy dishes and utensils stored away and carefully replaced with the Passover paraphernalia.

Every fall and winter, Papa would have brewed the Passover wine in our basement from juicy purple grapes, a process I always enjoyed watching and helping him with. Grapes would be piled into a large metal bucket, and with our bare feet thoroughly washed and scraped, we crushed the grapes and retrieved the colorful juices. Then Papa would fill a wooden barrel with those juices, add sugar and other mysterious substances, cover the top of the barrel with a linen cloth, and allow the wine to ferment in the heat of the basement. By the time it was ready for our Seders, Papa would have removed whatever furry scum had formed on top, tasted the wine, and pronounced it fit to drink. It was sweet and heady and always turned us all jolly halfway through the Seder with loud laughter and songs. Until my brother, Murray, was old enough, I was the one who had to ask the ritual questions, "Wherefore is tonight different than all other nights?"

I must also mention another of Papa's specialties. He made the most delicious sauerkraut, another chore where I was the helper. I've tried to duplicate his recipe, but somehow mine doesn't ever taste like Papa's. We would set his kraut out in a back pantry during the winter and bring in a plate full of cold, slightly icy sauerkraut whose taste I can still summon up in my memory.

It was a time of warmth, a time of love, a time of family, despite the adversity. We endured it all somehow—unaware of harder times yet to come.

CHAPTER FOUR

Sylvia, Danny— and Me

By 1925, when I was thirteen and in my final elementary-school grade, our family fortunes had improved. The country was doing better under our thirtieth president, Silent Cal Coolidge, who had stepped up from vice president upon the death of Warren Harding. Coolidge was a dour individual who seemed to have been weaned on a sour pickle, a conservative, taciturn New Englander. He was a good fiscal manager who cut taxes and costs and practiced economy with the belief that the less government did, the better the country would be. This policy worked for most of his presidency, and at its conclusion in 1929, he announced that he "did not choose to run" for reelection. That was undoubtedly a wise decision since his Republican successor, Herbert Hoover, got the blame for the country's crash into deep depression.

But in those earlier good times, my brothers were working as shoe salesmen in a fashionable downtown Brooklyn store on Fulton Street where, if I arrived before nine A.M. on Saturdays, I was hired for the grand sum of two dollars to act as "box boy." That meant that as soon as a salesman completed one transaction, he could turn to the next customer while the box boy raced with the lady's shoes and money to the cashier and wrapper, then delivered change and package to the lady. Often, if you were quick and smiled politely, you were rewarded with a ten-cent tip for your service. That Saturday's two and a half dollars was my weekly school allowance, and I endured a miserable, penniless week when I failed to get picked as a box boy.

Milk and ice were still being delivered by horse-drawn wagon, and Papa's business—shoeing horses, repairing wagons and carts—was doing well enough to add a helper. That income, plus contributions from my brothers' salaries, made it possible for Mama at last to realize a dream: to own her very own home. It was a two-story house on Van Siclen Avenue, down the street from our last apartment, and while we acquired much new furniture, I refused to part with my old upright piano. Some new strings and repairs had improved it, but not much. At the beginning of the fifth grade, I had transferred from P.S. 62 to P.S. 173, a mile and a half away, and I plodded back and forth, home for lunch between classes, in all weather, all seasons—like the proverbial mailman. Busing? No one had dreamed of free busing to school. Integration? That was hardly a problem. We were thoroughly integrated. Sheenies, polacks, micks, guineas, and niggers—those were our common names for each other, and they often sparked fistfights.

What set us apart was our willingness or unwillingness to abide by the rules both on the street and in school. "Cheezit—the cops!" was a warning to be feared, as was that blue-uniformed, baton-twirling symbol of authority. By today's standards, the educational process was undoubtedly limited, but most of the teachers were truly dedicated to their profession and held our respect. And we did learn! By the second grade, we could read, write, and spell, so those teachers must have been doing something right. We were such a polyglot group of kids, mostly speaking our parents' Old World languages at home. But in school, the common language was English, and we learned fast. I'm constantly amazed these days when I read that in some parts of our country there are debates about the necessity of Spanish teachers for Hispanic children and teachers versed in Ebonics to teach black children. Then there are the reports that many high-school graduates are unable to read, write, spell, or do simple mathematics. Something is terribly wrong with our present school system. Critics blame it on overcrowded classrooms and lack of discipline. It seems to me that our classrooms back then were always overcrowded, with kids having to double up in seats.

The teacher's hard ruler taught us discipline. In my day, we were in awe of our teachers, and many of them had the ability to recognize our various potentials—to stretch our minds, to instill in us a thirst for literature, science, mathematics, and the arts. Each class was graded A through D; the brightest pupils made it into the A group and thus were in competition with their intellectual peers.

It was in music assembly that I first discovered and developed a love for the classics, listening to symphonic recordings on scratchy Victrolas and learning to identify the great theme of each opus by singing its title. To this day I cannot hear that particular Schubert work without singing, "UN—FIN—ISHED SYM—PHO—NY—FRANZ SCHUBERT WROTE IT IN—B—MI—I—NOR!" And what joy when I first heard all those melodic, soaring themes of Tschaikovsky! They held a special empathy for me. They were Russian and sounded like many of the folk songs my mother used to sing around the house.

So there I was in 8-B, my final grade, editor of the school paper and a favorite of our teacher, Mr. Gainsborough (né Ginsberg). He thought well enough of me to give me carfare to his home to babysit his infant daughter when he and his wife were tied up with school activities. I was not entirely teacher's pet, however. There was a bit of rebel in me even then. Shortly before graduation day, I was dragged to the principal's office by the aptly named Miss Thew, an iron lady with a bosom like a bolster who supervised our school paper's editorial board. Indignantly, she reported to principal Bainbridge that I had gone against her wishes in writing and printing an editorial criticizing the establishment, our school administration, for certain practices with which I took issue. Miss Thew towered above me, all muscle, which I could feel in the grasp of my ear by her fist. Mr. Bainbridge, a kindly little monkey of a man, skimmed through my editorial and beamed at me.

"It's very well written. And you state facts that I can't dispute. I agree that we should institute some changes."

Miss Thew sputtered in rage. "That's not the point! The point is—this boy—he's too ambitious!"

"Well," said the amused little monkey, "you can't blame him for that." And with an inappropriate afterthought, he added, "So was Caesar—ambitious."

"Yes!" shot back Miss Thew triumphantly as she released my ear and turned to stalk out of the room. "And look what happened to Caesar!"

At any rate, on graduation day I was awarded first prize in the Declamation Contest, a bronze medal for my delivery of a bathetic poem by Robert W. Service called "Fleurette," the story of a French nurse in World War I who cares for wounded French *poilus* and loses her life in the sudden bombing of the hospital. All this declaimed with many a gesture and dramatic flair that I had perfected in the mirror in our only bathroom at home while my older brothers pounded on the door for entry. I also played the lead in our class play, the prophetic role of The Poet in an allegory titled *Hunger*, in which every character—The Poet, The Beggar, The Warrior, and The Maid—hungers for their own ideal and are philosophically advised by The Old Man: "Do not let your dreams blind you to the realities of life!" Pretty heavy stuff for thirteen-year-olds. And I delivered the graduation oration. "Here we stand on the threshold—and as we go forth into tomorrow . . ."

Of course, Mama and Papa sat there proudly that day and reported back to the relatives that it was almost as good as my bar-mitzvah speech, which they liked better because it was in Yiddish.

I cannot pass over those halcyon days of P.S. 173 without telling about a particularly close schoolmate, Sylvia Fine. It was the same Sylvia who, years later, married another neighborhood boy, Danny Kaye—né Kaminsky. His father was a tailor on my street, and Sylvia lived three blocks away. She was a somber child, overly serious, and bright, sallow of face, with a straight Buster-Brown haircut and bangs.

Her Viennese father was a successful local dentist, and her American mother was a Vassar graduate, two distinctions few families in our neighborhood could claim. Moreover, they occupied the upstairs and downstairs of their home while my family had to rely on an upstairs tenant's rent to defray expenses. But the crowning touch for me was the Steinway grand piano in the Fines' parlor. Sylvia was practicing to be a virtuoso pianist, and she and her best friend, Adele, a bucktoothed, big-bosomed girl, were expert duettists who often regaled our school assemblies with four-handed concerts.

Music is what drew Sylvia and me together. Every afternoon, it became my custom to walk her home from school while recounting our day's activities; I, carrying my imitation leather case, and she clutching two arms full of books to her white middy blouse. There was another great inducement to these daily walks:

the possibility of being invited inside her home. That Steinway drew me like a magnet, but it was a long time before I dared to confide to Sylvia that I had been writing songs for years.

Our friendship ripened as we graduated and went to Thomas Jefferson High School together. That was more than a mile-and-a-half walk from home every day, rain or shine, plus sloshing through deep snowdrifts in winter. It seems those winters were far more severe than the present ones. There was not a great attempt by the street-cleaning department to attack the snow piles along the street that were twelve feet high—or else I had not yet attained my full six-foot majority.

As I got to know Sylvia better, I eventually gathered up enough nerve to play her some of my songs. She was far from encouraging in her criticism. My lyrics were not too bad, she said, but nowhere near as clever as her favorites, Gilbert and Sullivan. Still—okay, for cheap, popular songs. My melodies? Well, what could be expected of someone who had no musical training or knowledge?

I argued, "Irving Berlin never had any musical training, either. He's a natural genius! How about that?"

"Well, Jack," she answered coolly, "you are hardly a natural genius. And I know what I'm talking about."

No, that didn't stop me from writing more songs, and whenever I found myself in the subdued, shade-drawn Fine parlor waiting for Sylvia to finish dressing upstairs so that we could get to some meeting or party, I would while away the time by noodling on the Steinway. Invariably, the Vassar lady of the house would appear in the doorway and call to me sternly, "Jack, stop banging. That's a Steinway, and it's just been tuned. If you want to play, take lessons."

Inadvertently, it was because of Sylvia that I was practically thrown out of school in my senior year. She and I had cooked up a little revue to present at one of the gym entertainments; she at the piano and I acting and singing. The details of that daring presentation escape my memory, but I dimly recall that one number required me to roll my pants up (yes, I was wearing long trousers by then), exposing my knobby knees and delivering some double-entendre ditty. We were a smash, and my next immediate booking was in the office of the dean of boys, where I was advised that I could finish my terms on probation; one more infraction and I would not receive a diploma. Sylvia was merely chastised by the dean of girls for having accompanied me. I was so upset that I quit Thomas Jefferson, found myself a job, went to evening classes at New Lots High (which was in the same building), and lost track of Sylvia for a number of years. In due time, I got my diploma and was valedictorian of my graduation class once more.

Years later, I was invited back to Thomas Jefferson High and presented to an auditorium full of kids as one of the successful alumni. I was there to deliver an inspirational address. Seated behind me was the principal, one or two of my old teachers, and that same, irascible dean of boys who had scared me out of school. I launched into my speech, sat down and played some of my songs, and concluded by telling the kids that I really had no idea what I was doing there—

and why I was not an alumnus of their school. The kids laughed and applauded, and my revenge on that dean was indeed sweet.

When I was going to night school, my day job was in Long Island City in the fuel-oil company that the Seven Schwartz Boys (my five cousins and two brothers) were operating. I had to rise at six-thirty every morning of that record freezing winter, drive to the oil plant with one of my brothers, and while he proceeded into office warmth, make my way to the work area alongside stinking, scummy Newtown Creek where the oil barges docked. The theory, as explained to me by my cousins and brothers, was that I was learning the oil business, which I hated, from the ground up.

In bulky, scratchy old clothes, I wrestled fifty-five-gallon steel drums filled to the brim and overflowing with gasoline. By noon each day, my clothes were sopping wet with perspiration and gasoline, and the smells, aches, and pains accompanied me home every night where Bobbeh and Mama would cluck over me sympathetically. I may have lasted about two months on that job until the gas spills produced burns and sores on my skinny frame, and Mama put her foot down.

That's when Papa made his famous remark about me. "He's too light for heavy work and too heavy for light work. Let him write songs!"

And I continued writing songs and saving them in my little rule-lined notebook. I began to feel like a line from a Coleridge poem: "A desert rose born to blush unseen."

CHAPTER FIVE

What Will I Tell My Heart?

There are two lines in the lyric of one of my hits, "What Will I Tell My Heart?" that I would like to quote because they are so appropriate to this chapter.

It's easy to lie to strangers . . .
But what will I tell my heart?

There's no easy way to gloss over what I have to say: I'm a homosexual. I have always hated the words "heterosexual" and "homosexual." They both sound obscene to me. And "gay" and "queer" seem equally repulsive. But since, to date, no better terms have been coined, I'll have to employ these old standbys. Most of the homosexuals I have known in my lifetime I would never label "gay." Many of my friends have been partnered in relationships that have lasted for more than forty years until separated by death. Mostly they are sober, hard-working citizens, usually involved in their communities, often devoting time, effort, and money to causes that might benefit their neighborhoods and mankind. It's odd that in all the reportage about homosexuals, very little mention is made about these long-term unions that have far outlasted many marriages. I feel quite strongly that at last, in some countries and even in a few of our own states, some civil and legal recognition is being given to homosexual and lesbian unions so that they now can enjoy equal-rights protection in all areas of life and death.

True, there are homosexuals who like to flaunt it, who love drag and street parades, who dance bare chested all night at discos. There are homosexuals who do drugs, who die of AIDS. But by the same token, there are equal numbers of heterosexuals who indulge in comparable behavior. Far be it from me to be judgmental. I was young once—young and frightened when I became aware of my homosexuality. I've described my Orthodox Jewish family and my immigrant parents. My two older brothers were five and six years my senior, closer to each other and very macho. In the parlance of the day, they were both known as big cocksmen. There was no one with whom I could discuss my feelings, so I tried to suppress them. I was thirteen when I first felt this overwhelming attraction to boys. At that tender age, I believe that most adolescents have homosexual tendencies, they indulge in soft-core pornography and mutual masturbation. In their youthful innocence, they see nothing wrong in such behavior. Some boys lose this innocence and age more rapidly than others. At least, that's the way it was in my youth. Perhaps none of this applies in today's life style of the young. I read about mere children, boys and girls, experimenting with sex, and thirteen-year-old baby girls giving birth to babies of their own.

Oh yes, I've been witness to many changes in the world during my long lifetime: telephones, airlines, radio, television, computers, space travel—and here we are in the twenty-first century. The prediction of things to come are mind boggling. So why should one be surprised at the changes in the world of sexuality? In my teens, it seemed as though everyone was in the closet. The words "homosexual" and "lesbian" were whispered, if talked about at all, and the media never printed them. There were titillating rumors about famous movie stars: Cary Grant, Ramon Navarro, Garbo; the list seemed endless, as did the explicit details of what these "queer" people did in bed. Guiltily, I, too participated in these rumors. Guiltily, because I had my own little secrets: an occasional tussle with school chums that I couldn't talk about, not even with the tusslee.

Unfortunately, we still live in a bigoted world where hatred is instilled by narrow-minded religious fanatics who have been known to beat young homosexuals to death. But I have been heartened to note a great change in the attitudes of educated young people. Many schools, colleges, and universities have programs today enlightening students about the world of homosexuality, explaining that it is not the illness it was once labeled, encouraging tolerance and approval of gay and lesbian gatherings. And I find that I am friends with bisexual men who, after years of marriage, divorce their wives and come out to their grown children without any loss of filial love or respect. None of these attitudes were possible, or even conceivable, in my teenage days. I created my own little secret world into which I could safely escape. I searched out and covertly read the few books that enlightened me, like Radclyffe Hall's lesbian novel *The Well of Loneliness*, and I shed empathetic tears at the heroine's trials and tribulations.

These were sad, lonely, angst-ridden years for me. I could not understand why I was born different from my brothers, different from boys my age. I crawled into and huddled in my little shell of a secret world. I felt no one would really understand what I was going through, and I cried in my loneliness. All these years later, I can still recall my feelings of emptiness and despair. I truly believed that somehow I had been marked and cursed, destined to a solitary life of misery. There was no one I could talk to, no one in whom I could confide. I tried hard to be like all the other boys.

Forcing myself into dating situations, I frequently found a girl for the weekend dances that took place in numerous neighborhood social cellar-clubs. Boys would get together and fix up somebody's available basement that had a street entrance. I tried hard to be one of the guys and join their activities. Furniture for these clubs would usually consist of discarded couches that the Sanitation Department had not yet collected. To create a romantic atmosphere, lighting was made extremely dim, and a Victrola or table record player would blast out all the songs of the day: "Ma! He's Makin' Eyes at Me," "Whispering," "When I Take My Sugar to Tea." Wonderful songs with a strong dance beat. We would sing along as we did spins and dips and acrobatic moves where you actually swung your partner up and off the floor. Of course, we held contests and awarded prizes.

Club members and popular girls never had to pay admission. Outsiders contributed a quarter, which entitled you to one Dixie cup of some sweetish concoction called punch. All the boys lied about their sexual conquests, including me. When you had walked a girl home after the dance and you had managed a French kiss and copped a feel of her budding breasts, the next night you would brag to the boys that she had "put out" for you. Based on these reports, girls were labeled "hot" or "cold." I had a lot of girl cousins my age, and I had to shlep them to these dances so that they could meet boys. But they were quickly dubbed "cold," so I usually ended up dancing with them all night. Some of the larger clubs could afford to pay an entertainer on a Saturday night. These were wannabe crooners or local talents trying out comedy routines. In retrospect, it was an innocent age—no drugs, no muggings, no murders. Maybe once in a while, the members of rival clubs would get into a verbal insult contest, but rarely into fisticuffs.

So there I was, living my double life, trying to be one of the boys and conforming to what was considered normal behavior. I was naïve enough to believe that my secret desires were unusual, that I was one of a kind, that I should feel ashamed. But it wasn't too long before I discovered two boys my age who were also suppressing homosexual tendencies and trying to conform. Finally, I had some chums in whom I could confide and discuss our mutual longings. The three of us had not the slightest idea where to go, what to do, or how to satisfy those longings. I was not sexually attracted to either of them. From my point of view, they were too effeminate. But they remained good friends and a comfortable outlet for frank discussions.

Then, at age seventeen, I found the hidden world I had been seeking—in Harlem! I had met an older man, all of twenty-three, who introduced me to what were known as "rent parties." These affairs were organized by either black or white gays who rented seedy apartments in Harlem for weekend gatherings. For seventy-five cents or a dollar, you gained entry to a dark living room furnished very much like my neighborhood cellar clubs, with sagging upholstered furniture and a record player. The admission fee entitled you to one watered-down gin drink and all-night dancing with the male guests. If you were lucky, you might meet an attractive number who invited you up to his one-room pad for sex. I have since learned that there were gay bars scattered around the city in out-of-the-way places, but I was not aware of them.

Harlem, however, was wide open. Whites and blacks mixed freely in places like the Savoy Ballroom. There was no dissension, no name calling, no fights, no resentments. At least, that's how I remember it. I frequented Harlem without fear. I walked the streets safely, unaware that there were wonderful small bars that had jazz groups and entertainers like Billie Holiday and handsome, honey-colored Jimmy Daniels, who liked men. But I did find the Apollo Theater and its amateur nights where many future stars were discovered.

And every Thanksgiving, Phil Black, an elegant colored man, gave a huge drag ball in an upstairs ballroom on Lenox Avenue. This annual event was famous and drew not only the gay world, but the downtown elite and sophisticates. Both white and black men would appear in the most elaborate feather boas, and tiaras and sequins were *de rigueur*. The highlight of the evening was the finale, a parade across the stage and prizes for the most flamboyant drag. Strangely enough, dressing up as a woman never appealed to me, although for those who went to great lengths and made their own elaborate costumes, it was wonderful fun.

I endured many a scolding for getting home to Brooklyn in the wee hours, sometimes late in the morning, and I became quite adept at inventing explanations. I should add that in those days, we indulged in sex freely, our only fears being gonorrhea or syphilis if we weren't careful. And crab-lice in the groin, no matter what precautions we took. But that dreadful plague, AIDS, would not be upon us for another fifty years.

The word "cruising" came into fashion at this time, and I exploited it. My next big discovery was Central Park at night where it was safe to cruise other young men who hid in the shadows, sending out signals from a glowing cigarette. The only fear was the occasional cop who patrolled the park. Another promising cruising spot I eventually found was the roof garden of the New Amsterdam Theater on Forty-second Street, which had been converted to showing films. The roof garden was set up in cabaret style with small round tables and bentwood chairs that were movable when you spotted an attractive face. One night a handsome gentleman moved his chair closer to mine. In due time, I learned that he was Belgian, had come to America as an actor, had played the lead on Broadway in *Seventh Heaven*, which was later made into a sweet Hollywood film starring Janet Gaynor and Charles Farrell.

My Belgian (I'll call him René) had decided to remain in New York and was now a successful antiques dealer. His apartment, on the first floor of a classic limestone building in the East Fifties, was also his showroom. The rear windows faced the rear of a speakeasy from which dance music emanated through the late hours. Years later I learned that this speakeasy had been the forerunner of what became Club 21. René was in his youthful forties, and I was an adult eighteen, but still Brooklyn naïve, a tall, gangly, wide-eyed boy who had read a lot and dreamed a lot and was completely open to life. I was like a sponge absorbing every new experience and reveling in it. Here I was, thrust suddenly into a world I'd never known, and René seemed to take great delight in introducing me—to French antiques and bibelots in his showroom, to fashionable cafés and restaurants in the city, to menus I had never heard of and which my high school French couldn't translate. He was a kindly, considerate teacher and an expert lover, and I drank it all in like a hungry child. For almost a year, I spent every weekend with my mentor in this new environment that had opened my eyes, my ears, and my heart.

I was tasting other worlds, other fruits, other lives, and choosing the best of it all with which to adorn my own needy existence. Yes, I was still living a double life, lying to my family and friends, going on dates with girls, pretending I was as straight as my brothers.

But I'm moving ahead of myself.

Although this "coming out" process seems to have happened overnight, it was really a long, slow, painful, doubt-ridden time with many highs and lows. At times I despaired about my homosexuality, cursed whatever it was that made me different. And at other times, I would feel as though what was happening to me was the most natural thing in the world. But all that is in retrospect.

Today it seems almost impossible for me to convey the pain, the torturous days and sleepless nights, the unhappiness and the tears. Worst of all was the loneliness, the knowing that there was not a soul I could talk to about my "affliction." For that is what it seemed to me, and nothing I heard or read made it appear anything less than an incurable disease.

Somehow, I learned to cope.

CHAPTER SIX

Jack of All Trades

It was shortly after that I met my first collaborator, Arthur Altman, who was a year my senior and lived not too far away with his parents, who ran a candy store. He was about as far advanced musically on the violin as was I on the piano. We both faked a lot.

He had been writing songs with a school chum who lived around the corner from me, Barry Hyams, the son of a local rabbi. Some years later, Barry married impresario Sol Hurok's daughter and became a publicity rep for his father-in-law. His son, Peter Hyams, has had a successful career as a film director and producer.

Arthur and I met as fraternity brothers. How that came about, I can't explain since neither of us had gone to college at that time. But it was an age of all sorts of fraternal organizations with initiations, rules, and dues. Not many of us could afford college, so we invented these local social clubs much in the manner of today's street gangs—but not with the same intent. As I mentioned before, these clubs existed in rehabilitated Brooklyn cellars, and their entertainment evenings spawned many a future star such as Phil Silvers and Danny Kaye, who went on to perfect their talents in the Catskills—or the Borscht Circuit, as it was commonly called. Why the Borscht Circuit rather than the Matzoh Ball Mountains, I never did discover. But it was an area close to New York City that had achieved great popularity with Jewish families in the early twenties.

The Borscht Circuit all started with what were known as *kuch-a-lains*, large farmhouses that rented out rooms to families who shared kitchen privileges. Mama would rent one of these rooms for the summer, take me and my younger brother, Murray, and Papa would come up from the city on weekends. In time, grand hotels to accommodate young people proliferated, like Brown's, the Nevele, and more elaborate conglomerates like Grossinger's.

I, too, had a fling at a Borscht Circuit job when I was about sixteen. I organized a band that consisted of piano, drums, and one fiddle and talked us into a summer stint at Schmuloff's Fallsburgh Hotel. Well, it was more a farm than a hotel. We were supposed to play for ten weeks through Labor Day and were promised fifty dollars each for the season plus room and board. Armed with this letter of employment, I made the rounds of all the publishers and collected free orchestrations—which did our trio very little good since none of us could really read music. But those orchestrations looked impressive and professional when spread out for playing.

We arrived at Schmuloff's and discovered to our disgust that our housing consisted of a cell upstairs in the barn, the downstairs being occupied by Schmuloff's cows and chickens. The hotel was a rickety wooden building, a potential firetrap that housed twenty-five families during season. The "casino" for concerts and dancing was merely the large dining room, which we had the job of converting by shoving all the tables and chairs against the wall after dinner—which was known as "suppa." We musicians were also required to act as busboys, carrying out the dishes, moving the furniture, and finally supplying the music and entertainment.

All those popular songs we had rehearsed went for naught. Schmuloff's clientele wanted only fraylachs, klezmer songs or Yiddish tearjerkers like "My Yiddishe Mama" or "Shtane, Shtane, Tiyurah Shtane"—which translates literally into "Stone, Stone, Memorial Stone (Once You Used to Be My Mother)." A heart-breaker!

To add to our woes, Schmuloff was having a bad, rainy season topped by a small fire. Just before Labor Day, we were tipped off by one of his relatives (a niece I had been summer romancing) that we were not going to get our promised money. The drummer packed and left, and I was stuck with a tearful fiddle player who called his father to come and take him home.

But I was the leader of the band and had to act. Fortunately, the hotel was booked to overflowing that last summer weekend, so I confronted Schmuloff, who wasn't aware that I had already lost my two musicians. Either we got our money in advance or we would quit. No pay—no play! Schmuloff screamed and threw things at me, but in the end, with many a Yiddish curse, he paid.

Many books and plays have been written about the Borscht Circuit and its hotels. They were the proving ground for singers and comics who went on to stardom. On our one night a week off from Schmuloff's, we would make the rounds of neighboring hotels like Grossinger's to catch new talents like Milton Berle and others known as *tummlers* (noisemakers), whose job it was to keep the guests laughing, introduce the acts, dance with the homely girls, and organize the day's activities. Anything and everything went as long as the guests were not bored. Young people did not come to the Catskills for a rest. Girls were looking for husbands, and boys were looking to make out. Aside from the *tummlers,* there were future doctors and lawyers earning tuition as waiters and busboys. Any passable youngster with strong gonads could sleep in a different bed every night as long as there were lonely wives and his stamina lasted. The 1930s in that mountain playground was an experience not to be forgotten.

My Catskill adventure helped considerably when Arthur and I teamed up and began writing songs, I at the piano, he at the fiddle, both of us harmonizing the lyrics. We made a thorough study of the popular music of the day, analyzing the construction of each song, trying to determine what made them great hits. My idols whom I studied assiduously were Larry Hart, Ira Gershwin, and Cole Porter. I admired their sophistication, the clever inner rhymes, the way each lyric told a complete story—beginning, middle, and end. Here's some smart inner-rhyming by Larry Hart, who wrote at that time with Richard Rodgers.

Once I laughed when I heard you saying
That I'd be playing solitaire,
Uneasy in my easy chair,
It never entered my mind.
Once you warned me that if you scorned me
I'd sing the maiden's prayer again
And wish that you were there again
To get into my hair again,
It never entered my mind.

And look how cleverly Ira Gershwin handles inner rhymes.

I could cry salty tears
Where have I been all these years?
Little wow, tell me now:
How long has this been going on?
Kiss me once then once more,
What a dunce I was before,
What a break, for heaven's sake
How long has this been going on?

Naturally, I tried hard to emulate their lyrics and despaired that I lacked the schooling and knowledge these college men had acquired. So I doubled my reading efforts and kept a notebook with phrases and ideas for songs. Arthur and I wrote a variety of ballads and novelty tunes and kept looking for some way into the music business. Once or twice, we got as far as a publisher's door, but were too intimidated to follow through. We felt we needed some personal contact.

By then I had found a new job as an usher in the rococo Brooklyn Paramount Theater, where I could watch all the latest films and vaudeville headliners every week. I confess that my sex life took a sudden spurt those days, what with the willing and attractive ushers who were my coworkers.

When I learned that a famous singer, Ruth Etting, was scheduled for an appearance at the Paramount, Arthur and I quickly got to work and dashed off a song that might suit her style. She had a low, velvety voice with a tear in it as she sang her hits, "Ten Cents a Dance" and "Love Me or Leave Me." Arthur and I were positive that our brainchild, "Easy Goin' Woman," would captivate her and start us on our careers. There was only one small hitch—how to get her to listen.

This seemed an insurmountable problem as I quickly discovered that the lady was well guarded. Her protector, known respectfully in gangland as "the Colonel" or Colonel Snyder (an appellation he had earned along with a permanently injured leg in gang wars) was better known to the police as "the Gimp." When the Colonel was not around, there were guards outside her dressing room. Daily I bided my time, watched, and waited for an opportunity.

One day I was rewarded. Miss Etting came in alone and smiled at me as she made her way to the dressing room. Nowhere could I spot the Colonel or his soldiers. Nervously I knocked at Miss

Etting's door, entered at her invitation, and held out my manuscript with the explanation that it had been written expressly for her. She was all graciousness, pretty to look at although a bit subdued in manner, and asked me to play the song on the spinet in her dressing room. I was halfway through the first chorus when the door burst open, and the Gimp stood there.

"Who the hell is this punk?" He scowled at me. "What're ya doin' here?"

"He's one of the ushers," Miss Etting tried to explain nervously. "He wrote this song for me. It's not bad . . ."

"Where're my boys? How'd ya get in here? What song?" growled the Colonel as he grabbed my manuscript off the piano. "EASY GOIN' WOMAN!" he barked. "Whaddya think Ruth Etting is . . . a HOOR? Git outta here before I . . ."

I never did hear what he intended to do to me because I was out of that dressing room long before the threat was uttered. For the remainder of Miss Etting's booking, I made myself scarce in the dark shadows of the upper balcony. I had visions of myself as one of gangland's casualties so frequently being reported in the *Daily News*.

It all came back to me vividly and clearly years later while watching Doris Day as a wholesome Ruth Etting singing all those wonderful songs while her fearsome protector, the Gimp, played by James Cagney, clomped around.

Our "hoor" song, "Easy Goin' Woman," never did get published, and my songwriting debut seemed as far away as a visit to Timbuktu. Yet I never lost faith in myself. I knew that some day I'd find the right key and open the right door to that world I dreamed about.

CHAPTER SEVEN

The Doors Begin to Open

Now that I had my high school diploma, my parents started badgering me to go to college. They wanted at least one of the four of us to become a professional something—doctor, lawyer, dentist, anything! I was the perfect candidate. Didn't I prefer books and learning to hard work? "Too heavy for light work, etc!" Wouldn't I like to be a professional somebody? I said all I wanted to be was a songwriter.

"A songwriter! A bum! So why can't you be a doctor or a lawyer and a songwriter, too? Meyer Gusman, the corner drugstore's brother—he's a dentist, and he writes songs on the side. He's got now a beautiful song, 'Underneath the Russian Moon.' So at least, go be a dentist!"

By 1931 our country had endured ten years of Republican presidents, starting with the corrupt administration of Warren Harding, followed by Calvin Coolidge, whose fiscal policies brought us to ruin with the Big Crash of 1929. Then we drifted along for another four years under Herbert Hoover. The country was in a deep depression, but that didn't deter my parents from urging me to become some sort of professional.

Arthur and I were having no luck with our songs. We couldn't even get past the front door of publishers' offices. Finally my parents' arguments wore me down when my brother, Joe, came up with a clincher that sent me back to school. Before the fuel-oil business, in his final years as a shoe salesman, he had organized their union and been elected president. Fastenberg's, the chic store on Delancey Street in Lower Manhattan where he was working at the time, had its own resident chiropodist, Dr. Arthur Gold, a handsome young man. From Dr. Gold, my brother had learned that chiropody was more than corn cutting. At that time, it took only two years to complete the course; it was a well-paying profession; and if I required further convincing, it was the saga of Dr. Gold's success. He had made a radical move from that shoe store to an office in Hollywood. In no time at all, one of his famous patients, the MGM star Jean Harlow, had taken a shine to handsome Arthur Gold and financed his ownership of a medical building in Beverly Hills. Immediately, I pictured myself as a white-coated doctor of chiropody, occupying a sumptuous suite of offices on Broadway with a Steinway grand in my antique-furnished reception room with a roster of theater stars as patients. In between corn-cutting appointments, I would be writing songs and sing my ditties to those stars before, during, or after treatments. A captive audience. How could I miss?

As a nineteen-year-old high-school graduate, I did not quite meet the minimum educational requirements of the First

Institute of Podiatry, which was located on 124th Street and Madison Avenue in Harlem. However, my brother, Joe, the b.s. artist with the gift of gab, was most persuasive. He pulled the proper strings on the admittance board, and I was enrolled. With the opening of the 1931 semester, I found myself making the hour-and-a-half subway trip from and to home each day. My curriculum was intense, but fascinating. Into a short, two-year course was crammed an entire medical training: pharmacology, osteopathy, anatomy, cadaver dissection at the morgue downtown, along with a second year of practical internship at the institute's free clinic. Today, to earn that same podiatry degree, it takes almost as long as a medical course.

In the limited time between classes, clinics, and studying, my collaborator and I kept meeting, exchanging ideas, and writing songs, constantly wracking our brains for some way to break into Tin Pan Alley. In those days, publishers, performing artists, and record companies were not at all receptive to neophyte songwriters. How different from the scene today. Youngsters squawking unintelligible gibberish have been petted, pampered, praised, and paid exorbitant sums once they show signs of becoming stars who sell records. Singers who can't sing are electronically produced by modern studio equipment. They are then diligently trained in acrobatic movements representing choreography so that they can make public appearances. Since their "choreography" must be perfectly coordinated, they can't possibly sing and jump around at the same time, so often they lip-sync to their recorded music, and kids who pay high prices to attend rock concerts really don't know the difference. Stars flash in the night, light up the sky, and disappear as quickly as a falling nova. Their overnight hits are soon forgotten.

In this category, I do not include true talents: Bob Dylan, Carly Simon, Paul Simon, Judy Collins. Jimmy Webb, and the Beatles, who have contributed everlasting standards that will long be loved and remembered. But how will the rap music of today enlighten the mind, add to our culture, and find its way into people's memories and hearts the way Gershwin, Kern, and Porter have? Or is this all part of the fifteen minutes of fame that Andy Warhol consigned to all of us?

I am cognizant of the fact that musical tastes have changed radically, that there is a great deal more freedom of expression lyrically than in my day, that rappers can vilify police and women and sell millions of records. But I doubt that today's output will ever replace the Golden Age of Rodgers and Hart or Hammerstein, and Mercer and Arlen, and one of the recent great talents to emerge on the Broadway scene, Stephen Sondheim.

Now that I've got that off my chest—back to my budding career in the thirties. Arthur and I tried every approach we could think of and followed any suggestion or slim lead, but to no avail. Manuscripts were sent to publishers and artists by the dozen, and when we remembered to include an SASE, our songs were returned unopened. When we heard of someone in our neighborhood who had a relative—no matter how distant—a singer, a bandleader, or anyone connected somehow to the music business, we wangled invitations to meet them. Unfortunately, no one in Brooklyn seemed to be related to any of the stars of the day like Rudy Vallee, Morton Downey, or Paul Whiteman.

Still, we kept writing. Even for shows being planned in union halls and synagogues. My Uncle Max tipped us off to one such show, and we met with the producer. He said he was looking for a minor-key torch song for a production he had in mind, so Arthur and I concocted a weeper.

> WHAT CAN I DO?
> I depended on you alone,
> Now that we're through
> Tell me what can I do?

The melody for those lachrymose words was a paraphrase of an old Russian tune Mama was always humming titled "Viyet Viyetri" or "Stormy Breezes." We were certain we had written a hit, but that union show never materialized.

One day my brother, Harvey, brought home a new date in whom he seemed interested: Bessie Liebowitz, a piano teacher. Mama gave her critique. "Is dyed blonde the hair! Her mother is fat? I'm not surprised. This kind girl gets fat after only one baby. Is only one good thing for her I can say—she's Jewish!"

Mama was definitely not interested, but I was, particularly when I learned that Bessie had a violinist friend on the staff at Columbia Broadcasting. Did she know him well? Certainly! She used to be his accompanist in Brooklyn before he joined CBS. Could she arrange an audition? No problem!

Too soon, Harvey's interest in Bessie cooled, so it became a bit more difficult to keep her to her promise. My constant nagging resulted in a definite date. Arthur and I settled on six of our strongest songs and nervously went to our appointment at CBS studios on the corner of East Fifty-second Street and Madison Avenue. A page ushered us into a small studio where four musicians sat around a table playing pinochle. They were a string ensemble, as evidenced by the violins and cello spread around the studio. This was 1932, and radio was in its infancy.

Bessie's friend called to us. "Wait'll we finish this hand, boys. Then we'll talk." He was an attractive man in his late twenties with a luxuriant mane of dark, wavy hair ending in a widow's peak on the forehead. He had a romantic look that fit his name and designation like a glove: Emery Deutsch, the Gypsy Violinist.

At the conclusion of the card game, Emery approached and explained that we were not to mind frequent interruptions from the control booth. In those early days of radio communication, remote pickup programs were not yet being timed accurately. For example, a speech from Washington was liable to end suddenly at any given fraction of the hour. For that reason, the home-base station of each network kept standby musicians or singers in a studio to fill in the time whenever the control booth gave a red signal. At such a signal, the standbys would drop whatever they were doing and start performing. In such a manner, Emery and his Gypsy strings might be called upon to fill in many incomplete hours. The group had an extensive repertoire of Gypsy czardas and light classics such as "Frasquita's Serenade," "The Glow Worm," "The Skater's Waltz," "The Bells of St. Mary's"—works they could rattle off from memory at the drop of a hat or the red alert. Emery cautioned us that when the red "ON AIR" signal flashed, we were to remain silent until they were through playing and the green "OFF AIR" flashed on.

"Bessie tells me you boys write great songs. Play some for me now. But remember, watch for the red light!"

At last! Our big chance! Quickly we launched into the first number—only to be cut off by the red signal after a few bars. We sat by silently while the Gypsy Strings performed. In this manner, it took us two hours to get through our six numbers. Those Gypsy Strings never repeated the same selection or played longer than ten to forty seconds. Finally we were ready for the maestro's verdict.

"I'll tell you, boys . . . you write nice songs. But I don't see how I can help you. Emery Deutsch and his Gypsy Strings have to play appropriate stuff. I don't play pop music. If you can come up with something—a song that fits our style—well, maybe I can at least play it for you."

Discouraging! But for us the most encouragement from a performing professional to date. And one that was on the air! We went home determined to create something for the Gypsies. That night I couldn't sleep. I was supposed to study for an important exam the next day. But instead of my *Gray's Anatomy*, rhymes, ideas, and tunes kept cluttering my head, each being considered and discarded.

Let's see, I thought to my sleepless self, Emery Deutsch and his Gypsy Strings—those schmaltzy tunes he was playing, mostly on the G string—sobbing, pleading melodies. We should be able to come up with something similar, a melody like that minor tune we wrote for the union show that never happened, "What Can I Do?" " I depended on you alone"—that's the kind of melody he'd like. Hey! What's wrong with that one? It sounds like a Gypsy song—except for the words. But suppose . . .

At three in the morning, I telephoned Arthur, woke his family, apologized, and got him out of a sound sleep. "I GOT IT! I GOT IT! Remember 'What Can I Do?'"

Arthur yawned. "Yeah, but that's not a Gypsy song . . ."

"Wait!" I shouted. "Listen to this!" I began to sing the lyrics I had been working on. "Play, fiddle, play . . . play my loved one a melody . . ."

"That's it, Jack! You've done it!" He was wide awake now. "We can give it a real Gypsy verse. That's it!"

"We can clean up the chorus and knock off a verse tomorrow. Make it early."

"But what about your anatomy exam?"

"Screw the exam! I'll call in sick. This is too important."

The next afternoon, we rushed to the CBS studios, eager to see Emery with our freshly baked Gypsy number. This was the verse and chorus:

> Now the Gypsy band rest their caravan
> Where the hills conceal the sun,
> Dusky magic falls, gypsy music calls,
> Calls to lovers one by one;
> A lover strums his fiddle while he hums this little
>   song . . .
> M mm m m m m m
> This is his song . . . mm mm mmm mmmm . . .

Chorus:
PLAY, FIDDLE, PLAY
Play my loved one a melody,
Sing to my love while the stars swing above,
PLAY, FIDDLE, PLAY
Sing my loved one a rhapsody,
Play on the strings of her heart,
The campfires are gleaming as red as the sun,

And my heart keeps dreaming, just dreaming of
   one,
So softly croon while the moon
Weaves our two hearts in harmony,
PLAY, FIDDLE, PLAY to my love.

It was an instant success with Emery and his Gypsies. They crowded around us at the piano, picked up their fiddles, and improvised an arrangement as we swung into a second chorus.

"Congratulations, boys. That song is for me!" said Emery.

"Can you get it published?" we asked breathlessly.

"Can I get it published? All the publishers owe me. I play lots of their music. All we gotta do is pick the right firm."

We left our lead sheet of the song so that he could have an arrangement made and floated home on the BMT subway to Brooklyn in a pink haze. Arthur was making plans to marry Matilda, his childhood sweetheart, and I was debating whether I even wanted to go back to the First Institute of Podiatry—much less finish the course.

"Whoa!" I said. "Maybe this song won't be as big as we expect. After all, a Gypsy song—and a waltz—that's kind of special."

"No matter!" said Arthur. "At least it will open doors for us. Anyway, I promised Tillie the day my first song gets published, we'll get married. You ought to find a steady girl, too. It's time you had someone."

I couldn't tell Arthur. Never had discussed my secret life with him. In those days, homosexuality was never talked about. And as close as we were, I somehow doubt that Arthur would have understood. He was a nice boy, but really kind of square. Had I confessed to him at that time, it surely would have shocked him.

So to cover up, I said, "Girls! Who's got time for that? You know what my family will say when I come home and tell them about today? 'Fine! So get your degree, and be a doctor. One song doesn't make a whole living. When you're not selling songs, you'll need something solid. A good profession!'"

More or less, that was, indeed, what my family did say when I came home bursting with the news. I returned to the institute. Besides, the course had been paid in advance by my father and brothers, and a dollar was a commodity we had been brought up never to waste. Yes, I did get my degree in 1932 and paid the two-dollar license fee that enabled me to practice. And although I never did open an office, year after year, while I kept writing and publishing hit songs, my mother kept renewing that license. Religiously, she never forgot to send that two-dollar renewal fee to Albany. Just in case! You never can tell when . . .

Before my graduation, my first song had a contract to be published. And even though I never practiced podiatry, you can call me doctor.

And my family was right—one song doesn't make a living. But my first published song introduced me to intricacies of the music business that very few young writers experience.

CHAPTER EIGHT

Published At Last

Nineteen thirty-two was a landmark year in all our lives, not mine alone. On my birthday, April 7, President Roosevelt made one of his most important campaign speeches and introduced the phrase "the forgotten man." In that same Depression year, he was swept into the White House on an overwhelming tide of votes as our thirty-second president. Almost immediately, once in office, he declared a bank holiday and instituted measures to stabilize the economy. That following year, Prohibition, speakeasies, and racketeering were done away with, and the country was singing "Happy Days Are Here Again."

Radio City Music Hall opened its doors to an Art Deco interior, and a man who was to play a vital part in my career, Walter Winchell, celebrated his birthday on the same day as mine and started his radio broadcasts to the public: "Good evening, Mr. and Mrs. America and all the ships at sea . . . "

And Emery Deutsch, the Gypsy fiddler who was going to lead Arthur and me to fame and fortune, quickly discovered that he was small fry in the music business. All those publishers he claimed owed him favors didn't seem to know it. He had neglected to tell us that many of them paid him a small stipend for playing their material, and in their minds, that canceled any debt. We three—Emery, Arthur, and I—made the rounds of music offices for months with discouraging results.

I recall some of the comments thrown at us. "Nobody dances to waltzes." "That kinda song is a ballbreaker." "A minor melody—and a waltz yet. Feh!" That should convey some idea of the classy publishers who ran the music business. Valiantly, the three of us continued, Emery even lugging his violin along to bolster our demonstrations.

The following is typical of the reactions we encountered. We were in a publisher's office. The firm was new and small. The man who ran it, George Marlo, was small of body and mind. The only big thing around was his oversized cigar, which he was able to afford due to his current, medium hit called "Home." We had just concluded our song—at least he had allowed us the courtesy of finishing, unlike other publishers.

George slowly removed the big cigar from his lips, flicked the ashes carefully on the floor, replaced the cigar, and spoke out of one side of his mouth. "What kind cockamamie song is that?

Who the hell is gonna sing about a fiddle? Bring me a song like—
and in a raucous voice he spread his arms wide and bellowed:

> "When shadows fall and boids whisper night is ending
> My thoughts are ever wending . . . HOME!"

He glared at us. "That's a song! That's what people wanna sing
about—wending HOME!"

Similar routines were repeated at other offices, the only varia-
tion being each firm's respective hit song. I was still in great awe
of these powerful tycoon publishers, little realizing what shallow,
crass, unmusical, but shrewd deal makers most of them were.
Traits they seemed to have in common: they were supersalesmen,
connivers, manipulators, and would have been equally successful
selling toilet fixtures—an area in which many of them would
have felt more at home.

All those months, while we had been making the rounds,
Emery and his Gypsy Strings had been playing our song at every
available opportunity when the red alert flashed and they took to
the air. As a result of these repeated performances, a strange phenomenon was taking place. Letters were trickling in to CBS,
some addressed to Emery, others to the station, all with the same
request. "What's the name of that song? Why don't you ever play
it all the way through? Why doesn't somebody sing it?"

Now Emery was truly frustrated. He felt he had a potential hit
on his hands, but his standby moments didn't permit him to fin-

ish the song or give its title. Finally, he was able to persuade two of CBS's singers with fifteen-minute programs, the tenor Ben Alley and Irené Wicker, billed as the Singing Lady, to sing "Play, Fiddle, Play." Those few airings brought even more complimentary fan mail.

Emery gathered all this mail and rushed off to an old-time publisher with a successful firm that bore his name, Edward B. Marks. Mr. Marks was a distinguished-looking man in his seventies who had been a writer and publisher since the 1890s. But this elegant, upright gentleman was not above chicanery, as I soon learned to my dismay.

E. B. Marks dealt mainly in concert songs and light classics by such composers as Rudolph Friml, Ernest Lecuona, and Fritz Kreisler. Emery, for a small, weekly bribe, performed much of this material, which is why he felt that this firm was his last hope. It was not our song that convinced Mr. Marks, but the letters Emery displayed. So finally, as a favor and with a promise from Emery to perform even more of the Marks catalog, our "Fiddle" song was taken for publication. Arthur brought me the good and bad news, which he had to deliver through the closed bedroom window of my house where I had been quarantined by the Board of Health. This twenty-year-old, about-to-be published songwriter had scarlet fever.

The "good news" was the impending publication of our song. The "bad news," Mr. Marks had told Arthur that (a) Emery Deutsch was more important than Arthur Altman and Jack

Lawrence combined, therefore (b) Emery's name would appear in larger type as the composer, and (c) our names would be lumped in tandem as the lyricists, and (d) Emery would receive two-thirds of the royalties, and we would split one third.

I screamed through my scarlet fever, "Never! I'm not giving our song away. Tell them both to drop dead."

But Arthur, tears running down his face, pleaded with me. This was our first big chance. We had waited so long. We would write many more songs. It was only for the first song. Then the *coup de grâce*. He and Tillie had already set their wedding date.

I fumed and fussed, but in the end I surrendered—with one stipulation: Either Arthur or I were to share composing credits with that bastard Gypsy fiddler. That was the only way that we could establish that we were capable of writing words and music. Outside my window, Arthur tossed a coin to determine which one of us would share the composing credit, and I lost, thereby becoming the lyricist.

The published version of our song came out late in 1933 with a huge blowup of Emery's face on the cover and his name twice the size of ours. How well I remember the excitement of those days and the sleepless nights when my family and I were literally glued to our new De Forest radio cabinet, switching from station to station and charting the number of times we caught a rendition of the song. From Columbus, Ohio! From Chicago! From Kansas City! My brother, Harvey, gave up all his girlfriends, temporarily, staying home nights while we both switched from channel to channel until we scored another performance. Big bands and their singers from every part of the country. "Play, Fiddle, Play" coming from all directions. The middle of the night was the best time for listening because then we were able to get direct broadcasts from the farthest distances: the Coconut Grove in Los Angeles and the Fairmount Hotel in San Francisco. These evenings at home were the closest relationship I had ever had with one of my older brothers. Joe, the oldest, had already married and was in his own home.

It's difficult for me to convey the excitement, the pride of achievement that the success of that first published song brought to me and my loved ones. But the ultimate thrill for Bobbeh, Mama, and Papa was when they heard Herman Yablokoff, known as the Jewish Minstrel, singing "Play, Fiddle, Play" in Yiddish!

Our song was selling well in both sheet music and recordings, and although we weren't earning much money, Arthur and Tillie got married, and I contracted for that Steinway rebuilt grand I had once promised myself. It was the beginning of a career, but far from the end of "Play, Fiddle, Play."

CHAPTER NINE

—And Sued!

Aplagiarism suit from out of the blue, especially when you know it has no merit, is the bane of any creator's existence. Literally anyone can bring such a suit against an inventor, an author of books, a producer of films, or a songwriter. There are many songwriter suits for plagiarism because everyone believes himself capable of writing a song. It's easy! You can make one up singing in the shower.

Laws that were written for the protection of the creator's rights inadvertently create injustices. Many a hungry attorney will take a plagiarism case on a contingency basis even when there is little or no reason for the suit, merely in hopes of achieving a nuisance-value settlement. Unfortunately, I have been involved in two such suits, neither of which had a valid claim, but still cost me money. Even if you win eventually, there are always attorneys' fees that escalate. Many writers I know have suffered similar traumatic experiences.

Here's an illustration of what can happen. Some guy in Pipsqueak, Wytona, makes up a song while performing his daily toilette, gets a musician friend to scratch out a lead sheet that is a single melody line, with or without chords indicated. He then Xeroxes fifty copies and mails them out to publishers and singers indiscriminately. Most of his copies are returned unopened if he has included an SASE. The rest wind up in the rubbish. One day a friend or relative hears a big, new hit on the air and rushes to the guy with the news. "Hey! I just heard your song! It's changed a bit . . . different words, too . . . but it sounded just like yours."

Oddly enough, very few suits are brought against songs that aren't hits. Our pipsqueak composer buys a copy of the hit song and by stretching his imagination, convinces himself that, indeed, they stole his opus. He then finds a lawyer who reads up on the copyright and plagiarism laws, agrees to handle the case on a fifty-fifty contingency basis, first insisting on an initial down payment and subsequent costs, all to be prorated when the suit is won. A smart lawyer then gets an injunction against the local radio or TV station prohibiting the airing of that hit song.

Many TV and radio stations are part of a network, so you can imagine what the results of such an injunction can be. The local station notifies the network, which puts the record company and publisher on notice, and panic ensues. It is not only unprofitable, but almost impossible, to stop the momentum of a hit until the lawsuit finds its way to a crowded court calendar in whatever town the suit has been instituted. The publisher must immediately indemnify the networks so that the hit remains on the air.

Then the publisher calls in the original writers and spells it out. "I agree that there's no basis for this claim—the other song sounds nothing like yours. But what are we supposed to do? Your song is hot now. Let's find out how little we'll have to pay the bastard to call him off."

A settlement is arrived at, and the writer discovers that the "we" the publisher referred to is "he." Since the contract he signed originally indemnified the publisher against all plagiarism suits, not only is the writer stuck for the full amount of the settlement, but sometimes he pays the fee for the publisher's attorney who made the settlement. There are shyster lawyers all over the country who specialize in such and similar cases, and there are paranoid wannabe writers who sue repeatedly.

One such paranoid "suer" of hit songs was an addled little man called Ira Arnstein who brought grief and loss of money to many legitimate songwriters in the thirties. This man would parade on Sixth Avenue in front of the ASCAP offices then located there with a sandwich sign that read, front and back:

I, IRA ARNSTEIN

Claim that my songs have been stolen by
the following ASCAP writers

VICTOR HERBERT	IRVING BERLIN
JEROME KERN	SIGMUND ROMBERG
GEORGE GERSHWIN	RODGERS AND HART
HAROLD ARLEN	HARRY WARREN

Well, he showed good taste! He had picked the crème de la crème of the music business.

In 1934 when "Play, Fiddle, Play" was at the height of its popularity, Emery Deutsch's name was added to that distinguished list by Arnstein. Our publisher knew that Arnstein was a nut who had never won a single case and decided to let the suit proceed. It did not reach the court until the following year, and then, unfortunately, it was set for the July calendar in the Federal District Court, presided over by a judge from Colorado who had been brought to New York because of a shortage of federal judges. Our song had become so big that the case attracted all the newspapers, and the judge from Colorado, who had never handled a plagiarism suit, enjoyed the publicity. He let it run almost a month.

While a writer is only as good as his last hit, a performer can become an overnight star with the same song. Emery Deutsch was now a star. Not only had he moved up to a network program with a large orchestra, but he had replaced a popular maestro, Dave Rubinoff, in the pit of the Broadway Paramount. Gypsies and fiddles were suddenly big that year. There was Rubinoff and Harry Horlick with the A & P Gypsies, and Phil Spitalny featuring "Evelyn and her Magic Violin." And they all performed "Play, Fiddle, Play." Our song even made its way into the all-star MGM blockbuster, *Dinner at Eight*, with Marie Dressler, Wallace Beery, Jean Harlow, John Barrymore, and more. And Arthur and I were still earning pennies as our share because of the unfair contract we had been coerced into signing.

Arnstein's suit was fascinating. He accused Emery and E. B. Marks of stealing his song and never mentioned Arthur or me, the true writers. However, Arthur was joined to the suit by virtue of being listed as cocomposer with Emery. Since legally I had been a minor at the time of the contract signing, my oldest brother, Joe, had signed for me. Arnstein had no claim on my lyric or title. His song was called "I Love You Madly."

So it appeared that I was out of it all. Then it developed that Arnstein proved that he had left his manuscript at E. B. Marks's offices and at CBS for anyone's consideration.

Arnstein had come up with a remarkable graph to try to prove that Emery had stolen his melody. On a screen, he showed a photograph of the treble (the melody line) and the bass (the accompaniment). By selecting certain notes from the treble and certain notes from the bass, he was able to construct the exact melody of our song. Naturally, the judge didn't know the difference; to him it sounded like the same song.

On the strength of our first big success, E. B. Marks had signed Arthur and me to a five-year contract for the publication of our entire output. A contract—but no money. We were too naïve to know what we were signing. Now, in preparation for the Arnstein suit, Marks's attorney called us all together for a war council. That one-third/two-third bad royalty deal still rankled, and I refused to cooperate in the planned strategy. An amusing news story in the long-defunct *New York American*, dated June 7, 1935, has such tongue-in-cheek overtones that I include part of it. The heading:

DISCORD IN COURT

Music loses its charms! Melodies lull judge to sleep! Pianist in tears!

In a cacophony of sour fiddle notes, tinny piano flats and sharps and a babble of highly excited voices, the Tin Pan Alley plagiarism trial against Play, Fiddle, Play ended slightly off-key yesterday. Judge J. Foster Symes confessed to a headache and reserved decision. Ira B. Arnstein, "songwriter," who sued E. B. MARKS MUSIC CORP. for $250,000, alleging that *Play, Fiddle, Play* was pirated from his song I Love You Madly, finally got his chance to play his piece. His playing on the cabaret piano in the courtroom brought tears to his eyes. The fiddling of Emery Deutsch, Gypsy King of radio, brought tears to many other eyes and muttered imprecations from Arnstein. Deutsch played both songs and Arnstein charged he deliberately fiddled Play, Fiddle, Play well and I Love You Madly badly. Deutsch resented that remark. They squabbled long and loud. Judge Symes finally opened his eyes, shook his head and restored temporary order.

There was a great deal more such nonsense. The case had turned into a comic opera, and Marks's attorney was quite perturbed. He decided that he could call for a dismissal of the case by simply putting Arthur and me on the stand to tell the truth: that we had written the song in its entirety and that Emery Deutsch was what is known in the music business as a "cut-in." This was a tough admission for that new Paramount maestro to have to make publicly, and it took hours of arguments to convince him that it was the surest way of closing the case in our favor. They finally wore Emery down. He agreed.

But they had reckoned without me. I announced that I would not testify.

Marks, his lawyer, Emery, and even Arthur were shocked. "Do you want to see the case lost and Arnstein get all the royalties and damages?" they demanded.

I shrugged my indifference. "All I have is half of one-third. The rest of you will lose a helluva lot more."

They stared at me blankly. All but old man Marks, who got the message and asked coldly, "What do you want?"

"Oh," I answered nonchalantly, "I might consider getting on the stand and telling the truth if the royalties were more favorably adjusted."

They were—and I did—and we won the case.

I had learned a hard lesson early in my career: When you've got the edge, chop before you get chopped. That lesson served me well in future years except once or twice when I was gullible and trusting. I adopted the old Hebrew adage as my guideline: "If I am not for myself, then who will be?" Twenty-eight years later, when renewals on my songs started coming due, unlike most other writers who dispersed theirs, I set up a holding corporation to collect all my copyrights. That enabled me to make a more advantageous deal for the *next* twenty-eight years.

My collaboration with Arthur Altman ended due to problems. Marks was furious at me for besting him, so he buried our songs that came to him under that phony five-year contract we had signed. Also, I was now in great demand as a lyric writer by established composers. I consulted an attorney for advice on the Marks contract, and he gave me a solution. The only way to get out of Marks's clutches was not to write with Arthur since we had been signed as a team. At that, old man Marks had the last laugh. Those royalty adjustments cost him nothing since they only affected the writers' royalties.

Much later I discovered that all the Marks contracts we had signed gave him rights in perpetuity. However, when I became the vice president of the Songwriters' Guild and was much wiser, we found loopholes in the Marks contracts that upset the perpetuity clause.

How did the music world react to Emery's admission that he had nothing to do with the writing of "Play, Fiddle, Play"? Not an eyebrow was raised. Cut-ins are a commonly accepted practice in our business. In my day, writers were always dependent on bands, performers, and record companies for exposure of their material. If the artist was important enough, a writer would welcome his name as a collaborator. In such a manner, many singers and bandleaders became ASCAP members and earned royalties.

Things are different these days since many a performer writes, publishes, and records his own material and controls it all. But in times past, some of the biggest hits had cut-in collaborators. Here are only a few famous performers who participated in this practice: Bing Crosby, Al Jolson, Morton Downey, Rudy Vallee, Ben Bernie.

Two of the worst offenders who accumulated marvelous catalogs and ASCAP ratings were Irving Mills, the music publisher whose name appears on Duke Ellington compositions, and Billy Rose, who ran the Diamond Horseshoe nightclub and added his name to songs written for his revues by other writers.

One of the most amusing stories of Billy Rose's chutzpah was told to me years ago by Ira Gershwin, who experienced it firsthand. Ira and some of the smartest young talents in the theater at that time were all contributing to a Fanny Brice revue that her husband, Billy Rose, was producing. Ira, Arthur Schwartz, Howard Dietz, Yip Harburg, Herman Hupfeld—the contributing writers—were all in New Haven at the Shubert Theater, working and revising up to the last minute before the break-in first performance. On opening night, Billy personally escorted all the writers to a reserved section moments before the rise of the curtain. One of the writers suddenly realized that they had been given no programs and would not be aware of the new running order. He dashed up the aisle, procured programs, and ran back to his seat just as the curtain rose. The writers had no chance to study the program until intermission in the lobby.

Then came the shock. Every single song on the program listed Billy Rose as a collaborator. The writers were fuming. Just then Billy swaggered over to them, pleased as punch at how well the show was playing.

"How'd you like it, guys?" he smiled at them. They looked at him with hurt expressions, holding out the program in accusation. "How could you do this to us, Billy?" He smiled sheepishly, extended both hands in a shrug. "Fellas . . . I just couldn't help it!"

CHAPTER TEN

How I Got to Hollywood

R adio in the early 1930s aired the battle of the crooners. Rudy Vallee and his Connecticut Yankees had actually come from Maine, where they developed their style and popularity playing for college dances. Rudy was a handsome All-American boy with a shock of blond, curly hair. When he picked up his megaphone (this was long before PA systems and microphones were in common use) and crooned, "I'm Just A Vagabond Lover," girls young and old sighed and swooned. He quickly became king of the airwaves. Another potent force at the same time was Guy Lombardo and his Royal Canadians. Their clean-cut look and rhythmic beat became a staple at the Roosevelt Hotel in New York and lured dancing couples by the hundreds.

Then along came two new crooners to challenge Vallee's reign. Bing Crosby stepped out of a Paul Whiteman vocal trio and boo-

boo-boo-booed his way to fame with "When the Blue of the Night Meets the Gold of the Day." And hot on his heels came Russ Columbo moaning "I'm Just a Prisoner of Love." A controversy raged as to whether Crosby or Columbo started the boo-booing style first, but it hardly mattered. They were both popular and attractive and had legions of female fans. It is interesting to speculate which one would have had the bigger career if Columbo had not died at an early age. At any rate, all three crooners answered Hollywood's call and started making films about the same time. Columbo lost the race tragically with his untimely death. He was either accidentally shot or murdered by a friend. Vallee made two or three films, but there was something stiff about him—perhaps too many cold Maine winters in his blood. He gave up Hollywood, or maybe vice versa, and went on to a long, successful career in vaudeville and radio. Bing proved to have the greater natural appeal despite thinning hair and jug ears. He made his first appearances in Mack Sennett two-reeler comedies, but quickly joined Paramount Pictures, where he went on to stardom and an Academy Award for *Going My Way* in 1945.

My career in the early thirties fell upon lean times after "Play, Fiddle, Play." In accordance with our contract, E. B. Marks had to publish five of our songs, which he proceeded to bury. In retrospect, I don't think those early songs were much good. Still, they enabled us to become members of the American Society of Authors and Composers. Age twenty at the time, I believe I was the youngest member to be inducted.

Just about then, I became friendly with Jack and Dave Kapp, who had been brought from Chicago by Columbia Records to run their Brunswick division. I hung around that recording studio daily and became sort of a gofer. This accorded me the thrill of meeting all the Brunswick record stars, especially Bing, before he moved to the West Coast permanently. Another new friend who took me under his wing was Victor Young, also brought out of Chicago by the Kapps.

Victor, a short man who grew into a music-business giant as a composer/arranger and winner of many Academy Awards, had already written and published songs such as the classic, "Sweet Sue." In the next few years, he was responsible for more great standards, including "Street of Dreams" and "I Don't Stand a Ghost of a Chance." Incidentally, Bing, who introduced it, was also a cut-in on that song.

Many evenings I would accompany Victor home to his New York apartment and partake of succulent meals his Russian wife prepared. Victor was then about thirty-five. His musical education had been acquired at the Warsaw Conservatory in Poland where he had been a concert violinist with the Philharmonic, toured Europe, and met and married an older woman to whom he was quite devoted. Along with that comfortable marriage, he had another relationship with a lovely, young singer who had a distinctive style, Lee Wiley. She, too, became a warm friend.

Victor encouraged my writing, made corrective suggestions about my lyrics, and even set some of them to his music when I could pin him down. We would then record the song on his home equipment. That was before the days of tape recording. "Demo" records were made by singing and playing into a microphone while a stylus scratched the result onto a wax-coated metal disk. Lee learned and sang our songs beautifully, but alas, we never got a Crosby rendition.

Al Jolson had become a big radio star on a weekly Shell Oil broadcast that originated in New York, and Victor was his conductor/arranger. Since the program used guest stars, Shell Oil decided to move the show to Hollywood where they were more readily available. Of course, Victor, his wife, and Lee were part of this big move. I was devastated at the thought of losing my new collaborator and friend. Then Victor, who knew how little money I had, came up with a solution. I could drive his Packard sedan to the West Coast. All it would cost me was food and overnight lodgings. I would be given a Shell Oil card, so gas would be free. My only responsibility would be to drape the sedan in a huge banner: SHELL OIL PRESENTS AL JOLSON EVERY THURSDAY NIGHT. Victor's wife had preceded him to the coast to find and set up a home while he and Lee Wiley followed on the Twentieth Century Limited. Victor assured me that on the coast he would have more time to write with me.

I was ecstatic at the prospect of my first trip to Hollywood and had to do some furious talking to convince my parents. I talked a gay friend into coming along to share the driving chores, and thus, in 1935, I made my Hollywood debut.

Some debut!

Not a soul outside of Victor and Lee did I know in that sprawling city that could best be described by Gertrude Stein's remark about Oakland: "There's no there there." Once I had delivered Victor's sedan, I had no means of transportation except the L.A. trolley car system that ran from the Pacific coast's Santa Monica to a dreary, shabby downtown Los Angeles. My driving partner took an instant dislike to the town, the people, and the long distances, and found another "share-the-driving" ride right back to New York.

Although I was miserably lonely, I found a cheap, small studio apartment, one room crowded by a closet kitchenette, a tiny bathroom and a Murphy bed that came out of the wall and covered the remaining space. The one big advantage was that I was living directly across from that well-advertised arch that spelled PARAMOUNT PICTURES. The gateway to Nirvana!

By this time, Jack Kapp had started a new label, Decca Records, and had signed up most of the Brunswick stars including Bing, Victor, and Lee. The West Coast recording studios were right around the corner from Paramount on Melrose Avenue, a short walk for me. Knowing all these people gave me access to recording sessions, and I soon became friendly with Bing's older brothers, who were in charge of his business affairs with offices on the Paramount lot. This gained me entry to the lot and Bing's suite of offices where I made a new friend, Dora Einzig, his secretary. She was the typical nice Jewish girl who kept inviting me home for dinner. And in my penny-scrimping state, I never turned her down.

The Einzig family had a comfortable home within walking distance and consisted of one older sister and two older brothers. The oldest, Lou, was a successful dentist, and I always suspected he was attracted to me, but he thought I was pursuing his baby sister, Dora. Anyway, Lou wasn't my type. But that family was warm and friendly and helped fill my lonely hours.

So now I could enter the Paramount lot, wander about at will onto the various stages where films were being shot, and meet and trick with an occasional gay extra. I should have taken advantage of all this and gotten some work as an extra myself, but I kept hoping that Victor would find time to work with me, and I wanted to be available. Aside from the Einzig family, I had no social life at all. I could not afford a car to enable me to cover the vast, spread-out square-mileage of Los Angeles, so I was restricted to areas that were within walking distance.

Naturally, on the Paramount lot, I got to meet rising stars like Dorothy Lamour, Ray Milland, and Martha Raye, but I was just that kid hanging around. One new star I met was a recent import from Denmark. Handsome Carl Brisson had been a pugilist, made a few European films, and then was signed by Paramount, who planned to star him in musicals. His wife, a formidable lady, handled all the business and left Carl free to be dashing and charming. Then there was Fred Brisson, who was always introduced as Carl's younger brother, but was really his son. Just when I thought I was on the verge of getting a song into the next Brisson film, Paramount dropped him, and Mr. and Mrs. went back home. But

Freddie stayed on, worked his way up as a Broadway and Hollywood producer, and eventually married Rosalind Russell.

One day I visited the MGM studio lot to see one of my New York music publishers, Jack Robbins, who had a large office there. While we were chatting, the door opened and a pudgy little girl bounced in. Even though she was wearing a kid's middy blouse and skirt, she already had substantial breasts. Robbins said, "You're in for a treat, Jack. Wait'll you hear this little girl sing."

She gave us a few bars of something a cappella. Not only was it a great treat, but it was my first introduction to fourteen-year-old Judy Garland.

I didn't see much of Victor in L.A. He had become twice as busy. Not only was he conducting and arranging the Shell Oil broadcasts and recording for Decca, he was also moving into writing film scores. In a few years, Victor would be in great demand, mainly as a film composer, and would gather a bouquet of awards. He was always friendly and pleasant when he saw me.

Despite my age, I must have been rather naïve. I recall one day talking with Victor when he was in a relaxed mood and the name of some well-known actor came up in our conversation. I let Victor in on a secret. "I hear he's gay for women."

Victor looked at me curiously. "Whaddya mean—gay for women?"

I said, "I hear he goes down on them."

Victor laughed and replied, "Doesn't everybody? Jack, you've got a lot to learn!"

My Hollywood days came to an abrupt end when a chance sexual encounter left me with gonorrhea. Penicillin had not yet been discovered, and I had no one I could talk to. I started going for treatment to a free clinic an hour's trolley ride from Hollywood in the downtown Board of Health offices. I was given frequent sulfur injections, the cure in those days, which didn't seem to be doing me any good. I had never had a close relationship with my two older brothers, the age difference kept us apart. But those sulfur treatments were not working, and my testicles blew up like a balloon. I was so frightened and worried about my condition that I broke down and telephoned my brothers. To their credit, when I told them what was happening, they immediately wired me the fare to come home immediately—by plane.

In those early days of cross-country transportation, propeller planes would make frequent landings to refuel. Flying was a brand-new experience for me. I had never been up in a plane before. I seem to recall that we had to climb some sort of ladder-staircase to enter the plane, which had a central aisle and about thirty seats. I don't believe that any food was served. I was assigned an aisle seat in the last row and behind me was the boarding door to the plane. Practically the last arrival was a smartly dressed, little old lady whom I recognized, a well-known character actress, Henrietta Crosman.

She took the window seat next to mine and immediately leaned back and closed her eyes. That prohibited any conversation I had in mind. Our first stop on this endless flight was Albuquerque, New Mexico. That's when my seatmate opened her eyes. I couldn't help but admire this stalwart, cool traveler. I said, "I envy you! You slept all the way. Flying must be an old experience for you."

She said, "Young man, I closed my eyes because I was scared to death! This is my first flight ever, and I've been praying silently for hours."

We both descended the ladder to the ground and went off to buy a sandwich and a drink. We continued the flight to New York in stages, and she felt more comfortable as we chatted about pictures and Hollywood.

Our plane arrived about eight the next morning. My brothers were there, and I was so happy to see them that I embraced them both. They took me directly to a Brooklyn urologist with whom they had made an appointment. On the way, they assured me with a chuckle that they could vouch for this doctor's expertise from previous personal experiences. "Welcome to the club!" they said. Fortunately, they didn't pry or ask how and by whom I had been infected. They just took it for granted that it had been some female.

My rating went higher in their esteem. But now I was back home in Brooklyn with Mama and Papa. My darling Bobbeh had passed on. She was given an honorable funeral, her casket carried by religious members of the congregation from our home to the little wooden *shul* where the head rabbi blessed her with the proper *bruchas*.

I had spent most of my "Fiddle" royalties and had to get busy on that elusive songwriting career or open an office to cut corns.

CHAPTER ELEVEN

Maine's Favorite Son, Rudy Vallee

So, back home in Brooklyn in 1935, I went to work writing lyrics with a new collaborator. Eliot Daniels had been a pianist for Freddy Martin's orchestra when we met during my Hollywood stay. Eliot was a great musician and had joined Rudy Vallee's band, which brought him in and out of New York. Whenever he hit town, we would have a writing session and one or two of our songs would be introduced by Rudy on his weekly broadcasts.

Rudy had a huge Park Avenue apartment where he kept his office and current paramour. He liked a definite type. She had to be dark complexioned, with long, dark hair, slinky, and slightly trashy. The one time his taste changed was when he hired Alice Faye as his band singer. She wasn't really his type, and the situation was solved when she was signed for movies.

He loved having an entourage, people to admire him and make him feel secure in his fame. As a good friend of Eliot's, I was often invited to join the party for the evening. One winter night, we all piled into Rudy's chauffered limo and drove to the Stork Club. All of us, guys and gals, were bundled up in heavy coats, and when we arrived at the club, Rudy announced, "Everyone leave your hats and coats in the limo. We're not paying any coat checks!"

Sherman Billingsley, who ran the club, knew how cheap Rudy was. Everybody knew. Nevertheless, we were greeted royally and had a great time.

I used to attend Rudy's weekly broadcasts, all of which were followed by the same routine when summer came. Rudy had a lodge on a large lake up in Maine close to where he had been born. After the broadcast, the entourage would pile into limos, drive to an airport where Rudy had charted a plane, and fly up to Portland. There we disembarked and got into more limos. The first stop in Portland was always at his father's drugstore where Rudy had clerked behind the soda fountain as a kid. Over the counter hung a huge oil portrait of Rudy, the star.

Then we would all be driven to the lodge, which consisted of two large buildings: the main house, where Rudy, his current girl, and the important guests stayed, and an annex for all the rest of us. It had a series of bedrooms and baths with twin beds in each, and on the night table a birch-bound book labeled "DO'S AND DON'TS FOR GUESTS." Inside, it spelled out the usual precautions:

water use, time for lights out, noise, rising time and breakfast hour, waste disposal, and so forth.

What I thought was wonderful was that each bedroom was named after one of Rudy's hit songs. Once I slept in "Deep Night" and another time in "I'm Just a Vagabond Lover," songs Rudy had made famous. I never got to sleep in "Betty Coed."

Rudy always had prestigious guests at these weekends. I remember meeting Walter Annenberg, who had just taken over his father's *Racing Form Journal* after the old man was jailed for some illegality, and Walter's new wife. Dinner was always a formal affair. Rudy appeared in his white flannels and blazer plus ascot. He sat at the head of the table and directed the conversations. It was always what he wanted to talk about, whether gossip or politics. After every dinner, we all adjourned to a large, comfortable salon where a screen had been set up to show Rudy's two or three starring films—the same ones each weekend!

When you rose in the early morning, as directed, and went to the main house for breakfast, you would first have to read the portable slate board that spelled out the day's activities: who was to play in the tennis foursomes and with whom, what time lunch would be served and where. Location was important

Let me explain about "location." Eddie Cantor, who also had a popular weekly program, took sick and couldn't make his broadcast one week. Rudy stepped in to replace Eddie that week, and in gratitude, Eddie bought Rudy a gift—a seventy-five-foot yacht, which he had delivered to Rudy's lodge lake. The lake was sizable, but by the time you got the yacht in motion, you had reached its end and had to turn around.

On nice weather days, the bulletin board read that lunch would be served on the yacht. That entailed a parade down to the yacht of all the household help with baskets, carafes, trays, china, and cutlery. All the guests would then troop down and take their assigned seats on deck, and then Captain Vallee would appear in full-regalia sailing uniform. Rudy always looked bandbox perfect. We'd get underway, hit the end of the lake, turn around and sail back, park in the shade, and be served lunch. Since Rudy took this all very seriously, nobody dared laugh.

Rudy Vallee was one of a kind. I doubt that he ever was aware of what a character he was with his strained New England mannerisms. Some years ago, when I was living on Sutton Place and owned and ran two theaters—one on- and one off-Broadway—I answered the phone and heard a voice say, "Jack, this is Rudy Vallee. How are you?"

I hadn't seen or heard from Rudy in years and thought someone was pulling my leg, so I kidded the voice. "Hello, Rudy, did you ever get Los Angeles to change the name of your street to Rue de Vallee?"

He replied, "As a matter of fact, I did. But that's not what I'm calling you about. I want you to put my one-man show into your small theater. You'll clean up! I do a very funny act. People fall in the aisles screaming. I'm going to send you a tape of my whole show, and you'll hear how funny it is. Call me afterward, and we'll discuss it."

I did get the tape and played it. It was truly embarrassing. Not funny. Pathetic. His act was a boring monologue backed up with clips from the films he had been in.

All this was followed up by a phone call from a young man who introduced himself to me as one of Rudy's relatives. He was making this call solely because Rudy had insisted. We chatted, and he confided that Rudy was not in the best of health physically or mentally and for me to pay no attention. Soon after, Rudy died. When I recalled his days of fame and this sad ending, I felt terrible.

CHAPTER TWELVE

A Song a Day

I n 1937 I teamed up with a new collaborator, Peter Tinturin, a small, effete man two years older than I, who had been educated at the Vienna Conservatory of Music and had come to America with his parents in 1929. Peter had a strong melodic sense and a passion for women. He was also quite persistent in pursuing me to write lyrics for his melodies. He had already had a few songs published and knew his way into publishers' offices in the Brill Building on Broadway and Forty-ninth Street. Every floor had music firms, and the hallways echoed with the sounds of writers demonstrating new material, singers rehearsing, record players blasting. It was a fascinating, lively world. In the halls or elevators, one would meet other writers who had either just contracted or had a song rejected. Publishers were all given ratings: "an easy mark," "a tough sell," "an ignorant shmuck."

Peter and I were meeting daily to write songs, and we managed to place a few with different publishers. One came through with a swinging recording by Fats Waller, who had an inimitable vocal style and played piano with a stride bass. Our song was called "Do Me a Favor," and Fats made it sound like great fun.

The day he recorded it, we were at the studio, and he was a delight to watch and listen to as he kept throwing in little interjections between the singing phrases—"Yeah! Yeah! Ya hear me talkin' to ya!"

> Do me a favor, marry me,
> Do me a favor, can't you see?
> I'm in a quaver to be middle-aisleing you;
> Do me a favor, tie the knot,
> Do me a favor, share my lot,
> Darling, don't waver and we will come smiling through!
> Say the word, dear, we'll do as other folks do . . .
> Raise two or three;
> It's absurd, dear, that I should have to coax you . . .
> Don't be that way, take a chance on me!
> You won't regret it when we're one,
> You won't regret it, we'll have fun!
> I won't forget it! Do me a favor . . .
> Let me do your favors for you.
>
> *Music by Peter Tinturin*

That song is still part of Fats Waller's retrospective albums.

Incidentally, the phrase Tin Pan Alley has been used for many years as an apt designation of the music business. That appellation was first applied at the turn of the century to a couple of blocks of Manhattan in the West Twenties where early music publishers had congregated. That area later became the city's wholesale flower market. These days that neighborhood has undergone another metamorphosis as Chelsea, the gayest area in Manhattan, with an infusion of art galleries.

However, back in those pre-air-conditioned days, when summer heat engulfed the city, everyone opened their windows for a breath of fresh air. The cacophony of sound that ensued from these publishers' office windows—pianos tinkling, bands playing, vocalists rehearsing, all those clashing harmonies—were dubbed Tin Pan Alley. So in due time, as theaters and the music business kept moving up to the West Forties, the Brill Building, with its plethora of publishers became the new Tin Pan Alley of the city.

Working with Peter Tinturin, I usually supplied the titles and lyrics. But one day, Peter came up with a great title: "What Will I Tell My Heart?" I wrote a torchy lyric for it and then had a bright idea. Instead of peddling the song to publishers, why not take it to my friend at Decca Records, Dave Kapp, and see if he would be interested in recording it?

Not only did Dave love our song, he proposed a deal. We could bring all our songs directly to him, and for each one he recorded, he would be our 10-percent partner. He had a similar deal with Lou Levy, he told us. (Levy would go on to become the manager of the Andrews Sisters.) If any of the recordings turned into a hit, he assured us the publishers would be running after us. That sounded wonderful to me since I dreaded the hours spent in publishers' outer rooms, waiting for those few moments when they deigned to call you into the inner office to put your heart and soul into a rendition of your new song while they took telephone calls and paid little attention. It was not only frustrating, but disheartening. So this idea of bypassing publishers was infinitely preferable.

Dave assigned "What Will I Tell My Heart?" to Andy Kirk and His Clouds of Joy, a well-known black band with a brilliant pianist/arranger, Mary Lou Williams. The vocalist for this band, Pha Terrell, had a terrific falsetto voice and put his soul into it as he sang in his appealing high tenor.

> I'll try to explain to friends, dear,
> The reason we two are apart,
> I know what to tell our friends, dear,
> But WHAT WILL I TELL MY HEART?
> It's easy to say to strangers
> That we played a game from the start,
> It's easy to lie to strangers.
> But WHAT WILL I TELL MY HEART?
> When I try to hide all the tears inside
> What an ache it will bring,
> Then I'll wander home to a telephone

That forgot how to ring!
I could say you'll soon be back, dear,
To fool the whole town may be smart,
I'll tell them you'll soon be back, dear,
But WHAT WILL I TELL MY HEART?

Music by Peter Tinturin and Irving Gordon

Peter and I were in the control room the day of the recording session, and everybody agreed that we had a potential hit. Decca was one of the few mainstream recording companies to prolifically record black artists like the Mills Brothers, Chick Webb and his band, and a brand-new vocalist who had been discovered at an Apollo Amateur Night—Ella Fitzgerald. Since I spent days at these recording sessions, I became friendly with all those wonderful performers.

I should add here that between professional talents, there was never any racial apartheid, although it was true in the early half of our century that discrimination existed throughout most of the country when it came to public acceptance of black people in housing, restaurants, trains, buses, and hotels. In the world of the arts, however, we were all equal, and talent was the primary door-opener.

The Andy Kirk record of our song had an electrifying success, and true to Dave's prediction, we were bombarded with offers from publishers. We made the best deal with Chappell Music, and I got to meet its legendary owner, Max Dreyfus. We followed this first success with about eight other songs, all well recorded by

Decca's artists. Unlike today, in those days, a hit song was usually covered by all the labels with their top artists, so it was normal to wind up with recordings of the same song by Bing Crosby, Ella Fitzgerald, and any number of big bands. I managed to be at many of those recording sessions, trading small talk with the musicians and vocalists, sitting in on rehearsals—particularly when one of my songs was being recorded. We got the royal treatment when we walked into publishers' offices. No more waiting around in the outer office. And when we ran into one of them on the street, we were greeted with "When are you guys gonna bring me a hit?"

We were hot!

All this activity got Peter and me a contract to Hollywood and Republic Pictures. We never regretted the deal we had made with Dave Kapp. What I did regret was what happened with "What Will I Tell My Heart?" When the song was at its height, we got called in by the ASCAP board of directors and accused of stealing the title from Irving Gordon, a writer I had never met. Gordon claimed that he had suggested that title to Peter with the intention of writing a lyric, but then never got around to it. Peter hemmed and hawed and finally admitted that it had been Gordon's title, but that he had never told me. In a strange ruling, the board decided that Gordon's name should be listed with ours on all sheet music, and he would receive one-third of the earnings. I, who was an innocent victim, was penalized.

In retrospect, I realize I should have argued my innocence. But I was still young, new to the business, and easily intimidated.

CHAPTER THIRTEEN

Hollywood Again . . .
But with a Contract

So once again to Hollywood—but this time under contract. I am grateful that my parents were there at the blossoming of my career and in a small way could enjoy the benefits of my success. In time, they became my staunchest defenders when people enviously remarked that I never seemed to work hard, that all material things came to me easily. But my parents knew otherwise. They had watched and dreamed and prayed along with me. One regret I still have is that they both passed away too soon before I could have done more for them.

That is why one of my pleasantest recollections is that of signing my first writing contract and going to Republic Studios in North Hollywood—usually referred to as "the Valley." Republic was known as the home of the Bs—grade-B pictures. The studio had made a fortune on Gene Autry's "hoss-operas" and had decided to upgrade its lowly image in the industry. To achieve this, a series of A productions was planned, musicals with star names. Those were the great days of screen musicals, Paramount's *Big Broadcasts of 1937* and *1938*, Warners' *Gold Diggers* series, and MGM's *Broadway Melodies*. Major studios like these had their star contract players singing and dancing, whether or not they could.

So there were my little Viennese collaborator and me about to compete with those superstar-studded films. Republic had started building its own roster of "stars"—such dubious talents as Phil Regan, the Brooklyn singing cop, an Irish tenor who had won some amateur contest, and Dorothy McNulty, (newly rechristened Penny Singleton and soon to star in the *Blondie* series), and former Warner Bros. contract-player Ann Dvorak.

To supply the hoped-for Hit Parade material, they had hired Peter and me for the munificent sum of $250 a week. That was good money in 1938, more than I had ever seen monthly. We proceeded to write the score for a great, forgotten bomb, *Manhattan Merry-Go-Round*, which was based on a popular radio program. The sheet music of this potpourri reads: "Star studded production with PHIL REGAN, ANN DVORAK, JIMMY GLEASON, LEO CARILLO, TAMARA GEVA, GENE AUTRY, HENRY ARMETTA, CAB CALLOWAY, KAY THOMPSON AND HER VOCAL GROUP"—(all less-than-stellar names at the time). Oh, more! Including JOE DI MAGGIO and TED LEWIS! Well, not too shabby for little old Republic.

Although their intended blockbuster somehow collapsed in the country's movie houses, that didn't deter Mr. Yates. He decided to bet his Autry earnings on another original musical, *Outside of*

Paradise, again starring Phil Regan. This was the story: Phil is a band leader in New York with such comedy stars in his band as Peter Lind Hayes, Cliff Edwards (better known as Ukelele Ike), Mischa Auer, and Bert Gordon, a comedian famous as the Mad Russian on Eddie Cantor's broadcasts. Gordon's claim to fame was that he could wiggle his ears together or separately while talking.

Anyway, Phil gets a wire advising him that a distant Irish uncle has died and left him a castle. Naturally, Phil and the band are excited and decide to go to Ireland to claim his inheritance. They arrive to find that the castle is a shambles and is being occupied by a comic caretaker and his feisty daughter, Penny Singleton. There is instant antagonism between Penny and Phil and—need I spell out the rest of the script?

The song titles will clarify the plot: "Shenanigans," "That Sweet Irish Sweetheart of Mine" ("Take the blue of old Killarney for the color of her eyes . . ."), "Outside of Paradise." That tired movie shows up on television now and then even today, and I'm thankful for the performance credits.

Oh well—Republic had another bomb. I never did understand why Yates had tried to make a star out of Phil Regan. He was attractive enough, had a nice tenor voice, couldn't act a lick, but had a huge penis that he loved to display. Phil loved to come out of the second-floor, makeup room onto the veranda in his robe, press up against the railing and drape his Irish salami over it, calling out, "Be careful down below! It looks like rain!"

After my first few months at Republic, when I sensed the job would last, I returned to Brooklyn in a newly purchased white

Buick convertible, picked up Mama, Papa, my cousin, Mary, and my youngest brother, Murray, and, with this full load, drove back to Hollywood. This was 1938, and in that prefreeway, preturnpike era, that was no small feat. It was a ten-day trek that involved roundabout distances, detours, terrible roads, and bad hotels, many on Route 66.

My parents had never been farther away than Philadelphia since their arrival from the old country, and I was determined to show them America—the Mississippi, Grand Canyon, Painted Desert, Rockies, and California. One problem I had not reckoned with was Mama's kosher orthodoxy. What food she had prepared and packed for the trip lasted about three days, and then we were forced to look for acceptable eating places. Imagine our arrival at some of those greasy spoons in western Iowa and Kansas, where waitresses' regional accents and our Brooklynese reached an impasse. After a fruitless perusal of the fly-speckled menus, the question "Whachyall like t' eat?" elicited a changeless response from Mama. "Two berled eggs, fife minutes, pliss!"

Mama trusted no restaurant food but hard-boiled eggs, which she could eat right out of their protective shells with her own spoon from home. Salt and sugar were acceptable since they could hardly be contaminated, but all other foods and dishes were suspect—they couldn't be kosher. Papa, on the other hand, was more adventurous and would order omelets, soup, cheese sandwiches—all frowned upon by Mama's disapproving eye. She resigned herself to watching the rest of us eating *trayf*—non-Kosher food—which was nothing new to Papa, who, after all, had once lived with a gentile family and served in the Cossacks. And we young ones had to keep up our strength.

We finally arrived and settled in North Hollywood in a large ranch-type furnished cottage that I had rented for eighty-five dollars a month from a Warner Bros. star, Glenda Farrell, who owned lots of real estate. The reason for such a bargain was the recent, devastating flood that had washed out most of Cahuenga Boulevard and left a thick residue of silt and mud over much of the San Fernando Valley. We had to scrape away layers of muck to make the inside and outside of the house habitable, although we never did clean out the mud-filled swimming pool enough to be able to enjoy it.

The first area Mama organized was the kitchen, scrubbing and scouring every inch, arranging all the pots and pans she had brought, along with newly purchased additions. The closest kosher market area at that time was Boyle Heights in East Los Angeles, many miles away. That subsequently became our weekly, all-day shopping expedition. Murray was enrolled as a freshman at UCLA, and with all these widely dispersed areas to cover, the Buick quickly accumulated mileage. I couldn't afford a second car. Unless you had been there in 1938, it would be difficult to conceive how far away North Hollywood seemed from the rest of the city. This was long before the maze of highways and freeways that now sprawls all over Southern California.

That valley ranch house soon became a Jewish enclave for studio coworkers and executives who vied to be invited to Mama's Friday-night dinners. They even drew numbers to attend the

Passover service at which Papa officiated. I recall Sol Seigel, one of the executive producers at Republic, coming to the first Seder night and talking about similar services his family used to have back east. Everyone raved about Mama's gefilte fish and Papa's sinus-clearing, hand-grated horseradish. Sol, who later became head of production at MGM, was in charge of Gene Autry's Westerns and his brother, Moe, was also a Republic producer. Cy Feuer, later of Feuer and Martin Broadway-producing fame, was somebody's relative and a quiet mouse in our music department.

Our studio office workers, many of them with secret ambitions of becoming actors, organized a group of which I became a member. The first and only play we attempted during my tenure was called *Butterflies and Ballots* and was written by a fey character, King Kennedy, who later married Louella Parsons's daughter, Harriet, as a cover-up—he was gay, and she was a lesbian. Years later, Harriet and I became close friends. I can't recall how the butterflies mixed with the ballots in that play, but I recall that I was cast as a gas-station attendant who had designs on the heroine, who wound up with King, the lepidopterist.

Our director was Ralph Byrd, an actor who played the lead in Republic's Dick Tracy series, and we decided to mount our effort in a small theater right off Hollywood Boulevard. We had planned a three-night run and sold tickets to all our friends. Our opening night was struck with a huge cloudburst that washed through Cahuenga Boulevard once again. The city was practically blacked out, but a few stragglers managed to make it to the theater. In true "the show must go on" spirit, we lit candles and presented the play. That was our first and last performance.

I had always been interested in theatricals. As a kid, I wrote and produced shows in the cellar of our home in Brooklyn and charged two-cents admission. Then, in my fifteenth summer, I gathered a few of my schoolmates and put on three one-act plays in a lecture hall connected to Grand Central Station. The small, bare stage was used for sales presentations and had no curtain or stage lights, but that didn't deter me. Somehow I scrounged a curtain and some makeshift lights and printed up elegant black tickets with gold lettering that read: WE MODERNS PRESENT. I played the villain purely because I was the tallest in the group; my leading lady was all of five feet tall, which made it rather awkward for six-foot me to grab her and force a kiss. It was a French costume play, and I managed to get knee britches and powdered wigs for free, too.

I've digressed. Meanwhile, back at the ranch house in the valley, both my older brothers, Joe and Harvey, came out to stay with us on their vacations. Joe had been divorced and was living back at home in Brooklyn with my folks. All three of my brothers were proud of my accomplishments by this time, and it somehow brought us closer than we'd ever been. Despite our closeness, however, I still could not bring myself to discuss my homosexuality with them. I went on pretending.

Harvey and Joe, after an unfraternal disagreement with the five Schwartz brothers, decided to open their own fuel-oil company with my financial aid. Now that royalties were rolling in on a regular basis, I was happy to help them. As I've indicated before, brother Joe had a true gift of gab, and with him as the contact man on the outside and Harvey on the inside running the day-to-day business, they made wonderful progress as the newly formed Whale Oil Company, a name I had dreamed up for them. They developed a large plant in the Brooklyn water basin, which they sold years later for a small fortune.

My father at that time in North Hollywood was about fifty-six, although a long, hard work-life had added years to his appearance. He now was a tall, quiet, gentle man with a seamed face and a shock of thick white hair bristling in the Prussian fashion he had worn all his life. At my insistence, he had sold his last business—a gas station—and was retired. He loved to take long walks around that burgeoning neighborhood in the valley where there were still large stretches of desert land, observing the orange groves that were fast giving way to tract developments.

One evening at the dinner table, he stated quietly that if only he had two thousand dollars, there was a nearby corner he would like to purchase as a site for a gas station. The next day, we all went over to inspect that corner, and I pooh-poohed Papa's idea.

"Pop," I assured him, "nothing much will ever happen out here at Laurel Canyon and Ventura boulevards." Oh yes, I was a wise young man of vision. Not! Looking forward was never my forte. But now, in my nineties, looking down that hill of yesterdays . . . how clear the view!

Unfortunately, our stint at Republic Studios didn't result in one real hit despite many recordings of all our film songs. While Mr. Yates was faced with the undeniable truth that he wasn't capable of competing with the majors, he still had to utilize our services as we were still under contract. We were thereupon instructed to write songs for all the hoss operas. A stranger combination couldn't be conceived of—a Jewish guy from the wilds of Brooklyn and a Viennese-trained composer.

So we collected a lot of cowboy-song folios and copies of Autry's vocals, studied them religiously, and came up with some fairly good ersatz material: "Dust Over the West," "The Man From Music Mountain," "At the Old Barn Dance." I think we used the same three chords for every song and just changed the lyrics. Oddly enough, those "oaters" are still being shown on television somewhere in the world today, and ASCAP, which pays writers and publishers for performances, lists and credits all these international screenings.

Peter and I were on the lot when Gene Autry went on strike because Mr. Yates refused to up Autry's salary, simply taking the position "I made you a star—I can do the same for someone else!" He plucked a young, attractive lad out of a singing group known as the Sons of the Pioneers. This youngster, Len Slye, was an all-around improvement on Autry—years younger, better looking, and actually able to play the guitar, sing, and ride a horse at the same time.

And so Roy Rogers was born. He, his wife, Dale, and Trigger, his hoss, became immortal not only through films, but a chain of fast-food restaurants. Roy was a soft-spoken, sweet man who used to come to our little cottage office to rehearse the songs we wrote for his pictures. He was always respectful, easy to get along with, and overwhelmed by his unexpected good fortune. Yates eventually made peace with Autry, who continued with many more Westerns for Republic and began investing his earnings in ball clubs, real estate, and television stations. He died just a few years ago, a very rich man, at age ninety-two.

But Herb Yates still kept hoping to give those giant studios real competition. One day we were told he was considering signing Ramon Navarro, who had been a silent superstar at MGM, but was now on the way down. Mr. Navarro was brought to Peter's and my little music bungalow to listen to some of our new songs. I vividly remember this swishy, pretty man being ushered in and the overpowering scent of his cologne. I gazed at him in wonder—how could anyone that effeminate have become a screen heartthrob? He was so obvious. Some years later, this poor man was bludgeoned to death in his own Hollywood home by two hustlers he had picked up.

Our writing chores at Republic left us with idle time on our hands. My folks went back east, and I moved into a Hollywood apartment with all the amenities. Peter and his wife lived nearby, but we didn't socialize much—we had different life styles. I had some amusing experiences in my new apartment. There was a gay telephone operator on our switchboard who, I'm certain, listened in to all conversations. It's probably true that "it takes one to know one." We became phone friends, but nothing else.

Our small apartment building had a basement garage, and on many occasions, I would find myself going up the elevator to my floor with film stars like Kay Francis or Marlene Dietrich. I asked my switchboard spy whom they were visiting, and he told me, "A big queen down the hall from you. Andy Lawlor. Watch out for her. She's a piranha!"

Well, one afternoon when I pulled into the garage, my elevator companion was a pleasant, bald-headed, friendly chap who chatted me up and invited me to his flat on the same floor for a drink. I said I had to pick up my messages and would drop in a bit later. Naturally I grabbed the phone and asked who my neighbor was. "That's Miss Lawlor! Big mouth Andy, they call her. Just be careful!"

I knocked at Andy's door and entered to find that he had already changed into a robe that was more like a silk peignoir. He gave the unnecessary explanation that it was too hot. Seating me in a large, overstuffed armchair, he served me a drink and asked if I would like to see some photographs. He laid a big leather album on my lap and sat down at my feet. The album was filled with erotic pictures of nude men and women, everybody doing what to whom. Andy watched slyly, and when he noticed the first stirring in my pants, he pounced.

He was a master of oral sex. Later I discovered that he had taken out all his dentures, upper and lower. He even bragged about his technique and showed me a gold cigarette case given to him by some Scandinavian royalty and inscribed: "To the greatest mouth in the world."

To avoid Andy's frequent calls, I had to warn my switchboard spy never to admit I was home. Andy had been an actor in silent pictures. Now he was an agent and close with many AC/DC film stars. He was very social, and I ran into his star visitors often.

With time and empty days on my hands, I found myself at home noodling on my rented spinet, going back to my beginnings, writing music to my own words. One afternoon, my old friend, Eliot Daniels, stopped by. He was still with Rudy Vallee, traveling the country. I got up enough nerve to play him one of my solo efforts. I didn't tell him that I had already mailed a lead sheet of this song to Dave Kapp at Decca.

Eliot heard the song through and paused before answering. "Jack, you know I'm your friend. You know I think you're a helluva lyric writer. I wouldn't bullshit you!"

Then a BIG pause. "Jack—forget it. It stinks!"

Oh well! To paraphrase: One man's stink is another man's rose. So I tried the song on my next visitor, Archie Bleyer, a successful arranger and eventual discoverer of the McGuire Sisters. Archie's reaction: "I think it's commercial, Jack. But you're making a terrible musical mistake. You start in one key and end in another. Let me show you what I mean."

He sat down at the piano and demonstrated. My song ended with a high musical phrase, but he insisted that it had to end low to be in the right key. I didn't really like his version as well as mine, but not wanting to be called a musical ignoramus, I asked Archie to write out his ending. Quickly, I mailed it to Dave at

Decca with the explanation Archie had given.

I got a very prompt reply. His wire read: RECIEVED YOUR MUSI-
CAL CHANGE TOO LATE. STOP. SONG ALREADY RECORDED BY A
NEW GROUP CALLED INKSPOTS. IF I DIDN'T CARE IS A SMASH HIT.

Months later, when the whole country was singing "If I Didn't
Care," I ran into Archie, who shrugged and said, "Well, you
could have used either ending." When I met Eliot again, he
shook his head and said, "It still stinks!"

I laughed all the way to the bank. With that song I came into
my own. Here's the song Eliot thought would never make it.

IF I DIDN'T CARE
More than words can say,
IF I DIDN'T CARE
Would I feel this way?
If this isn't love
Then what makes me thrill?
And why does my head go 'round and 'round
While my heart stands still?
IF I DIDN'T CARE
Would it be the same?
Would my every prayer begin and end
With just your name?
And would I be sure that this is love beyond compare?
Would all this be true . . .
If I didn't care for you?

CHAPTER FOURTEEN

Welcome to Tin Pan Alley

My short Hollywood contract was over in 1939, and I returned to New York, where I basked in the glory of "If I Didn't Care," my first solo effort. The years 1938 through 1946 were—to quote Andy Warhol—my fifteen minutes of fame. In that period, I had sixteen songs on the Hit Parade, some weeks three at a time. The Inkspots' recording of "If I Didn't Care" truly established my reputation. That was the Golden Era of Big Bands like Glenn Miller, Claude Thornhill, Billy May, Tommy and Jimmy Dorsey, Duke Ellington, and Sammy Kaye, all of whom I got to know, some better than others. The orchestrations were brilliant, and the band singers superb: Jo Stafford, the Eberly Brothers, Vic Damone, Tony Bennett, Anita O'Day, Helen O'Connell, Bea Wain, the incomparable Ella Fitzgerald. And I was fortunate enough to have most of my work recorded by this array of talent. It was not unusual, when you had a hit, to wind up with six to ten cover recordings. I was well enough known by now to take my new songs directly to these singers or their band leaders.

Not only did I have a welcome mat at Chappell Music and Max Dreyfus's office, but Walter Winchell, the most widely read columnist of the day, had fallen in love with the Inkspots' rendition of "If I Didn't Care" and kept writing about them frequently, quoting lines from my lyric:

> If this isn't love then what makes me thrill?
> And why does my head go 'round and 'round
> While my heart stands still?

Hanging around the Decca recording studios, I inevitably became friendly with their entire roster of artists. Ella was a shy, young girl who had won an Apollo Theater amateur contest at age sixteen and was immediately signed up as a vocalist to Chick Webb's orchestra. Chick was a small hunchback who sat propped up smack in the center of his band, beating out an incessant rhythm on his drums. Ella would sit on the side waiting for a signal to sing, then take center stage. Every time I went to the Savoy Ballroom in Harlem, when they were appearing, I would get a great welcome from the band, and when Ella spotted me, she would give me a shy smile and waggle her fingers discreetly.

At break time, I would usually buy her a lemonade; that's all she drank. She was a chunky little girl, uncommunicative, with a lack of social graces, but a warm, lovable smile that made her endearing. She seemed so grateful for anyone's attention. Once you knew her background, all of this was understandable.

Ella was an orphan at fifteen, homeless and friendless on the streets of Harlem, when she decided to try her luck at one of the Wednesday night Apollo Theater amateur hours. Her vulnerability could not mask the innate talent that won her that evening's prize. Fortunately, the orchestra leader for the night was Chick Webb, and he was so impressed by her that he signed her up as his band vocalist and practically adopted her. Even at that tender age, the poor girl was afflicted with the diabetes that practically blinded her in later life and resulted in her always wearing long dresses that covered her thickened limbs. Tragically, her diabetes also led to the amputation of both her legs in 1992. Despite all this adversity, Ella had a fantastic career that lasted almost six decades and earned her thirteen Grammys, numerous doctorates from universities, and a Kennedy Center honor. I was privileged to have known her all those years.

Musically unschooled, Ella, nonetheless, possessed a voice that had true pitch and a lingering resonance. As her performance career progressed, she absorbed the essence of jazz music from all the great black musicians with whom she worked. Her ability to scat, I'm convinced, came from listening to jazz instrumentalists doing variations on a written tune. The trick of this kind of playing or singing depends on a firm sense of harmony and the ability to create interesting variations on the chord structure of the song.

I once asked Ella, "How did you learn to scat? When you do that, you sound like Louis Armstrong's trumpet. Where'd you learn that?"

She looked at me and gave me her shy smile. "Listening to Satchmo!"

Eventually, Decca started using Ella as a solo performer backed by a small band. She made some wonderful records of my songs by herself or occasionally with the Mills Brothers, who also became good friends. This four-man singing group had an individual style and imitated instruments vocally. Although they billed themselves as the Four Mills Brothers, they were really three brothers and their dad.

When one considers Ella's development and eventual importance to the scene of American popular music, it's almost beyond belief. This untrained, unwanted little orphan left her everlasting mark on the world of entertainment and will never be forgotten as long as Gershwin, Porter, Kern, Arlen, and the other musical giants of the last century are remembered. She did homage to them all, and I'm grateful that a little bit of me was included. Even today, when I listen to Norman Ganz's collection of Ella's Great American Songbooks, I listen in awe of her talent. How wonderful that when a group of ex-band vocalists like Ginny Mancini, Bea Wain, Helen O'Connell, and other West Coast singers got together to form the Society of Singers some years ago, their first annual honor was conferred on Ella Fitzgerald. Since then, every successive year, their honored choice is awarded the ELLA statuette.

Mary Lou Williams, a fabulous pianist and an even better arranger, was another chum with an incredible background. By the age of thirteen, she had played carnivals and vaudeville shows and had married the leader of her band, reed man John Williams. When Williams left, she hired Jimmy Lunceford to replace him and Andy Kirk to front the band, for which she made arrangements and played piano.

With her serene, sculptured face, she looked to me like an Egyptian princess, and we developed a warm friendship. She liked me enough to ask me to write lyrics to a couple of her compositions. One was an oddly constructed blues with tricky phrasing that I wrote up as "What's Your Story, Morning Glory?" The day it was set for recording with Andy Kirk and his band, Pha Terrell, their vocalist had difficulty mastering the tricky tune.

Mary Lou spoke up. "Jack knows it. Let him sing it!" Here's what I sang:

> What's your story, Morning Glory?
> What makes you look so blue?
> The way that you've been acting . . .
> I don't know what to do,
> 'cause I love you!
> Sure as one and one make two!
> What's your story, Morning Glory . . .
> If I guess it, darling, will you confess it?
> Oh won't you tell me that you love me, too?

Say, what's your story, Morning Glory?
You've got me worried, too . . .
The postman came this morning
And brought a note to you . . .
Did you read it?
Then you know that I love you!
Got a feelin' there's a lot you're concealin',
Oh won't you tell me that you love me, too!
                    Music by Mary Lou Williams and Paul Webster

It was not the beginning of a singing career. I did an adequate job, and Dave Kapp kidded about putting my name on the label as vocalist Spade Lawrence. But the record was released with no vocalist mentioned. And alas! Nobody asked, "Who was that?" However, that song became a blues classic and garnered some great recordings, Glenn Miller and a blockbuster by Jimmy Lunceford, arranged by Mary Lou.

I kept in touch with Mary Lou for years. She went on to do arrangements for Earl Hines, Benny Goodman, and Duke Ellington. She also made solo appearances in the best nightspots of America and Europe. In the midfifties, she left music for a while, entered the Catholic Church, and became ultrareligious. By the time I saw her again in the sixties, she had grown paranoid about people, publishers, and record companies. Everyone, she felt, was out to cheat her. She became a recluse and died in 1981. But she is not forgotten by those who heard her play or listened to her band

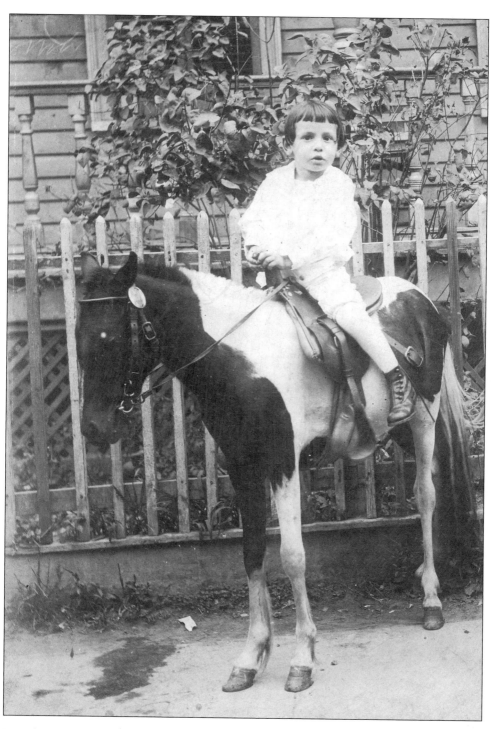

Me, three years old; the traditional pony picture. I look like I'm about to cry.

Right: Me, five years old in Brooklyn. The coat Mama made was a hand-me-down from my older brother. She said I would grow into it. *Below:* My brothers, Joe, 13; Harvey, 12; and me, 5 years old in 1917. The youngest brother, Murray, had not yet arrived.

Papa as a Cossack in the Russian Army *c.* 1890s, before he married Mama.

Mama in her mid-fifties, enjoying Miami for the first time. My treat.

Mama and I posed in my New York apartment for a newspaper story about "Yes, My Darling Daughter," based on a folk song she used to sing.

Above: Brother Joe's wedding photo. Harvey, on the left, was his best man. Mama, in her beaded glory, sits next to Papa. Where are the bride and I? (1928) *Right:* Me in the service, in summer whites, 1943.

Me and my dear friend, Walter, having fun in Coney Island, 1945.

My dear friend, Walter, enjoying a winter scene, upstate New York, 1954.

Me as seen through the lens of Bruno of Hollywood, 1946.

V.P. advertising executive 1969 Richard H. Debnam before he became Richard D. Lawrence. (Photo by Fabian Bachrach.)

Four brothers (left to right): Murray, Joe, Harvey, and me at my house in Bel Air, California, 1977.

Me surrounded by works of art in the living room of the Sutton Place apartment Richard designed, 1983.

 the piano in Sutton Place, New York, 1983. (Photo by Al Gilbert.)

Left: Richard, now my son, in a professorial and pensive mood, 1989. *Below:* Richard and me in St. Thomas, Virgin Islands, 1983.

Bella Linden and me in my Connecticut home, 2001.

With Michael Feinstein at the Weill Hall Tribute to Jack Lawrence in 2002.

Sutton Place, New York, 1982. (Photo by Al Gilbert.)

arrangements or her compositions like "Camel Hop," "Roll 'Em, Trumpets No End," and "In the Land of Oo-Bla-Dee."

Another Decca pal was Connee Boswell, who spent most of her life in a wheelchair as a result of polio. She had studied piano seriously and was the musical brains of one of the first famous girl trios, the Boswell Sisters. There was Martha on cello, Vet on violin, and Connee, in her wheelchair, on piano. The girls started out in New Orleans as blues singers with Connee's clever arrangements. Eventually, in 1931, when they played the New York Paramount, Jack Kapp signed them to a record contract with Decca.

As a trio, they had quite a career, appearing with Bing Crosby on radio and in films. Their success was disrupted by marriages and the subsequent retirement of Martha and Vet, but Connee went on for quite a while as a single. Despite her physical handicap, she was always cheerful and bubbling. Since I was a frustrated vocalist, I always envied Connee's honey-smooth delivery. Visiting her at home one day, I asked, "Can you give me some advice about breath control? When do you stop to breathe?"

She laughed, "When I run out of breath!"

On another occasion, she asked me if I knew a particular Hungarian march, which she proceeded to play for me. She explained that it had been one of her teenage exercise pieces that helped develop octave dexterity of her hands. When she finished playing, she said she had always thought it would make a great rhythm song. I agreed, and the result was "Never Took a Lesson in My Life (But I Still Know How to Make Love)." When the time came to record the song and publish it, Connee refused to use her name as cowriter and insisted on the nom de plume Diana Foore. She didn't want people to do the song just because it had her well-known name on it as a writer. We did three songs together, and she was always Diana Foore. This warm and talented lady passed on in 1976 at the age of sixty-nine.

As I mentioned, this was a most active period in my career. So many of my songs had started as Decca Records that publishers pursued me, feeling that I could get anything recorded because of my connection. I was in constant demand. Often I was called in to supply an English lyric to some foreign hit the publisher had acquired. Many times I found inspiration in old folios I had picked up, piano solos or art songs. I was writing more of my own music to my lyrics.

I came across a folio of art songs published by Schirmer Music and written by a lady named Clara Edwards. One of her lovely songs, which was well performed, was "By the Bend of the River." In the book was another song, only sixteen bars long, with a marvelously descriptive title: "With the Wind and the Rain in Your Hair." It had a very "arty" lyric and according to the publication date, had been in print for at least ten years. The way I envisaged the song should have been written began to take shape within my head. Unwittingly, I made changes, added a verse and release to those sixteen bars and, of course, an entirely new lyric.

To say the least, this was presumptuous of me. I was tampering with a published work, I knew nobody at Schirmer's, and had no idea whether or not Clara Edwards still existed. But with the brashness of youth, I carried on. I persuaded a publisher to contact Schirmer's and make a copublishing deal for my version. It developed that Ms. Edwards, in her midfifties, lived in New York, and was furious at the knowledge that I had dared to rewrite her published composition. My publisher, who felt he had a potential hit, persisted. Once he had convinced Schirmer's, they went to work on Ms. Edwards and changed her mind. The new copy credited words and music to both of us.

> Last night we met and I dream of you yet
> With the wind and the rain in your hair,
> I held you tight as we whispered goodnight
> With the wind and the rain in your hair,
> Now it will be my fav'rite memory . . .
> That vision of you standing there;
> There in the mist as you sighed when we kissed
> With the wind and the rain in your hair.
>
> *Music by Clara Edwards*

When the song played week after week on the Hit Parade, Ms. Edwards suddenly discovered fame and more royalties than any of her other compositions had brought her. Now even her "art songs" were in greater demand. The final cap was when the song was used in a very important film starring Henry Fonda and Barbara Stanwyck, *The Lady Eve.*

Ms. Edwards and I finally met. She invited me to tea at her Riverside Drive apartment, not only to thank me, but to offer me her entire catalog of published songs, just in case I could discover another sleeper. Ah! The Hit Parade plus money! It was such a leveler.

In another folio, a book of piano solos published by Chappell Music, I found an intriguing waltz by Eric Coates, an English composer unknown to me. Again, I acted on my own because I couldn't get the melody out of my head. Coates's title was "By the Sleepy Lagoon," so I stayed with that, just eliminating the first two words. I took my completed song to Max Dreyfus at Chappell, and he approved of what I had done, but was a bit dubious. He said, "I don't know how Sir Eric Coates will react to your writing a lyric without his consent. Besides, right now England is under a blitz, [it was 1939], and I don't know if we can get through to him. But I'll try!"

It took months before Chappell and I received a reply. Sir Coates wrote a special note to me that I still treasure: "Congratulations! You have fit your words to my music so perfectly that it sounds as though I wrote the music to your lyric."

Signed: Eric Coates.

Another big Hit Parade number! And it became England's number-one song during the height of the war. It was equally big in our country thanks to a brilliant trumpet solo recorded by my friend, Harry James.

> A sleepy lagoon, a tropical moon
> And two on an island,

A sleepy lagoon and two hearts in tune

In some lullaby-land;

The fireflies' gleam reflects in the stream,

They sparkle and shimmer . . .

A star from on high falls out of the sky

And slowly grows dimmer . . .

The leaves from the trees all dance in the breeze

And float on the ripples,

We're deep in a spell as nightingales tell

Of roses and dew;

The memory of this moment of love

Will haunt me forever!

A tropical moon, a sleepy lagoon

And you.

Music by Eric Coates

Harry James and I developed a good relationship, and he asked me to write new lyrics to an old Italian street song he was using as his theme, "Ciribiribin." I had a ball writing words to fit Harry's swinging arrangement, and among the many records we gathered was a fun version by Bing and the Andrews Sisters, which is one of my favorites. I had known these three Greek sisters, Patty, Maxene, and Laverne, from the early days when Lou Levy discovered them and became their manager. Laverne sang alto, the other two soprano, but Patty had the most personality and became the lead singer. Lou became an integral part of their lives, married Maxene, started a successful publishing business, and made many film deals for the sisters. After a few years of marriage, Lou and Maxene were divorced, and she came out of the closet. Later on I got to know Maxene and her girlfriend rather well. Laverne, who was the oldest, died in 1967, and shortly after that Maxene and Patty became estranged.

I was now in demand from many quarters, either to write lyrics or for my latest words-and-music effort. It was wonderful to be in a position to pick and choose and call the terms. I wrote a lyric to a lilting instrumental composed by bandleader Frankie Carle. "Sunrise Serenade" stayed on the Hit Parade forever and had innumerable recordings, one of the best vocals being done by my friend, Connee Boswell.

SUNRISE SERENADE

Good morning, good morning, you sleepy head,
It's dawning, stop yawning,
Get up and out of bed!
Say, the air is full of silk, it's time to get
  that morning milk,
Wake up, get out of bed!

Chorus:
Look at the grass, silver in the sun,
Heavy with the dew,
Look at the buds, you can almost see

How they're breaking through!
Look at the birds feeding all their young
In the sycamores;
But you better get on with your morning chores!
Just take a breath of the new mown hay
And the sugar cane;
Looks like tonight there will be a moon
Down in lover's lane!
There you go day-dreaming
When it's time that you obeyed
That sunrise serenade.

Music by Frankie Carle

Dave Kapp suggested that I should have a follow-up song for the Inkspots after their first hit, so I wrote one to fit their style: "It's Funny to Everyone But Me." Dave suggested that I drive to Philadelphia where the group was appearing and let them hear my new song. It was an unexpected and disappointing encounter. They listened in silence. I asked them what they thought, and I was taken aback by the response. They felt that they had given me a tremendous hit with "If I Didn't Care," which earned me lots of money——in which they hadn't shared! I pointed out that as a result of my hit, they had become a successful group with solid bookings. I didn't resent their success nor did I expect to share in their earnings. We parted on unfriendly terms.

Naturally, I reported this encounter to Dave Kapp whose reaction was, "Those ungrateful bastards! They'll record what I want them to record!" They did and had another hit. The song went on to be covered by Harry James and Frank Sinatra, among many others.

During this time, I became reacquainted with a couple of brothers who had also grown up in my old neighborhood, East New York. (Come to think of it, there may have been something in the water we drank that turned so many of us to a career in music.) A short walk from my home, there was David's Delicatessen, with two sons in the family who also attended Thomas Jefferson High. Mack David was my age and wrote a number of successful songs: "Candy," "Sunflower," "On the Isle of May," English lyrics to "Lili Marlene" and "La Vie en Rose." His younger brother, Hal David, was even more successful, going on to write many popular songs with Burt Bacharach and win Academy Awards.

Also within neighborhood walking distance was Warnow's Music Store, which sold radios, pianos, instruments, and sheet music. The two sons in that family became quite famous. The older one was Mark Warnow, who conducted an orchestra at Columbia Broadcasting and was associated with many large shows, chief among them "Your Hit Parade." His younger brother, Harry, had studied at Juilliard and not wanting to trade on Mark's reputation, changed his name to Raymond Scott. He played piano in Mark's and other orchestras and began writing music seriously. He did a lovely score for a Broadway show that starred Mary Martin, *Lute Song*. Then he organized an ensemble that he dubbed a quintet (although it had six members) and wrote and recorded many original instrumentals. He asked me to contribute lyrics to these compositions and trusted me to make any necessary musical changes. I truly enjoyed turning the following instrumentals into vocal songs: "Boy Scout in Switzerland," "Huckleberry Duck," and "In an Eighteenth-Century Drawing Room." I had fun putting a lyric to Mozart's exercise:

I found an old musty book
Long lost in some far forgotten nook,
In the book a faded picture
And the scent of faint perfume,
Two old-fashioned lovers
In an eighteenth-century drawing room;
Nothing is ever new, ever since love began,
See her two eyes of blue flirting behind her fan!
Look at his silk and lace . . .
Isn't he debonair?
And the smile on his face
Tells of the love they share
Hear their two hearts softly beat . . .
One moment more and their lips will meet!
What a sweet and charming picture . . .
Love in glory, love in bloom,
Don't you wish that you were
In an eighteenth-century drawing room?

Music by Raymond Scott and Wolfgang Amadeus Mozart

My career was really shaping up. I even had a lover in my life!

CHAPTER FIFTEEN

Bye-Bye Brooklyn

In the winter of 1939, it gave me extreme pleasure to be financially able to drive Mama and Papa down to Miami and rent a two-bedroom apartment for them right on the beach. It was their first visit to Florida, and my plan was for all my brothers to take turns spending time with them. Joe and Harvey were now operating their own fuel-oil business, and Murray was still in school.

President Roosevelt and his "New Deal" had improved our economy and put people back to work. Our country was on a high. Broadway was booming with a variety of great shows: *Life with Father*, *The Boys from Syracuse*, and *The Man Who Came to Dinner* were filling theaters. Hollywood was turning out some of its greatest films, including *The Wizard of Oz*, *Wuthering Heights*, and *Gone with the Wind*. We were slowly coming out of the Great Depression and, as Irving Berlin succinctly put it, "Nothing but BLUE SKIES" did we see.

Miami Beach turned out to be a new experience for me, too. My third night there, I wandered into a gay bar and met someone who would prove to be a turning point in my life.

Maury Harris was a prominent Manhattan allergist also on vacation in Miami. He was fifteen years older than I, a soft-spoken gentleman with a Boston brogue and a bubbling laugh. He looked enough like me to be taken for my older brother. It was an instant attraction for both of us. I've since learned that there are times when the heart tells you what's right for you.

Maurice Coleman Harris came from an old Massachusetts Jewish family that had been well assimilated over the years. He was not religious, but attended Unity Church on occasion. I sensed that Maury was a different breed from my show-biz friends and acquaintances and that there was much I could learn from this man. He lived gracefully, he was obviously cultured, he could talk theater, art, politics, social mores—all subjects about which I had a smattering of knowledge and a desire to learn more. Maury was a true educational force for me, right from that very first night—which I spent in his hotel suite.

I had no hesitation in introducing him to my parents. Their background and accents didn't faze him in the least. He was charming, and they took to him like *schmaltz* to chicken liver. This was one friend they approved of completely: a successful, practicing doctor, who could sympathize with Mama's aches and pain—and perhaps even prescribe! There was not even the slightest chastisement when I started to spend every night at Maury's hotel.

Such a wonderful feeling! I was relaxed—I was in love—and I knew he loved me in return. For the first time in my twenty-seven years, I was not ashamed of my homosexuality. Fate had brought me Maury, a man I would be proud to introduce to anyone. Life had taken on a luminous glow. Each day began with great anticipation, and each night ended wrapped in each others' arms.

We had met two pretty girls from New York, both in their early twenties, a niece and her young aunt. We spent days on the beach with them or bicycle riding, stopping by to introduce them to my parents, who smiled approvingly. Nights we took them dining and dancing. I told Maury that Florence, the aunt, would be a perfect mate for my brother, Harvey, and I piqued her interest in his imminent arrival.

Maury and I had made plans to return to the city together the day after Harvey arrived. I greeted my brother with the news that I had found his future wife and introduced them. I was a wise matchmaker. Harvey and Florence enjoyed a long, happily married life, and produced a son and daughter who gave them grandchildren.

Once Maury and I were back in New York, it was inconceivable that we should part or that I would continue to live in Brooklyn. Maury had been living in a hotel suite with one bedroom on East Forty-eighth Street. It was convenient to his office and adequate for a bachelor.

Of course, it became a bit tight when I moved in.

That happened before my parents returned from Miami. In retrospect, it amazes me how easily my entire family accepted my move into Maury's life. They were truly fond of him, and I don't believe any one of them suspected the true nature of our relationship at that time.

Maury had become involved with a group of scientists who met regularly and debunked fakers and fortune-tellers who dabbled in psychic phenomena. He had also studied and perfected the art of hypnosis, which he used occasionally to treat recalcitrant patients who were not responding properly to medication. He became so expert at hypnosis that he enjoyed demonstrating this art at public meetings, which I attended and watched with great interest.

While we were still living at the Middletowne Apartments, I invited some of my friends for drinks and to meet Maury. But unfortunately, he was called away for medical consultation, and I played the solo host. My date for the evening was the young comedienne, Mitzi Green, who had made quite a splash in the Rodgers and Hart Broadway musical, *Babes in Arms*. Among my other guests were Harold Rome, who was enjoying the fruits of his first Broadway success, the revue *Pins and Needles*, and his charming new bride, Florence. During the evening, I got to talking about Maury's proficiency as a hypnotist, describing some of his demonstrations. Mitzi and Harold were so intrigued, they voiced their disappointment at Maury's absence, and both expressed a desire to be hypnotized. Mitzi wanted to be given posthypnotic suggestions to lose weight, and Harold wished to be hypnotized into getting ideas for a new show.

In my brashness, I stated that I had watched Maury perform so frequently that I was certain I could do the same. It didn't take much urging by my guests for me to agree, so I started with Mitzi. I began with all the repetitive vocal cadences that I recalled Maury using, and to my amazement, Mitzi quickly went into a comalike sleep. She willingly reacted to all my suggestions, holding her arms outstretched, doing some dance steps, and singing.

Harold was so excited, he said, "Me! Do me now!"

I directed Mitzi to sit down and relax, giving her a posthypnotic suggestion that when I clapped my hands, she would awaken, stand up, and sing. Then I went to work on Harold. Never having tried this maneuver, I was completely overwhelmed by my success. And doubly so when I succeeded with Harold, getting him to sit at the piano and start composing. Florence became quite excited. "He's playing a tune I never heard before! Will he remember it?"

So I gave Harold the command that he would recall everything that happened when I awoke him. Then suddenly, I panicked. Suppose I can't wake Mitzi and Harold?

With great trepidation, I clapped my hands. Mitzi stood up, opened her eyes, and began belting out a song. Harold woke and said, "I remember . . . I remember everything."

And he did recall the tune he had been playing. By the time Maury came home, the guests were all gone, and I told him what had happened. He was quite upset with me and made me promise I would never attempt hypnosis again, that it was too dangerous in amateur hands. I have never tried it since.

Harry James proved to be a good friend. He asked me to write a lyric to an old Italian street song he had been using as his theme whenever he broadcast. We used the original title, "Ciribiribin," which I never quite understood, except that it had a cheerful, happy sound. I tried to capture that humor in my lyric.

When the moon hangs low in Napoli
There's a handsome gondolier,
Every night he sings so happily
So his lady love can hear;
In a manner so bravissimo
He repeats his serenade . . .
And his heart beats so fortissimo
When she raises her Venetian shade.

Chorus:
Ciribiribin, Ciribiribin, Ciribiribin . . .
Ciribiribin, he waits for her each night
Beneath her balcony,
Ciribiribin, he begs to hold her tight,
But no! She won't agree!
Ciribiribin, she throws a rose and blows
A kiss from up above;
Ciribiribin! Ciribiribin!
Ciribiribin, they're so in love!
                    Music by Harry James and Alberto Pestalozza

This vocal was instantly recorded by every band with a record contract, but none compared to the brilliant pairing of Bing Crosby and the Andrews Sisters. It was a megahit, making Harry, the publisher, and me ecstatic.

Some months later, Maury and I decided we needed a larger apartment and moved into a spacious penthouse on East Fifty-ninth Street with two terraces, one facing the bridge and the other downtown New York. My songs were earning money, so I insisted on paying my share. It felt so good to know that my career was ensuring me a comfortable income. It felt better to know that with my first royalties I had helped my brothers, Joe and Harvey, to split away from my cousins and establish their own fuel-oil business.

Our penthouse was beautifully furnished. Maury had excellent taste, which I absorbed by osmosis, and it was amazing to realize how much I had learned about décor from my Belgian friend, René. We entertained often. Maury had a large circle of straight and gay friends, many of them mature professionals. I was warmly included and never felt out of place in this new world. We mixed socially with Manhattan's elite.

I started to date the daughter of the Schinasi family, who lived in an incredible limestone mansion with a *porte-cochère* on a corner of Riverside Drive in the Eighties. There was even a tunnel leading from the house to the Hudson River, where their yacht was docked. The Schinasi wealth had come from manufacturing and importing. One of their many products was Fatima cigarettes.

It had been a second marriage for Ruby Schinasi, who was now a beautiful and wealthy widow. Dinners at the mansion were most impressive. A white-gloved butler in full regalia stood behind each chair. After dinner, when we were a small group, we would adjourn to madame's elegant dressing-room, which faced the river. The chandelier glowed, not only with crystal, but with rubies and emeralds, and madame loved sliding out drawers of a nearby cabinet to display all her jewelry, precious stones, and gold meticulously arranged in made-to-order compartments.

I became pals with Leonora, Ruby's daughter (from a first marriage) who was fondly known as Bubbles. She was recovering from a disastrous marriage and divorce to the young film star, Wayne Morris, who had left her with an infant. I helped her get settled in a small apartment and took her shopping for fireplace utensils on the Lower East Side. Bubbles was a sweet and lovely young girl, and some years later, she married Arthur Hornblow Jr., the famed Hollywood film producer, which resulted in a long and successful union.

One of Maury's gay friends was a widely known East Side dentist in his fifties who had been married and divorced, but remained friendly with his grown daughters. Elmer had had a brief fling with Tyrone Power during Power's early days. Power was now a rising 20th Century-Fox film star, and whenever he came to town, he made it a point to see Elmer. On a couple of occasions, Maury and I were invited to dine with them in some quiet, out-of-the-way restaurant. Tyrone was incredibly handsome, quite reserved in manner, and very discreet. Elmer's avuncular relationship with him lasted a long time. He was a sounding board for that young man's surpressed problems.

CHAPTER SIXTEEN

How I Rewrote Cole Porter and Made a Star of Dinah Shore

I was twenty-eight years old in 1940, and my career as a songwriter was in full blossom with a string of hits: "Play, Fiddle, Play," "Foolin' Myself," "Ciribiribin," "If I Didn't Care," "Sunrise Serenade," "What Will I Tell My Heart?" and recordings by Bing Crosby, Billie Holiday, Benny Goodman, the Mills Brothers, Fats Waller, Ella Fitzgerald, Nat Cole—all the top stars of the day. Hardly a week passed without at least two of my songs on the Hit Parade. That was the most glorious era of the music business: the sound of the Big Bands, the memorable voices of the boys and girls who sang with them.

And the songwriters of the day—Johnny Mercer, Jimmy Van Heusen, Sammy Cahn, Jule Styne, the Gershwins, Porter, Berlin, Arlen, Kern—were the creators and suppliers of unforgettable words and music. Each hit garnered at least a dozen recordings, unlike the music business of today, where most songs are written by their performers, whose meager vocalizing is then electronically enhanced.

In my day, the Tiffany of the music business was Chappell, Incorporated, with offices in London and New York, owned and managed by the Dreyfus Brothers, Max and Louis, who specialized in publishing all the great Broadway musical scores. Chappell had published a few of my songs, including a current hit for which I had written both words and music, "If I Didn't Care." So I was that year's fair-haired talent in their roster, and I had a good relationship with Max Dreyfus, whose frail body and ashen face gave the impression that he might not last the day. As a matter of fact, he lived another twenty years.

One day, Mr. Dreyfus (I never felt enough on equal terms to address him as Max—that privilege was reserved for his star writers: Jerome Kern, Oscar Hammerstein, Richard Rodgers, Cole Porter, and the Gershwins) to repeat, Mr. Dreyfus summoned me to his office in Radio City where his Bechstein grand piano sat in splendor. In this hushed atmosphere, Mr. Dreyfus often donned bedroom slippers to ease his aching feet and a cotton dust jacket, such as those worn by old-time clerks. Rarely would he invite you to be seated while he sat behind his huge desk, aimlessly shifting about papers and objects and never looking at you directly while talking.

The reason for the summons finally became clear. Cole Porter's newest musical, *Leave It to Me*, starring William Gaxton, Victor Moore, and Sophie Tucker, had just opened on Broadway. It introduced a pretty young thing named Mary Martin, who had taken the town by storm, wrapped in a mink coat with very little underneath, while singing a typical Porter whimsy titled "My Heart Belongs to Daddy." However, an unforeseen snag had developed. The media was being attacked for allowing suggestive lyrics to be aired (so what else is new?), and as a result, the networks and record companies were censoring songs and refusing to broadcast the big hit of Cole's show.

What an age of innocence the forties seem to have been. Cole couldn't have cared less. His song was filled with his usual witty double entendres and therefore was being censored. That hardly bothered Cole. He wrote what he pleased without regard to the carping of narrow-minded bigots and was already at work on a new score. But Max Dreyfus hated to lose the financial rewards inherent in any hit song—and so, my summons.

Here is Cole's original lyric, which was then being labeled "highly suggestive."

> *Verse*:
> I used to fall in love with all
> The lads who call on young ladies,
> But now I tell each young gazelle
> To go to hell! I mean Hades!
> Since I began to care for such a sweet millionaire . . .

Chorus:

While tearing off a game of golf

I may make a play for the caddy.

But when I do, I don't follow through,

'Cause my heart belongs to daddy!

If I invite a boy some night

To dine on my fine finnan haddie,

I just adore his asking for more

But my heart belongs to daddy!

Yes, my heart belongs to daddy,

So I simply couldn't be bad,

Yes, my heart belongs to daddy,

Da da da da da da dad!

So I want to warn you, laddie . . .

Though I think you're perfectly swell.

That my heart belongs to daddy

'Cause my daddy, he treats it so well!

As you can see, it's Cole's usual mischievous, clever wordplay for which he was so famous. However, once Cole had finished a score and the show was produced, he was through with it. He hated to rewrite anything. So Mr. Dreyfus asked me if I would like to rewrite the lyric to make it a more acceptable and less censorable song. *Would I*! A nice, young lad from Brooklyn who had nurtured himself on all those famous writers who were my heroes! I would gladly have *paid* for such an opportunity. Instead I was assured that if I delivered an acceptable lyric, Cole Porter would pay *me*! Naturally, I also had to agree that I would receive no credit and keep my contribution a secret.

Here are the changes I made:

Verse:

I used to fall in love with all

Those boys who call on young cuties,

But now I find I'm more inclined

To keep my mind on my duties,

Since I began to share in such a sweet love affair . . .

(You see, for starters . . . I'm making this a "love affair.")

Chorus:

While teeing off a game of golf

I may get a play from the caddy,

But when I do, I don't follow through,

'Cause my heart belongs to daddy!

(See? She's only playing golf and being faithful to her B.F.)

When some good scout invites me out

For wine and some fine finnan haddie,

(Well, there aren't that many rhymes for daddy! And this is simply an innocuous dinner date.)

I just adore . . . keep asking for more,

But my heart belongs to daddy!

(She's just crazy about finnan haddie!)

Yes, my heart belongs to daddy

So I simply couldn't be bad,

Yes, my heart belongs to daddy,

Da da da da da da dad!

(No double entendres there . . . just double words!)

So I want to warn you, laddie,

To be careful right from the start,

'Cause I'm gonna marry daddy,

For my daddy belongs to my heart!

(All wrapped up with love and marriage. What a good girl she is!)

With my whitewashed, goody-goody version, the song gathered many recordings, was a huge hit, and a moneymaker for Porter and Chappell. I was paid the munificent sum of $250 for my work with a check signed by Cole. That would have been the end of this story, but for my friends at Decca Records and Walter Winchell. Decca decided to record my version of "Daddy" with Ella Fitzgerald, and when the record was released, under Porter's name they added in small print: (Special lyrics by Jack Lawrence). After Winchell had fallen in love with the Inkspots' recording of "If I Didn't Care," he often mentioning my name and quoted parts of my lyric. Now he began crediting me with the success of "My Heart Belongs to Daddy" and writing that I was being deprived of proper credit.

Another summons to Mr. Dreyfus's office.

I entered apologetically, expecting to be chastised because of Winchell's revelations, and eager to explain that I was not to blame.

Instead, I was greeted with the news that Cole wanted to see me. I was to go that very afternoon to the Waldorf, where he resided. I asked why I was being invited. Perhaps Mr. Porter wanted to berate me personally? Mr. Dreyfus said he didn't know the reason for the invitation, but assured me not to worry. "Cole is bigger than that! He must have some special reason for wanting to see you."

Off I sped to the Waldorf Towers, gave my name to the concierge, who called up to announce me, and rose in the elevator to the penthouse. I was ushered in by a valet and seated in a sumptuous living room. The valet disappeared while I studied my surroundings: lovely antiques, impressionist paintings, an air of quiet elegance.

"Someday," I thought to myself, "someday I'll live like this!"

And at that moment, Cole Porter was wheeled in by his valet. He had fractured both legs some years before in a fall from a horse, and despite the fact that he suffered terrible pain and agony and had undergone repeated surgery with eventual amputation of one leg, this brave, talented man had continued turning out legendary scores for musicals.

He must have sensed my awe and unease, offering me a drink and quickly making me feel comfortable and relaxed. He complimented me on my lyrics for "Daddy" and—would you believe?—he knew practically all my songs, and he never mentioned the Winchell columns.

Finally, he got to the reason for his invitation. Would I like a weekly job of rewriting lyrics of the song Sophie Tucker sang in his show? The song called "Tomorrow" dealt with the headlines in the daily news and constantly required updating. He was already working on a new score for a musical called *Mexican Hayride*, to star Lupe Velez. He confessed that he detested having to rework lyrics and would happily compensate me for each one I delivered.

Did I accept? YES!

I had been there perhaps an hour, finishing my cocktail and rising to leave, when Cole asked had I written anything new? If so, he'd love to hear it. I said that as a matter of fact, while working on "Daddy," I had been reminded of a similar Ukrainian minor melody—a folk song my mother used to sing. I had developed that basic tune into a song. He pointed to the piano. I sat down and performed my new opus.

Verse:

I've got to be good or mama will scold me,
Yes! Yes! Yes!
I asked her and this is what she told me . . .
Yes! Yes! Yes!

Chorus:

Mother, may I go out dancing?
YES, MY DARLING DAUGHTER!
Mother, may I try romancing?
YES, MY DARLING DAUGHTER!

What if there's a moon, mama darling,

And it's shining on the water . . .

Mother, must I keep on dancing?

YES, MY DARLING DAUGHTER!

What if he'll propose, mama darling,

When the night is growing shorter . . .

Mother, what should be my answer?

YES, MY DARLING DAUGHTER!

All this was followed by an interlude and second chorus.

"I love it!" Porter said when I finished. "I wish I had found that old Ukrainian folk tune. You know, I love minor melodies. Every time I write a new one, Irving is on the phone . . ." (Irving? The only one I knew of was Berlin!) ". . . on the phone kidding me. 'So I hear you've written another Yiddish melody!' And he proceeds to sing a rabbinical, liturgical version of 'My Heart Belongs to Daddy.' He goes 'di da de da . . . di da de da . . . Di dydle de dydle de dydle!'" Cole laughed uproariously. "Then Irving says, 'Cole, are you sure you haven't got a little Hebrew boy writing those Yiddish melodies? You know, like the little pickaninny who they say writes my songs?'"

As I was about to leave, Cole called out, "By the way, have you played your new song for Max? No? I'm going to call him right away to tell him about it. Be sure to go directly to his office."

By the time I got back to Chappell Music, Mr. Dreyfus's secretary, Irene, was waiting for me with the door open. Mr. Dreyfus beckoned me in, pointed to the Bechstein, and said, "Let me hear the song Cole says is a positive hit!" I happily complied.

Mr. Dreyfus spoke. "Irene, call in Eddie Wolpin!" His general manager promptly appeared. "Eddie, Jack has written a new song which is going to be our number-one plug. Let him hear it, Jack."

Although my relationship with Wolpin had been amicable, I sensed that this procedure rubbed him the wrong way. He was used to being the one who first heard new material and brought it to Mr. Dreyfus's attention. This reversal did not sit well. However, contracts for my song were drawn that very day.

Six months, nine months passed during which time I repeatedly asked Eddie what was happening with my song. Nothing! He said he was having difficulty getting a recording. I pleaded with him to tell Mr. Dreyfus about his difficulties so that I could reclaim my song, but this he refused to do. I was tempted to call Cole, who had been paying me the established $250 per for my updated lyrics on "Tomorrow," but I decided that I must fight my own battles.

The scene shifts! Almost a year later, I was in the general manager's office of the Leo Feist Music Company, one of the firms owned by MGM Pictures, where I had a current hit riding, "A Handful of Stars." In a sense, Cole Porter and Sophie Tucker were responsible for this song. Because of those updated lyrics Cole had me writing for Sophie's "Tomorrow" song, I decided to catch her act at the Latin Quarter club on Broadway one night. Her long-time accompanist was an old songwriter named Ted Shapiro. Sophie was a veteran trouper, and her act was a polished diamond.

At the halfway mark in her show, she would always stop to plug her autobiography, which she offered to sign personally with each purchase. She managed to sell a lot of books. During her sales pitch, Ted would softly noodle on the piano in the background. I became conscious that he was always playing a most distinctive riff, so when he joined me for a drink, I asked him what he had been noodling.

"Just filling time," he said. "I play that whenever Sophie's doing her shtick." I asked him for a lead sheet, and that time filler became "A Handful of Stars," recorded by Johnny Mathis, Jimmy Dorsey, Glenn Miller, and, best of all, Nat Cole! Ted Shapiro was delighted. It had been years since his last hit and I was really proud of this lyric.

> I recall a story, a night of love and glory,
> A night that left my heart romantic scars . . .
> We stood so near to heaven that I reached clear to heaven
> And gathered you a handful of stars;
> Sweet remembered hour when love began to flower
> With moonlight through the trees like silver bars
> And as the moon grew older, I reached across your shoulder
> And gathered you a handful of stars;
> I placed my fingertips upon your lips
> And stars fell in your eyes,
> Moon-glow made a halo of your hair . . .
> Suddenly you looked at me

And dreams began to rise . . .
Oh, what words unspoken trembled in the air!
Our hearts were madly beating and then our lips were meeting
And Venus seemed to melt right into Mars!
And while we stood caressing, blue heaven sent a blessing . . .
A shower of a handful of stars.

Of the multiple recordings that song gathered, my favorite was Nat Cole's version.

So here I was in the office of the general manager, Harry Link, congratulating him on the great job he was doing on my song. As I was sitting around shooting the breeze with him, I decided to ask his opinion of the song Eddie Wolpin couldn't get recorded. When I concluded my rendition of "Darling Daughter," Harry jumped up all excited.

"You get that song back from Chappell today. I'm leaving for Hollywood tomorrow. Give it to me, and I guarantee it will be in Judy Garland's next film!"

Now, at that time, I wasn't aware that Harry was known to the old-pro writers as Link the Liar. Harry had a peculiar nervous habit of twisting and torturing his white linen handkerchief while in conversation with anyone. When he was telling whoppers, Harry would usually shred the handkerchief to rags. I just assumed at that moment that the shredding was due to his enthusiasm and excitement about my song. Harry called in one of his rehearsal pianists, Ticker Freeman, asked him to listen to my song and to suggest which of the singers he worked with should make a demo.

"Ticker, I want it done today so that I can take it to the coast tomorrow. Who can you get?" Ticker listened and said he had the perfect girl who was due in shortly for a rehearsal. "Okay!" said Harry. "Jack, get moving! Get that song back from Dreyfus, and we're in business!"

I rushed over to Chappell Music, pleaded with Wolpin once more to help me get my song released. He refused! I stormed into the old man's office, practically shouting, "Mr. Dreyfus, my song has been here over a year. Eddie Wolpin hates it, says he can't get a record. You have to give it back to me!" Mr. Dreyfus, behind his desk shuffling papers, said mildly, "I never give any songs back!" He then sent for Wolpin, who started making halfhearted excuses. "Tell him, Eddie! Tell him you hate the song!"

Eddie mumbled a few words and was dismissed by Dreyfus, who kept shuffling papers and muttering, "I can't give you back the song. Cole said it's a hit. It will be a hit with some other firm."

With tears in my eyes, I called upon my chutzpah. "Mr. Dreyfus. I've given you some big hits in the past few years. If you don't return this song to me, I'LL NEVER come to your firm again!"

It worked! He gave me a release then and there, and I rushed back to Harry Link, where Ticker was waiting with a pleasant, but mousy-looking Southern girl. She had a thick accent, stringy hair, and a mile-wide gap between her two front teeth.

"Jack, meet Fanny Rose."

"Ticker!" she said. "Ya know my name's Dinah now!"

"Yeah . . . Dinah!" said Ticker. "We've been rehearsing, and she knows your song pretty good now." We proceeded to a recording studio where I directed and coached her on a proper interpretation, and we made the demo, which Harry did take with him on his departure the next day. I sat around checking off the days and praying. "Judy Garland! MGM! My song!"

About ten days went by when I got a phone call from my Southern songbird. "Jack!" She was breathless. "You'll never believe what happened! I auditioned for Eddie Cantor—with your song! Not only does he want to sign me for his weekly program, he plans to introduce me as his newly adopted daughter singing your song as a duet with him for the next few weeks!"

"Forget it, Fanny . . . Dinah . . . whatever your name is!" I said. "That song is going into Judy Garland's next picture. Harry Link promised, and I'm waiting to hear."

"But Jack," she cried, "this is my big break. If I can't do that song, Cantor may not want me."

I remained adamant. Two days later, I got a call from the head producer of the Cantor show. After a pleasant introduction, he suddenly screamed at me, "Who the fuck do you think you are telling Eddie Cantor he can't use your song?"

I tried to maintain my dignity. "The song belongs to me. It's going into Judy Garland's next picture. Harry Link promised."

"Bullshit! You're gonna trust Link the Liar? It ain't going into any picture. I spoke to Harry on the coast, and he said we could have the song for our show!"

I was shocked. And furious at Link's betrayal. I said, "In that case, you'll have to pay me for the use of the song as special material!"

"Pay?" he yelled. "Writers pay Cantor to do their songs! We'll find another song!"

"Okay, find yourself another song." And I hung up.

Two days later, another call from Mr. Producer. "Okay, Jack, how much do you want?"

I had to think fast. I'd never been confronted with a similar situation. The only criterion I had for payment was what Cole Porter had paid me per lyric. I swallowed nervously and muttered, "Two hundred and fifty dollars per performance."

I knew I'd sold myself cheap when he quickly replied, "Okay! You've got a deal!"

The entire family and I were glued to the radio the night Eddie Cantor introduced his new protégée, Dinah Shore, with my song "Yes, My Darling Daughter!" In a babushka, he played the mother to her daughter, and that first broadcast earned her a contract with Victor Records. Naturally, her first recording was my song, and she was on the road to stardom.

How many weeks did Cantor pay me that $250? One! Because my song was rushed into general release, it was then available for everyone's use, and Cantor no longer had to pay me. Regardless, we all did well. Except Max Dreyfus, who never let me forget the favor he had done.

P.S. Dinah and I remained buddies through the years, and she recorded many of my songs.

CHAPTER SEVENTEEN

Losses

In 1941, Mama, who had never smoked a cigarette in her life, was diagnosed with lung cancer. Maury Harris arranged for her to see the most highly regarded physicians and surgeons, and the conclusion was surgery. Chemotherapy had not yet been put into practice.

After the surgery, Mama was given little chance of survival. Maury had recommended a hospital to which he was attached so that he could monitor her treatment. As the end drew near, the pain was unbearable—for her and for us who watched. I took Maury aside and without telling my family, begged for a favor—to end her suffering. Tearfully, he promised he would. I will be ever grateful to him for that gesture.

Mama's passing was a tremendous loss to my father, brothers, relatives—and especially to me. I was devastated! I had been the closest to her, and I missed her wisdom and love. She had always believed in me and encouraged me in my darkest hours. She died a few days before Pearl Harbor and the subsequent declaration of war by America. She was fifty-four years old and was gone before I could shower her with the fruits of my earnings. I'm delighted that she lived to see a part of my success. When "Yes, My Darling Daughter!" became a big hit and I was asked to do interviews, I brought Mama into the city and told how I had converted a folk tune she always hummed into a hit. They ran the story in the *Daily Mirror* with a photo of Mama beaming at me, both of us seated on a piano bench.

My parents also had the pleasure of seeing me on stage as part of an act called "Songwriters on Parade," which toured the Loew's circuit. Four grand pianos on stage with a songwriter at each keyboard: Fred J. Coots, writer of "You Go to My Head," "Santa Claus Is Coming to Town," "For All We Know"; then Peter De Rose with "Deep Purple," "Wagon Wheels," "When Your Hair Has Turned to Silver"; then a real old-timer, Jean Schwartz, who was married to one of the Dolly Sisters and wrote many early Broadway shows plus "Chinatown, My Chinatown." Our MC was Charley Tobias, author of "Two Tickets to Georgia," "Little Lady Make Believe," "Somebody Loves You." And then—the youngest member of the group, me, playing and singing some of my repertoire.

When we reached the Loew's State on Broadway, many writers used to drop by to catch our performance. Tobias would always call them up to the stage and have them do their hits. One evening, Charley spotted Irving Berlin in the audience and coaxed him on stage. After a few pleasant remarks, Berlin concluded with "All these old guys—they don't bother me! The one I'm worried about is that kid!" pointing to me.

Hey, Irving, you needn't have worried.

Shortly after, in 1941, Maury and I discussed the imminent draft, for which we were both possible candidates. He decided to accept a commission in the U.S. Navy, and since I didn't have a degree that would entitle me to a commission, I decided to enlist in the Coast Guard.

Before entering the service, Maury and I decided to give up our penthouse since we had no idea how long the war might last. A lady friend who was a real-estate broker persuaded us to store our furnishings in a smaller penthouse that she would rent out, rather than put it all in storage. When we were both in our respective services, she notified us that she had sublet our new apartment to John Latouche, a brilliant young lyricist who had just written the hit Ethel Waters show, *Cabin in the Sky*, with Vernon Duke.

Maury went to sea and saw active service as a doctor on a battleship that plied the Pacific. By the time the war ended, he was a full commander. But those four years we were apart had taken their toll. We had both lost what we once treasured—love for each other. When Maury retired from the navy, he decided to remain on the West Coast, where he resumed his practice and published many books on allergy. After some years had passed, we started a correspondence, particularly at Christmas time. We met cordially three or four times over many years. Sadly, I learned in the summer of 2000 that Maury, age ninety-eight, had passed away quietly in his retirement home in the Southern California desert. His charm, his wit, his urbanity are still with me.

CHAPTER EIGHTEEN

How I Fought World War II and Saved Nelson Riddle

A few years ago, a biography of Nelson Riddle by Peter Levinson titled *September in the Rain* hit the bookstands. An early chapter mentions my involvement with Nelson and how I was partly instrumental in starting him on his brilliant career as an arranger. Reading that story brought back a flood of memories about those long-ago wartime days.

At the time of the Pearl Harbor debacle in 1941, I was twenty-nine years old and a ripe candidate for the draft. Enlisting seemed the best recourse. But in what branch of the service? Not being a macho patriot, I gave careful consideration to the army, air force, and navy and concluded that the Coast Guard looked like a safe bet. All I knew about it was that it guarded our coastlines, so I wouldn't be too far from home. Down I went to their recruiting office and presented myself.

Since I had no university degree, I was not eligible officer material, but in filling out the questionnaire, I listed my many hit songs and my affiliation with the world of entertainment. Lo and behold, the Coast Guard grabbed me eagerly, enlisted me as a chief petty officer, and sent me to their newly opened training station in Sheepshead Bay, Brooklyn. (Back to my hometown that I had so happily and recently left.) I knew nothing about boats and was looking forward to being turned into a seaman. But the Coast Guard had another immediate need of my services. They appointed me welfare and morale officer and asked me to recruit musicians for both a parade and dance band. Immediately I envisioned myself in a snazzy uniform, leading a parade band for military occasions.

It suddenly occurred to me that I knew nothing about conducting a band, so I rushed off to my good friend, Mark Warnow, the orchestra conductor of the popular "Your Hit Parade" programs on CBS. Mark laughed at me when I explained my problem, put on a recording of Sousa marches, stuck a baton in my hand, and said, "All you have to do is give the band a downbeat. That's all there is to it!" he laughed. "Once you give the downbeat, the tempo never changes in a march. You don't even have to wave the stick anymore. Just wait for the finish, and be sure to end with the band."

"Yes, but what about 'The Star-Spangled Banner'? That's not in strict tempo. It's got all those retards and holds."

So my next lesson consisted of conducting a recording of our national anthem until Mark said I was passable. "Okay, you're ready. Now go out, and fight the war!"

When I finally got to the Coast Guard base in Sheepshead Bay, I started making telephone calls. My first recruit was another good friend, a sallow-faced night owl, Cy Walter. He was a great pianist who had played all the best boîtes as soloist or accompanist to great chanteuses like Mabel Mercer. In a Coast Guard uniform, poor Cy was a sad-looking sack. Nothing seemed to fit.

I can't let this moment pass without a few words about Mercer. She was an elegant mulatto lady who had been born in England and spent innumerable years performing in Europe. She was a matronly, soft-spoken, polished grande dame in her thirties when she immigrated to the States and began appearing in the chic, intimate East Side clubs where I met her. She did not have a huge voice, but what she did possess was an understanding of sophisticated lyrics and phrasing that kept her singing well into her seventies. Wherever she appeared, she was a treasure, a cult figure. Her fans were legion and loyal and sat there enraptured as she told her song-stories, always elegantly gowned and coiffed, always gesturing with a long, chiffon handkerchief, adding emphasis to a phrase. We were friends for years, and when she visited my homes, she never drank anything but champagne.

Mabel died nearly twenty years ago, but she is still venerated as the doyenne of the cabaret circuit. Frank Sinatra, among other great singers, always credited Mabel as the one who had taught him how to interpret a song. Today, singers like Bobby Short,

Barbara Cook and Julie Wilson, and a whole new generation of cabaret performers keep Mabel's memory alive.

Okay. Back to the war. Now I had a pianist, Cy Walter, but no piano. So I called another friend, the famous columnist Ed Sullivan (he had yet to become a TV host), who obliged with a small squib in one of his columns. "Jack Lawrence, CPO now in the Coast Guard, desperately needs a piano so that he can provide entertainment for our brave seamen." In short order, I was inundated with offers of pianos and wound up with a dilly of a Baldwin grand. Meanwhile, I had been raiding and recruiting musicians from all the big bands.

There I was, fighting the war—in Brooklyn!—in my navy whites, waving a baton in front of a hastily collected group of quirky musicians who griped constantly about having to march with their instruments and prayed they would never feel the deck of a ship under their feet. Their one enjoyment was tootling away at the nightly entertainments I organized with local bobby-soxers who were bused in as dancing partners for our men in training. I had about twenty-five professional musicians, all of whom had brought their own instruments. Music publishers gladly supplied us with printed arrangements of their hit songs. After a few weeks of these nightly soirees, I noticed two frequent visitors, a naval captain and his wife, who sat on the sidelines observing. One night, he beckoned me over and introduced himself: Captain Wauchope, in charge of a huge base under construction practically next door to us in Manhattan Beach. This was to be a training base for the U.S. Maritime Service and in time would house thousands of young lads being readied to replace the merchant seamen delivering food and goods to our allies, who were being knocked off by German submarines.

Captain Wauchope said that he had been watching me for some time and liked the way I was doing my job. "How would you like to switch to my base and be in a similar capacity?" he asked. "We'll need lots more musicians for our huge base."

I stammered, "B-b-but I'm in the Coast Guard. And my superior says that I'm due for a promotion to ensign."

"No problem!" said the captain. "I can get you transferred, and you'll come in as ensign. And if you do as good a job for us, I can guarantee you a quick promotion."

Well! I'd have been a fool to resist such blandishments. When I told my Coast Guard superior, he was quite upset. He told me that he'd been ready to promote me to ensign, but he couldn't refuse the U.S. Navy's request to release me. He let me go with the warning that he hoped I wasn't making a big mistake.

My next two years (fighting the war, you know) at Manhattan Beach were both fruitful and harrying. Imagine being in charge of 110 crazy musicians from all the big bands who had joined the Maritime Service under the illusion that they would never have to go to sea. Many were New York City guys and couldn't understand why they weren't allowed to go home every night after the dance and come back the next night for the following gig. To them, being in the service was just like playing a gig—except they couldn't smoke reefers on the base.

Guy Lombardo, the Dorsey Brothers, Sammy Kaye, Glenn Miller—all of whom I knew—had pleaded with me to take their best musicians into the Maritime Service before they could be drafted into the army or navy. What a talented group I assembled. Dave Terry had been chief arranger for Andre Kostelanetz. Philip Lang had worked with my pal, Morton Gould, as an arranger. I had Glenn Miller's talented bass player, Doc Goldberg, and Sammy Kaye's pianist and arranger, Ralph Fleniken, (after the war, I changed his name to Flanagan, and he fronted a big band). I had Charlie Barnett's trumpet player, Lyman Vunk; clarinetist Willie Schwartz, also from Glenn Miller; George Arus, trombonist with Tommy Dorsey and Artie Shaw; and in our string section, Zelly Smirnoff, formerly concertmaster with the NBC Symphony; and from the Metropolitan Opera orchestra, Freddy Buldrini. One of our drummers was Nat Polen, who went on to become a big soap opera star on "One Life to Live." And I mustn't forget Alan Shulman, a fine cellist and arranger from the NBC Symphony.

And this is where Nelson Riddle comes into my story. Nelson grew up a quiet, introverted boy in New Jersey and played trombone in the Ridgewood High School Band. As a teenager, he made his way from one small band to another until he finally joined Charlie Spivak. By that time, Nelson had made friends and fallen in love with Bill Finegan's great charts for Glenn Miller, so he decided to try arranging. Age twenty-two in 1943 when he knew the draft was about to swallow him, Nelson joined my Maritime conglomeration. He was very much a loner and always seemed to be in deep thought, probably dreaming up musical combinations in his head. He quickly realized that this was his grand opportunity—to pick the brains of all our well-known arrangers and write charts for the thirty-eight musicians who made up our dance band. Those charts he produced were an incredible new sound. In retrospect, there's no doubt that Nelson Riddle was a talented genius. Even today, his orchestrations for Frank and Ella and Rosie sound as fresh and innovative as the day he wrote them.

That passel of crazy musicians was a handful for me, and some days I almost wished they would be shipped out to sea. Instead, they would spend all their leave time hobnobbing with other cats in New York bands. They couldn't understand why they had to make an appearance at eight every morning, why they had to be there on Christian and Jewish holidays, why they couldn't take home the girls who came to our dances. I was always interceding for some musician who had broken the rules or been caught smoking pot.

I divided the men into two large groups: a swinging dance band under Dave Terry, who wrote lush arrangements that made me sound really good when I sang with the band, and a parade band under Phil Lang, who wrote ringing martial charts that brought out your pride in being American. Phil was an extremely talented fellow who came into his own after the war as an arranger in great demand for top Broadway musicals. He and I worked together again when he did an artful job on my Broadway score, *I Had A Ball*, which I wrote with Stan Freeman. To this day, when I play the original cast album of that forty-year-old score, it still sounds fresh and new.

By this time I had written a spirited march, which Phil arranged, titled "Heave Ho, My Lads, Heave Ho (It's a Long, Long Way to Go)." It ended with a great climax: "Damn the submarines! We're the men of the Merchant Marine!" This became the official Maritime Service song, made its way into a few Hollywood war films, and is still played annually on Maritime Day. Through my show-biz connections—and to aid recruitment for the Maritime Service—CBS gave my band a full hour on a coast-to-coast hookup. I fronted the band as leader and vocalist.

During that time, I was able to lure some of Hollywood's biggest names as guest stars: beautiful Madeleine Carroll, Jack Benny and his wife, Mary Livingston, my ex-Brooklyn neighbor and schoolmate, Sylvia Fine and her husband, Danny Kaye, George Burns and Gracie Allen, sexy Carole Landis, and many more. Every week brought another glamorous star. They would each do their shtick and end with a plea to America's young men to join the Maritime Service.

I must confess, I loved it all. It was all show biz, and I was making my small contribution to the war effort. And I had been promoted to lieutenant, junior grade. On that Manhattan Beach base, the word was "Here you can get a promotion quicker than you can say Jack Lawrence." Naval Academy men had no great love for me. But all the protocol and paperwork kept me occupied seven days a week.

Sad to say, my glory days ended too soon. My protector and promoter, Captain Wauchope, asked for and was given command of a navy ship and sent into action. I begged him to take me along, but he said, "Jack, I'd like to. But you've had no sea training. What would you be able to do on my ship?"

I got his point and decided I had to get off that base. There were too many Damocles swords hanging over me, wielded by officers who resented my fair-haired-boy status. I took leave of all the good friends I had made in my band, assuring talents like Phil Lang, Ralph Flanagan, and Nelson Riddle that we would certainly work together after the war. I was transferred from that base at my request. Where to this time? Another battlefront! The old Chelsea Hotel on West Twenty-third Street in Manhattan, where the navy had leased a number of floors to house Maritime-trained pursers waiting for ships. In charge of this operation was a Naval Academy senior lieutenant who lorded it over me and handed me the impossible task of babysitting these young pursers. They lay around idly all day with nothing to do but gorge on their three daily meals, all at government expense.

Something had to be done. I got a bright idea and called up all the shipping companies who were involved in the war effort. Since the government was paying these kids while they lay about, I offered them to the shipping companies gratis. In that manner, I disposed of most of the boys. Suddenly they had daily jobs to go to, and eventually each company would place them on ships when an opening occurred. I did such a good job that after a year, Washington HQ transferred me to Boston to run a shipping-out station there. I was head honcho in complete charge of that operation.

I enjoyed a comfortable existence in my new post, found a smart, furnished apartment right off the Charles River Basin, acquired a circle of old Boston family friends, and was a welcome figure trimly turned out in my navy whites that summer.

Naturally, I still led my closeted, secret life. After a social evening, in the late hours, I would drop into a nearby hotel bar where servicemen of all ranks cruised. I recall stumbling home about three one morning, full of martinis and good cheer. As I was passing a dark niche between buildings on the basin, in the shadows I noticed a sailor peeing. I walked past, and he quickly caught up to me.

"Sir, sir, can I ask you something? Is there any place to get a drink this time of night?"

I looked him over. Blond hair tumbling down his forehead, little white hat askew on his head—he was cute and appealing, although staggering a bit.

I knew I shouldn't be getting involved with a sailor. I held an important position. But it was the middle of the night, and my libido was charged. I led him around the corner to my flat. Before we got into bed, he asked me to set the alarm. He had to leave by 6 A.M. to report back to his ship. I can't remember anything that happened or how I would rate it on a scale of one to ten. I didn't even stir when the alarm went off. I woke at about eight and reached for my watch. It was gone! Reached for my pants. They were gone! I found them hanging in the bathroom, but didn't remember putting them there.

I went through the apartment in a panic. My money, my identifications, my wallet—all gone. There was not a trace of that sailor left behind. I had no idea what ship he was on, what his name was. Besides, there were too many ships in the harbor, so even had I known his name, it would have been difficult to track him down. I spoke to a gay officer friend, hoping for some advice, but neither of us could think of any solution. My friend advised that discretion was the primary consideration. So all I could do was write off my missing money and replace the identifications. I cursed that sailor from here to the last of the seven seas and was quite circumspect—for the next week or so.

CHAPTER NINETEEN

I Do—and I Didn't

One evening, Bernice and Ken Roman, two good Boston friends whose home was always open to me, invited me to dinner at the Ritz Hotel. For entertainment, there was a singer named Bernice Parks who had gotten some good reviews. She was attractive, sexy, vivacious, put on a good show, and flirted with me outrageously. Naturally, I sent her a note inviting her to join our table for a drink, and when we took the floor to dance, we made an eye-catching couple, I in my summer whites. I loved to dance, and she was a perfect partner.

My friends the Romans thought she was enchanting and urged me to go for it. So I made a date for the following night. Bernice's show finished rather late, and she suggested we find a quiet place for a drink. I suggested my apartment. Without going into explicit details, I'll simply say that the sexual satisfaction I enjoyed that night—and for many nights to come—was as great as any I had experienced with men. This girl had been around and knew a few tricks. By the close of her engagement at the hotel, we were seriously involved. But she told me that she was determined to have a career, and therefore marriage was secondary. She had appeared in a revue called *Meet the People* on the West and East coasts and garnered good reviews. My feeling was that finally I had found a girl who could excite me sexually, who could share my musical life, and who was also Jewish. I knew that would please Papa, my brothers, and our relatives.

Bernice's father had died recently and left her mother in charge of a chain of popular Chinese restaurants in Washington, D.C., New York, and Boston called Ruby Foo, named for the Chinese lady who had been the original owner. Her mother and younger sister were living on Park Avenue in a large apartment. When her mother came to Boston, we met, and she seemed to be pleased at the prospect of our union. From my point of view, in my thirties, I felt that this was my big chance for marriage and what I really wanted—children. I hoped Bernice felt the same.

I had never been in analysis, never felt the need for it, and truly didn't know if I could change my sexual orientation and my life, but I wanted to give it a shot. I had known other men who married, had children, and then eventually returned to a gay life. As usual, I had no one to talk to about this drastic change I was contemplating, but I hoped for the best. Meanwhile, Bernice and I continued having great sex. We were inseparable, and my Boston friends all approved and entertained us.

Then I received orders that I was being transferred to run a maritime station in Panama. Bernice and I had a tearful parting, promised to write frequently, and made plans to be wed as soon as I was out of the service. She had bookings on the road again with more singing engagements. I knew that I had to pack everything I would be taking with me to my new station in Panama. At last . . . I was going overseas.

I started packing a huge steamer trunk that I used as a traveling closet. When spread open, the left side contained all my hanging clothes and the right side was a series of drawers for foldups. I had worked my way down to the bottom drawer when I reached in and got the surprise of my life. There was my lost wallet, with all my ID cards and money!

That drunken night with that cute sailor whom I had cursed so furiously . . . well, I had had enough of my wits about me, even in my sloppy stupor, to safely stash all my belongings. The next morning, I had completely blocked it out of my mind.

Bon voyage, little sailor!

I hated the year I was stuck in Colon, Panama. It was rightly named—the asshole of the world. I was surrounded by army and navy personnel, the weather, the flies, the boredom, my nonsocial life—all of it dull and dreary. It was like living in a goldfish bowl—there was absolutely no privacy. But what was I complaining about? Men were dying in battles all over the world, and I was living in comparative safety. My social nights out were occasionally fun, with unlimited liquor and marijuana. I was able to send and receive mail and even make calls directly to Bernice and my family.

She wrote loving letters in answer to mine. We missed each other. Her mother had decided to buy a brownstone on East Seventy-second Street off Madison Avenue and convert it into duplexes for herself and us. We were counting the days until we could be together. Then D-Day. By 1945, I was free to return to civilian life.

All this time, I had held on to the penthouse on Washington Square that was a sublet. Over the years, through correspondence, I had written Maury about Bernice, and he had told me of his decision to remain on the West Coast after the war. So we made a deal for me to buy out his share of the furniture and apartment. He wrote about my plans with Bernice, and he wished me all the best. I have always believed that my plans were what caused him to decide on staying in California.

Bernice knew about my penthouse in the Village, which John Latouche was subletting with a new bedmate he had taken in, the sexy, young film actor William Eythe. They were notified that I would be reclaiming my apartment, so they vacated, leaving an enormous unpaid phone bill and stains all over my bedspreads. Bernice and her mother went to inspect the apartment and quickly let me know that there was nothing there they liked, wanted, or approved of. In their estimation, it was all junk and not to be considered for our forthcoming duplex.

Bernice was there to greet me on arrival and whipped me off to her family's Park Avenue home, where we shared her roomy bedroom with mother's approval. After all, we were scheduled to be married. I finally met Bernice's younger sister, who was rather strange. The two girls hardly communicated, and I soon recognized that her sister was a lesbian.

What a farcical situation. Me pretending to the lesbian that I was a straight guy who was going to marry her sister.

A couple of months later, when my bride-to-be was on the road again, I found myself in the apartment with sister. She stopped in the middle of a conversation we were having and said, "Jack, you're too nice a guy for Bernice. I have to warn you. Don't marry her. You'll regret it!"

By now I had brought Bernice to meet my family and relatives in Brooklyn. Papa and my Aunt Rivka and her children all were impressed with her. My brothers approved, particularly when I took them to Ruby Foo's in Manhattan and they met my future mother-in-law, a quite imposing woman. So the wedding date was set, and the brownstone was being renovated. We were to have the first two floors and her mother, the top two. An elevator was being installed and the strange sister, who was rarely home, would have an apartment on the roof with great privacy.

I hated the renovation plans, and I disliked the furnishings Bernice and her mother were buying for our duplex. It was all shlock, glitzy, fake Chinese reproductions, and I wondered how I could remain quiet and live with it. When I ventured an opinion, I was told that I didn't appreciate what was good. But by now, I knew better.

We were still living in the Park Avenue apartment, still having thrilling sex when my fiancée was off the road and at home. One night when we had just completed an exciting and satisfying union, Bernice turned to me and said, "You know, Jack, you haven't been using condoms."

"No. I thought you were taking precautions."

"I was," she said, "but I guess I slipped up somehow."

"You mean . . .?"

She nodded. "I think I'm pregnant."

I hugged her close and said, "Great! Let's move up the wedding day!"

"Oh no!" said Bernice. "I've got club dates to play. William Morris says that I'm on the verge of an important career. I can't stop now to have a baby!"

"When do you think you might have time for children?"

" Well, once my career is established—maybe in two or three years—I can take time off and then . . ."

Suddenly I realized this marriage was never going to work out for me the way I wanted it to. I didn't picture myself escorting a possible son to his bar mitzvah when I was fifty years old. Or a daughter to her wedding when I was in my sixties. I tried to reason with Bernice. "Darling, you can play your club dates at least for the next five months. Then you can take time off, have the baby. We'll get a nanny. You'll be back on the road in no time."

"No!" she said. "I won't jeopardize my career. I'm going to get an abortion."

I could tell by the set of her jaw she was determined. "Okay. I'll ask around tomorrow—see if I can find the right doctor."

"No need," she said. "I know one." And then she confessed that she had already had an abortion four years ago.

"Who . . . what . . .?" I stuttered. "No! Don't tell me. I really don't want to know."

"But darling," she smiled, "you didn't think I was a virgin, did you?"

I didn't answer what I was thinking. No! Not a virgin. Many men before me had taught her all those moves. Maybe that's why her sister was warning me off. Right then I knew we were saying good-bye to marriage, to children—and to each other.

"I'll pay the doctor," I said.

"You don't have to."

"I DO have to! I insist!"

She turned out the lights, curled up, and went to sleep. I didn't shut my eyes that night. I was making plans, knowing what I must do in the morning. I got out of bed at 6 A.M., packed my bags, and left the apartment while everyone was still sleeping. Of course I left a note on the bed.

"Bernice, I'm going back to my apartment. I need some time to think about all this. Please send me the doctor's bill."

She did, I paid, and we never communicated again. Her sister was delighted and phoned me to say that her mother was inconsolable. The duplex was practically fully furnished, and Bernice refused to tell them why we had split. I realized that my dream of a married life was a fantasy, that it never would have worked out. Bernice's ego, her vanity, her selfishness would have turned me off eventually. I was relieved that she had never had our baby. She was not cut out to be a mother. And besides, I truly hated that pseudo-Chinese apartment I never got to live in.

I was also delighted that I hadn't disposed of my Village penthouse and all the furnishings, despite the insistence of Bernice and her mother. Was it perhaps a subconscious desire, a premonition I had suppressed that my marriage was a mirage? I don't know. But happily, I moved into my apartment, freshened it up, and began to enjoy my solitude.

I phoned old friends and acquaintances I had been avoiding. Slowly, I reclaimed my life.

I had done very little writing the last couple of years. Even with my musical spouse-to-be, I had not been inspired to write anything except some material for Bernice's act. So now I went at it full tilt, writing my own words and music or collaborating: Hoagy Carmichael, Johnny Green, Oscar Levant—I was in demand again.

I had become friendly with a public relations man who wrote a weekly theater-news column for the *Herald Tribune* and knew everyone in the world of theater. We decided to make a trip by car to the West Coast with stops on the way in various cities to visit actors and authors who were friends of his. Irving Drutman was erudite, amusing, and a pleasant traveling companion.

In Beverly Hills, he introduced me to Ira Gershwin with whom we spent some enjoyable days that included afternoons at the racetrack with Ira's wife, Leonore, who loved to gamble. Ira, in his dry, wry manner, was a great raconteur of Broadway and Hollywood inside stories. He was still not reconciled to the sudden death of his beloved brother, George, but had not yet reached the state of depression that befell him some years later.

One afternoon, we visited another of Irving's friends, director-producer-screenwriter Albert Lewin, on the set where he was filming his current production, *The Private Affairs of Bel-Ami*. Al had a penchant for costume and period films, which he turned out with consummate taste. (His best-known was *The Picture of Dorian Gray*.) Irving introduced me and ran some of my credits by Al, who responded with "Great! I could use a song for this film if you guys can come up with something fast."

So off we went, found a piano to work on, and dreamed up a lilting French waltz called "My Bel-Ami" that told the story of this roguish philanderer being played by George Sanders. Herewith our song:

> *Verse:*
> So many women adore him,
> So many women . . . they bore him,
> I'm just the woman who's for him . . .
> If only he . . . loved only me . . .

> *Chorus:*
> Who am I dreaming of
> Each time I dream of love?
> MY BEL AMI!

Who clinks his glass with mine
Each time we're drinking wine?
MY BEL AMI!
Whose arms romance with me
Each time they dance with me?
It's plain to see . . .
Whose love is deep?
Whose love is strong?
Whose love will keep?
But not for long!
Who has my heart and lips
Right at his fingertips?
MY BEL AMI!

Al Lewin loved the song and said he had a perfect spot for it in the film: a scene in a nightclub where a young French girl was making her first appearance. This turned out to be Angela Lansbury, still in her teens and delightfully innocent looking.

For some reason, Al decided that Angela couldn't do the song justice, and he would have to find someone else to dub her voice. Whereupon I suggested a Hollywood friend with a great voice, Peg La Centra. So Peg got the job singing while Angela mouthed the lyrics.

Those few weeks we spent in Hollywood resulted in a second film job, *The Bachelor's Daughters*, starring Adolphe Menjou and Claire Trevor, for which we wrote "Twilight Song." It turned out to be a profitable trip.

CHAPTER TWENTY

What Comes First— the Chicken or the Egg?

I t's the age-old question that songwriters are constantly asked.

"What came first—the music or the words?"

Well, there's no set rule. Many times I have been presented with a *fait accompli*—a foreign song that has been acquired by an American publisher who calls me in to write an English lyric. In that case, I have to fit my words to an existing, established melody. Other times, I have suggested an idea and title to a composer who comes up with an appropriate melody, sometimes based on just the title, other times created around a few lines of lyric I may have given him.

The process is even stranger when I write my own words and music. I may be sitting at my desk, dreaming—and suddenly a title or a line or two will flash in my mind.

And I start hearing a melody in my brain to accompany the thoughts. Other times, I may be sitting at my piano just idly strumming, and I hit a melodic strain that captivates me.

I follow its development instinctively to a conclusion. Then I decide to write a lyric to fit. So which is the chicken and which is the egg?

Now, some words about some of my collaborators are in order. John W. Green, whose great songs "Body and Soul," "Out of Nowhere," and "I Cover the Waterfront" are still being performed, was a brilliant musician known to all in the business as Johnny. He had graduated from Harvard, become a band leader, conductor of musical comedies, and a successful songwriter. That's when he was known as Johnny Green, living in New York, and married to Hollywood starlet Betty Furness. We wrote a few songs together that were recorded, but never reached the top. One, recorded by a dear friend, Bea Wain, was "The Lady Who Walks Alone." Poor "Lady" never made it.

Bea and her husband, Andre Baruch, and I remained friends over the years. She's a warm and wonderful lady who still misses Andre. These days we stay in constant touch via e-mail. Bea lives in Beverly Hills and has been very involved with the Society of Singers, an organization that does a great job of taking care of those singers who've fallen on bad times and need help.

However, back to Johnny Green. Quite a few years after our collaboration, Johnny divorced Betty, who eventually became a successful TV spokeswoman for Westinghouse. Johnny went to

Hollywood and worked his way up as head of the MGM Studios music department, scoring important pictures. We met again on the lot in 1953 when I was writing songs for a Lana Turner epic, *The Flame and the Flesh*. He caught me up short when I greeted him with, "Hello, Johnny!"

"Nobody calls me Johnny. My name is John W. Green."

Johnny succeeded in placing a lovely ballad we had written together in our early days, "The Trembling of a Leaf," in two different MGM films, sung by Mario Lanza in one and by Lena Horne in another. But as happens once in a while, our song was cut out of both movies. Years later, when Ted Turner bought and began to release all the music that had been cut out of MGM pictures, I finally acquired the CDs of both Lanza's and Horne's superb renditions of this song. Despite the fact that it never made it to hit status, it has always been one of my favorites because its lyric is so poetic and John's music makes it soar.

THE TREMBLING OF A LEAF
The budding of a rose,
The clinging of a blossom to the vine,
The budding of a dream,
The trembling of your hand on mine;
The whisper of the wind,
The singing of the sea,
The silver mist that lingers on the hill,
The singing of our love,

The whisper of a promised thrill . . .

Be still! My delirious heart,

You are pounding away like the boom of a drum,

Stand still! Time and heaven and earth,

This night must never, never go

And dawn must never come!

THE TREMBLING OF A LEAF,

The blooming of a rose,

The starlit waters kissing moonlit shores . . .

The blossoming of love,

The trembling of my lips on yours,

THE TREMBLING OF A LEAF,

The trembling of my heart and yours.

Music by John Green

Yes, John Green was talented, but so pretentious! I am reminded of another incident. He, Henry Mancini, and I and some other West Coast writers went to Washington to meet with our elected representatives to persuade them to vote favorably on a new copyright extension bill. Daytimes we toured offices, meeting senators and congressmen; evenings we met at parties where we entertained them, each writer doing his shtick. I had just finished singing and playing my medley, ending with a rendition of "Tenderly." I believe that I've already stated what a poor pianist I am. I fake a lot. Before I could rise from the piano bench, John W. Green spoke up.

"Poor Walter Gross, who wrote that beautiful melody, is probably spinning in his grave at the way Jack massacred it. I would like to let you hear the way that melody really should be played."

Whereupon he sat down and played a concert version. He finished with a flourish and turned to the audience for applause. The audience seemed embarrassed, so I spoke up quickly. "I would now like you to hear my interpretation of Mr. Green's 'Body and Soul.'" Everyone laughed, and that broke the tension.

Henry Mancini was my seatmate on the return flight to L.A. He asked, "Why did Johnny do that? It was in such poor taste!"

"Oh well," I replied, "it's all part of the John W. Green aura."

Incidentally, over the years, we songwriters made frequent trips to Washington to lobby our elected representatives for various causes, and we became quite professional at it. On one occasion, a group of us headed by Oscar Hammerstein spent a few days there educating congressmen about the music business. Democrats were usually partial to our positions, but we had a harder time with Republicans. A Washington hostess who was also a newspaper reporter invited us to a dinner at her home so that we could meet a few important Republicans socially. There were three writers, Burton Lane, Arthur Schwartz, and me, and she had placed us at three separate tables with senators and their wives.

There was a lot of imbibing before and during dinner.

I do not recall the names of all those loud and boisterous solons except for one: Barry Goldwater. To cap the evening, we three writers planned to serenade them with our songs and then make our pitch for support of a new copyright bill. As the youngest of the group, I was the first to play and sing my repertoire—to a far-from-attentive audience who had been drinking liberally. Burton Lane followed as the liquor flowed copiously, and he received a respectable hand. The last was Arthur Schwartz. The moment Arthur sat down at the piano and ran an arpeggio, a jovial Senator Goldwater rose to his feet.

"Listen!" he said. "Can you play 'Tea For Two' in stop-time?" Arthur obliged. Goldwater grabbed one of the other senators. "Come on! Let's show 'em our tap routine!" And the two clowns proceeded to fall all over the floor, whooping and laughing.

After they picked themselves up and sat down, Arthur, still at the piano, turned to the guests with a smile and said, "You'll be interested to know, ladies and gentlemen, I studied the law, passed my bar—and then I told my father that I planned to be a songwriter and write for the theater. My father was shocked. 'The theater!' he said. 'You'll meet such a terrible class of people!' Well, folks, I just wish my father could be here tonight."

Would you believe those senators madly applauded Arthur?

Another collaborator of mine was Oscar Levant. Max Dreyfus had asked me, as a special favor, to write some songs with Oscar. This was before he had become nationally famous as the savant on the "Information, Please" game show. Oscar had written some serious music and a few popular songs, including "Lady, Play Your Mandolin" and "Blame It on My Youth." He had been very close to George Gershwin, but very envious of Gershwin's phenomenal success and was known for his barbed remarks. George would monopolize the piano and play his songs for hours at every party. He once asked Oscar, "Do you think my music will be played years from now?"

Oscar, without missing a beat, replied, "Sure! As long as you're around!"

How wrong Oscar was. Recently I attended the George Gershwin centennial celebration at Carnegie Hall. Michael Tilson Thomas conducted the San Francisco Symphony, Audra McDonald and Frederica Von Stade sang, and the George and Ira Gershwin evergreens sounded as exciting and thrilling as upon first hearing.

Oscar's caustic remarks and dry wit made it fun to work with him. I would make dates to meet him in between my other appointments. When I gave him a title or a couple of lines, he was very facile and would quickly produce a melody. Each time we completed a song, Oscar would insist that we show it to Mr. Dreyfus first. He would barge into the office with no announcement and say, "Max, we've got a winner for you!"

Oscar could get away with being irreverent. He would sit down at the Bechstein and sing out silly words we hadn't written. "LOVE STAINS IN THE CLOSET!" he would bellow, and Max would wince. After he'd had his little joke, we would do our song. Some Max would take, some he rejected; then we would make the rounds of other publishers. We kept placing songs and getting records, but no hits.

Oscar would complain, "I don't understand it. You go off and have hits with yourself and other composers and write all these dogs with me."

Without a doubt, Oscar was one of the sloppiest, dirtiest men I've ever known. His clothes were one big stain, his ties a wrinkled mess, and his fingernails black enough to plant potatoes. And yet he had a terrible phobia about germs. When we would stop at a drugstore counter for a quick bite, he always ordered a fried-egg sandwich on white bread, then rip the crust off with his dirty fingers (never using any flatware because it might have germs), and stuff hunks that he tore off the sandwich into his mouth.

He lived at what was then called the Park Central on Seventh Ave. and Fifty-sixth Street, in a single room that held a bed, a desk, and a spinet, as well as masses of books and periodicals that overflowed everywhere. One day when we were working in this crowded space, I watched him spray the phone with a detergent before he spoke into it. If I had to go to the bathroom, I would not be allowed to use his. He made me go all the way down to the men's room in the lobby.

There's a wonderful story told about Oscar and *Show Boat* author Edna Ferber, who was also germophobic. They were seated next to each other at the famous Algonquin Round Table for lunch. Oscar's order, a pasta plate, arrived before Edna's, and she remarked that it looked delicious. Whereupon Oscar twirled some of the pasta on his unused fork and offered her a taste. She demurred, but he kept shoving it at her lips until, finally, she opened her mouth and oh-so-delicately removed the pasta from his fork with her teeth—no lips touching the silverware. Immediately, Oscar turned and called, "Waiter, a clean fork, please!"

Our hitless collaboration ended when Oscar became a regular on "Information, Please." He was brilliant, witty, and caustic, and knowledgeable about the most arcane trivia. His curmudgeonly manner captivated the entire country. He went on from television to films in Hollywood. Unbelievably, he married a great beauty who managed to clean him up and make him socially presentable.

Oscar's wit was what made his outrageous behavior stick in one's mind. Tallulah Bankhead and Ethel Merman were the same way. Frank Loesser told me about one of his celebratory parties for *Guys and Dolls*, at which Merman and the show's female lead, Isabel Bigley, were draped over his piano having drinks. Isabel was bragging that she had gotten her leading role in Frank's musical entirely on her talent and merit.

"As a matter of fact," she boasted, "nobody ever threw me on a casting couch."

Ethel, sipping her cocktail, seemed unimpressed.

"You tell her, Frank," Isabel continued. "Didn't I get my part purely on my talent?" Frank nodded yes. "The truth is," said Bigley, "I've still got my cherry!"

Ethel took another sip, started to walk away, then turned back for her parting shot, "That's nice, dear, but doesn't it get in the way when you're fucking?"

Then there was Mae West. But that's a chapter in itself.

CHAPTER TWENTY-ONE

Sin-Sationally, Mae West

One day in 1945, I had a phone call from Abe Lastfogel, who was then the head of the William Morris Agency in New York, asking me if I would be interested in writing an album of songs for their client, Mae West. She had made a tremendous reputation in Paramount Pictures and had practically brought that studio back from insolvency during the Depression. But her film career was now over, and she was starring in her own comedy in theaters on the Shubert circuit.

Naturally, I was intrigued at the idea of meeting her and writing songs. She was a living legend. It was arranged that I would drive down to Philadelphia where she was appearing at the Forrest Theater in her little opus, which she called *Come On Up*. The plot involved Mae as a solo USO hostess who drops notes out her window to attractive servicemen inviting them up to her apartment—and not for a spot of tea!

I drove to Philadelphia in a blinding rainstorm with a friend and arrived just before curtain time. We were sure the theater would be far from full on such a stormy night and were surprised to see that it was packed—mainly with what looked like hausfraus. A young man stepped out in front of the closed curtains before the lights dimmed to announce that Miss West would be delighted to personally sign autographs to all ticket holders after the show.

Then the curtain parted on an all-white set, a black maid was dusting and arranging flowers. The maid answered phone calls, muttered a few lines—all a long buildup for the star's entrance. Finally, Mae West, in an all-white, down-to-the-floor peignoir, sashayed in and flashed her ivory smile at the audience, who applauded her madly for a few minutes. She was fifty-three at the time, matronly of figure, and well corseted.

At last, the play began. She threw her one-liners, her zingers, swayed up and down the stage, patted her artificial blonde coiffure, and waited for all the laughs. It was old hat, ersatz, single-entendre sex—but, corny as it was, it was fascinating to watch.

We had been instructed to remain in our seats after the final curtain. When all the stragglers had departed into the continuing rainstorm, the curtains parted, and there was Miss West in her white, flowing outfit, posing in the bend of the white baby grand, waiting with poised pen for the autograph hounds. Finally, two little old ladies, completely rain soaked and dripping, edged in through the stage-door entrance. They stood there shyly, afraid to approach the legend.

Miss West smiled, patted her wig, and said, "Come on in, ladies. I don't bite!"

The ladies giggled, came closer, held out their programs, which she signed with a flourish, and left. There was a long wait, but no one else came through the door. The stage manager spoke apologetically. "Miss West, the rain is still fierce out there. That's why they're not coming."

Miss West spoke up sternly. "They're not coming because the Shuberts haven't advertised us properly. People don't know we're here IN PERSON. They think we're still a movie." And she swept off stage.

We were then invited to her dressing room, where she sat and made chitchat with us until she finally got around to the reason for my visit. She would love to have a batch of new material to make up an album. Between Philadelphia and some theater in New Jersey, she would be in the area for the next six weeks. On her Sundays off, her chauffeur could drive her into Manhattan to my apartment.

Could she come in time for lunch? I asked. She said that would be nice, although she never ate much. So it was arranged, and we left.

Came Sunday . . . came Miss West! You will note that I never call her "Mae." She referred to herself in the third person and never spoke a four-letter word in all the time we were together. That first Sunday's lunch was a cold cucumber soup and a shrimp salad, which she devoured. As I soon discovered, she was a hearty eater. Our conversation was pleasant. I don't know how it happened, but we got around to all the Mae West jokes. I would tell one that I had heard, and she would top it with "Did you hear the one about Mae West in church . . .?"

She enjoyed it all, and she was fun to be with. It didn't matter whether the stories she told about her early days in the theater were true or not—how men constantly showered her with diamonds and expensive gifts, how single-handedly she made sex palatable and profitable. You could take it all with a grain of salt and still enjoy it.

I recall one Sunday I was telling her about a performer named Carrie Finnell I had seen at the Blue Angel. Carrie was a zoftig woman with a peach complexion, a baby face, and dimples. She appeared wearing a soft, loose gown with a plunging neckline and began with some innocuous song. After about a minute, something flashed in and out of her low neckline. The audience looked at each other puzzled. They weren't sure exactly what they had seen. Whereupon Carrie, with a mischievous smile, pointed to a ringside table and asked, "Did you see that? You're not sure? Well, watch!" Then with a wiggle of each shoulder, out and in popped the right breast—followed by an out and in of the left breast. Throughout all this, Carrie kept giggling with enjoyment, and the audience laughed with her.

Carrie said, "Oh, you wanna know how I do it? Watch this!" Her two breasts began popping out and in almost to a martial beat. It was a great performance and hardly pornographic. I described all this to Miss West, who wasn't surprised in the least.

"That's nothing new!" she said.

Whereupon she shrugged each shoulder separately and within her dress each breast popped up and down. "I learned that years ago. It's all muscular control." And she demonstrated with more up-and-down jiggling maneuvers. "You know Leonard Lyons?" He was a popular *New York Post* columnist and a big tit man. "Well, when he interviewed me, I told him about my grandmother. She had . . ." indicating her breasts, "three of them! It's true. Three!"

All those Sundays, I was having a ball, but I soon discovered that Miss West had a tough time learning new material. So I made a demo record of all the songs for her in order that she could listen and learn. We met for a couple more Sundays, then she was out on the road and too far away for meetings, and we lost contact.   About a year went by. I was reading that week's *Variety*, and in the theater section, there was a review of a new Mae West play. This time she had come up with a new gimmick. She was surrounded by a number of musclemen. Toward the bottom of the review, the credits were listed. Once again, Miss West was the sole playwright—*and* she had even written all the songs she sang. *My* songs!

I phoned Abe Lastfogel at William Morris and told him what I had just read. "Oh, my God, she's doing it again!" he moaned. "She always claims she wrote everything including the *Gideon Bible*. Let me talk to her."

Abe called me the next day. "I forgot to tell you—Mae fell in the shower, and bruised herself badly. Now the Shuberts have temporarily closed the show. She's recuperating at the Park Central and would love to see you."

Off I went to the hotel. I was admitted into her suite by a muscleman and shown into the bedroom. There was Miss West, fully gowned in her usual white peignoir, the blonde artificial Hadassah hairdo immaculately arranged. She was propped up on top of the bedcovers beaming seductively at me.

"Jack, it's so nice to see you. Sit over here!" She patted the bedspread, and I sat down. She nestled a bit closer. "About your songs . . . I'm so sorry! That was an oversight. I told them to give you credit. From now on, we'll correct it."

"Thanks," I said. "But how long has this oversight gone on? I should be getting paid for the performances."

"Oh, Jack—that was only our first week. And now I'm incapacitated. But I assure you, when we go on . . ." She put her hand on my thigh. No doubt about it, I was being vamped by Mae West! Then she cooed, "You know, dear, I don't think I've ever given you an autographed picture of myself. Why don't you pick the one you'd like? There, on the dresser."

I went to a pile of photographs on the dresser, all those airbrushed, doctored shots with the Paramount Pictures logo at the bottom that they had sent out for publicity purposes years before. She had the entire stock. I finally chose a typical head shot, Mae looking directly at you, flashing that 100-watt smile. I brought it to her on the bed.

"Ahhh!" she sighed. "That's my favorite, too! Let's see, what should I write? Something very special . . . for you!"

She thought for a moment and then, as though struck by a brilliant idea, began to write. She finished and handed it to me triumphantly, and I read:

SIN—sationally yours,

Mae West

She never resumed the road tour with the musclemen, and I never received one cent in payment for performances, before or since. Mae is flying around in heaven somewhere, and I'll bet she's taking credit for all God's decisions.

CHAPTER TWENTY-TWO

More Collaborators

Working with composer Sammy Fain proved to be a most pleasant experience. We had been hired by Walt Disney Studios to write a score for the animated version of *Sleeping Beauty*. Sammy was a prolific tunesmith with a natural talent for great melodies. Just a few titles of his tremendous output should give you the picture: "I Can Dream, Can't I?," "I'll Be Seeing You," "Love Is a Many-Splendored Thing," and "That Old Feeling." His songs earned him three Academy Awards.

Sammy was a true pixie, always smiling and sunny. He had only one failing—he loved to play the horses. If the racetrack had supplied bed and board, he would have lived there. I would arrive at the Disney studio on time every day and have to make constant excuses for Sammy's absence. How many sick mothers and funerals can you invent? I would spend my time at story meetings or dreaming up song ideas, waiting for Sammy's eventual arrival. But he was so facile, so quick—he could take my few lines of lyrics, sit down at the piano, and pour out a singable melodic line in moments.

We had finished about a dozen songs to accommodate the story line being developed when Walt Disney decided he wanted the film to take an entirely different tack. His intention was to stay close to the original Tchaikovsky score written for the *Sleeping Beauty* ballet. All he wanted was a lyric to Tchaikovsky's main ballet theme. This was a terrible blow to both Sammy and me. They were discarding our entire inventive score.

Sammy was truly upset. "I try not to steal from anybody, and they want me to take Tchaikovsky's well-known theme and turn it into a pop song. That's a job you can do easily, Jack—without me. I don't want any part of it."

I said, "Sammy, this may wind up being the only song in the picture. They've been paying us for weeks. We might as well have something to show for it. Let's write what Walt wants." So I wrote a lyric called "Once Upon a Dream," and Sammy made the appropriate melodic changes in Tchaikovsky's theme. Not only was this song given a lovely presentation in the finished film, but it has become a well-performed part of my catalog. Thanks, Peter Ilyich!

A few years before, Walt Disney asked me to write another lyric to a tune written by Frank Churchill. This was a most pleasurable assignment. Let me explain why. In 1937 Disney made the first full-length animated feature, *Snow White and the Seven*

Dwarfs, for which Frank Churchill wrote a classic score. Shortly after, Disney had talked about doing an animated version of *Peter Pan,* and Churchill had written a few melodies for it. However, Churchill died in 1942, and Disney abandoned the project for ten years. Then he put it into preproduction with a different team assigned to do the score. The only Churchill melody retained was used as a background theme for the crocodile in the film.

I loved Churchill's melody. It made me chuckle each time I heard it, and I tried to imbue my lyric with the same tongue-in-cheek spirit. Here it is.

NEVER SMILE AT A CROCODILE

No, you can't get friendly with a crocodile,

Don't be taken in by his welcome grin,

He's imagining how nice you'd fit within his skin.

NEVER SMILE AT A CROCODILE

Never tip your hat and stop to talk a while,

Never run! Walk away!

Say Good-night! Not Good day!

Clear the aisle and never smile at Mr. Crocodile.

Music by Frank Churchill

I don't know if this next event can be referred to as a mere collaboration. It happened late in 1946. At a publisher's office one afternoon, I ran into a good friend, the singer Margaret Whiting, who was visiting from the West Coast. She asked if I knew Walter Gross. I had never met him, but was aware that he was a widely known jazz pianist.

Maggie said, "Walter has written a fantastic tune, and you're the one guy who can bring it to life with the right words." She picked up the phone and called Walter, who was then employed at Musicraft Records a few blocks away from where we were. She spoke briefly with Walter, hung up, and said, "He wants us to come right over. Now Jack, Walter's kind of strange. But never mind. Just listen to his melody."

She was right. He was strange. He seemed spaced out. I later discovered that Walter was an alcoholic and high most of the time. He was far from friendly, but sat down at the piano and played a gorgeous melody. I loved it and asked for a lead sheet, which he reluctantly scribbled out. He also gave me his home phone number.

Walter had written this melody as a waltz with a healthy range. It was magnificent, and I couldn't get it out of my head. It kept repeating over and over, and inevitably, I started adding words to that music. It had a sensual, sexual quality that called for the most romantic expressions I could conjure up.

The evening breeze caressed the trees
TENDERLY . . .

Once I got the lyric for the first eight bars, the ensuing words seemed to flow like a golden stream.

The trembling trees embraced the breeze

TENDERLY . . .

Then you and I came wandering by

And lost in a sigh were we,

The shore was kissed by sea and mist

TENDERLY . . .

I can't forget how two hearts met

Breathlessly!

When I got the last, inspired phrase:

Your arms opened wide and closed me inside.

You took my lips, you took my love

So tenderly . . .

Music by Walter Gross

I was certain that I had written a classic! I have always believed that this sparsest of lyrics, in its way, embodies the most sexual affair that I have ever described in a song. Particularly those last few lines.

This lyric had come so freely, so effortlessly, that I hesitated to call Walter Gross too soon for fear that he would consider my lyric "off the cuff." So I waited patiently ten full days before I phoned him. He sounded as though he had just gotten up—or had never been to bed. I mustered a great enthusiasm.

"Walter," I said, "I've got it!"

"Yeah?" he replied. "What's the title?"

"'Tenderly,'" I crooned. "TEN—der—ly!"

There was a dead silence. Finally he spoke. "That's no title. That's what you put at the top of the sheet music—'Play tenderly!'"

I was deflated. I concluded the conversation by telling him I would send him a copy of my lyric. Weeks went by and not a word from Walter Gross. Meanwhile, my song, "Linda," had been a recent hit at Morris Music. Paul Barry, the head song-plugger there had heard my rendition of "Tenderly" and loved it. So one day he asked me to let the president of the company, Buddy Morris, hear it.

Buddy said, "It's good, but it's a ball breaker. With that vocal range, it'll be a bitch to get recordings. Anyway, get it if you can."

Paul said, "I've been trying to sign it up, but Walter Gross insists that he wants a big advance and a number-one plug."

Morris said, "Forget it! No advance. No promises."

About eight months had gone by without a word from Walter Gross. One day he phoned me to ask what I thought of E. H. Morris as publishers. I said I had been pleased with their performances on my recent songs. He said they wanted to publish "Tenderly," but refused to give an advance or promises.

I asked, "So who else is interested in the song?"

That seemed to decide him. He had no other offers and agreed to let Morris publish it. Through his Musicraft Records connection, Morris was able to get Sarah Vaughan for the first recording. The Divine Sarah, as she was known, gave an incredible, bravura performance. But that seemed to establish the song as a jazz classic, and every recording that followed—and there were many—treated it as holy jazz.

Months had gone by, and Walter Gross was appearing at a small East Side place called The Little Club. I had had little contact with my "collaborator" all this time, but I said to myself, "I guess I should make an appearance. After all, both our names are on this song." Since I was living on the East Side, I walked over to the club. It was a tiny room, but packed, and I had to stand at the bar. Gross was the only performer, and the moment he sat down at the piano, the crowded room yelled, "Play 'Tenderly.'"

Sometime during his performance, I caught his eye and waved to him. He nodded his head in return, but otherwise never acknowledged me. I got the feeling that he would have been happy if the floor had opened and swallowed me. When he finished his spot, he left the room and never came out to greet me. So I left.

Shortly afterward, I discovered that a number of lyric writers had taken a crack at Walter's melody—including Johnny Mercer, one of my heroes. But Walter had turned down all their lyrics. If I had been aware of all that, I would never have agreed to take his manuscript. I didn't realize it was a competition. In retrospect, I wish I knew what Johnny had written.

The song kept attracting attention and gaining recordings, but mostly by jazz interpreters who would make recordings that ran eight and ten minutes with all their variations on the main theme. There were so many jazz recordings by bands and vocalists that I was convinced this song would never become a big hit, that it was destined to remain a cult song. Then a surprising thing happened. It was a recording by Rosemary Clooney.

CHAPTER TWENTY-THREE

Remembering Rosie

The playwright John Guare wrote a fascinating play, *Six Degrees of Separation*, based on the premise that everyone's life is connected to other lives through various links and circumstances. This was true of Rosie Clooney and me. We first met when she and her sister, Betty, came to New York as vocalists with Tony Pastor's band.

The arranger/pianist of the band was Ralph Flanagan (from my Maritime Service days), whom I had known in that same capacity with Sammy Kaye's orchestra in the forties.

In 1946, when we were both out of the service, Ralph served as my pianist on a series of vocal recordings I made for Langworth Transcriptions and Rainbow Records.

It was through Ralph that I met the Clooney Sisters, sixteen-year-old Rosie and thirteen-year-old Betty, from the small river town of Maysville, Kentucky. They were first discovered on local radio and joined Pastor's band in 1945. After a few years of touring, Rosie was signed to Columbia Records by Manny Sachs, the head of artists and repertoire, in 1950, and sister Betty retired to Kentucky.

Naturally, I was eager to get this new Columbia recording star to do my songs. But I soon discovered that she had little say over her choice of material. The new head man at Columbia, Mitch Miller, had a classical-music background, but was embarking on strange musical choices. His preferences tended toward either country music or gimmicky novelties.

I always had the feeling that it was envy on his part that gave him pleasure, in his official position, to turn down songs by reputable composers. Rosie fought against most of the songs he picked for her; she felt they would not advance her career. But Mitch always prevailed. When she refused to do a quasi-Armenian pseudo-folk song, "C'mon-a My House," he told her, "You record it. Or you're out!"

Now here comes another link in my relationship with Clooney. The man who played the jangly harpsichord part on that record date was Stan Freeman, a friend of mine with whom, a few years later, I would collaborate on the score for the Broadway musical, *I Had a Ball*. Stan did a couple record dates with Rosie and admired her as much as I did.

Mitch Miller showed his real power with this recording Rosie hated. He released 400,000 records of "C'mon-a My House," flooded the market, persuaded and paid DJs to play it, and created a hit that catapulted Rosie to stardom. But this talented girl was truly unhappy with her status as a novelty singer. She knew she was capable of better material and kept pleading with Miller to let her record standards and ballads. Finally, she wore him down, and he agreed to let her do "Tenderly"—but he put that song on the B side of the record. Unfortunately, I do not recall what his A side was.

My song had been written about four years before and despite all its interesting recordings, had never broken out. Rosie's pure and simple version, in her natural voice with no vocal tricks, backed by Percy Faith's arrangement, emphasized the nostalgia of the music and lyrics and brought it universal recognition as a real love ballad. Years later, Rosie told me that she was certain that recording of "Tenderly" changed her life and career. Without it, she might have remained the "C'mon-a My House" girl. Her version of "Tenderly" catapulted the song into its standard classification, and to date, it has achieved more than 350 recordings.

In 1951, when Rosie came to Paramount Pictures for her first film role, we met again. I was working at one of the Hollywood studios and living in Beverly Hills. As proof of John Guare's theory of the degrees of separation, there were a couple more links in our relationship. We ran into each other at Paramount when I went to visit my pal, Bing Crosby. Hollywood was a brand-new and glamorous experience for Rosie and a bit scary.

Her agency had found her a secretary/companion named

Jackie Sherman, and they were temporarily living at the Beverly Hills Hotel. I introduced her to a real-estate broker, and we found her a house on Bedford Drive in Beverly Hills as a rental befitting her new star status.

Then came another link in our connection. I took Rosie to the Richard Whiting home to meet his daughter, Margaret, who had instituted Sunday open house for all the young musical stars of the day. In those years, all the major studios were making big, splashy musicals for which they had signed many promising Broadway musical talents.

Maggie's father Richard Whiting, who had passed on, had left a great treasure-trove of wonderful songs: "Beyond the Blue Horizon," "Breezin' Along With the Breeze," "Hooray for Hollywood," "My Ideal," "Sleepytime Gal," and many more.

Maggie by now had her own successful recording career. That Sunday afternoon, Rosie met Johnny Mercer and his wife, Ginger, Mel Tormé, Mickey Rooney, Debbie Reynolds, Kathryn Grayson, Gloria De Haven, June Allyson, and even Judy Garland.

Bubbling, fresh, young talents kept dropping in, some staying a short time, others remaining to sing a song. It was Hollywood at its best, and Rosie's eyes sparkled with excitement. The connection she made that day with Maggie was furthered years later, in 1977, when Rosie's career had hit a downturn. She joined up with Maggie, Helen O'Connell, and Rose Marie for a show called *4 Girls 4* that went on to become a hit national tour.

Rosie's fourth film at Paramount was the apex of her career, *White Christmas*, with Bing Crosby, Vera-Ellen, and Danny Kaye. Danny, of course, was another old link with me.

Rosie was pursued by and married José Ferrer, who at that time was at the height of his film stardom. I always felt that he was responsible for destroying the great acting career she might have had. First, he kept her away from her many old friends. Then he made sure she remained in a state of perpetual pregnancy: five children in quick succession. And all the while, he very publicly carried on his infidelities. Fortunately, Rosie continued to make some great recordings in spite of these disappointments.

A further link between Rosie and me. In 1956 she met Nelson Riddle, who created brilliant arrangements for her albums. He and Rosie not only clicked musically, they fell madly in love and carried on an affair for seven years. Nelson was ready to leave his wife for Rosie, but was advised against it. He was not earning enough money to support Rosie's five children and his own brood of five. And unfortunately, he was not even able to take credit for all he had contributed to Rosie's wonderful album because his recording contract prohibited him from working on outside jobs. He had to use a pseudonym on his charts—Joe Seymore, arranger—and allow Frank Comstock to take credit for the conducting.

Just listen to the brilliance Nelson and Rosie achieved in their recording of "Come Rain or Come Shine."

When they broke up, Rosie's world went into a tailspin. Not

only did her professional future come to a standstill, she became hooked on prescription drugs. By the time she regained control of her life in the midsixties, she was no longer that slim, sexy girl. She and Ferrer divorced, remarried, and divorced again. She devoted herself to being a good mother to her children.

At the start of her marriage, Ferrer had purchased a Spanish-style house directly next door to Ira and Leonore Gershwin, with whom Rosie became close friends—another link in our relationship. And still another: Michael Feinstein, who has become a cherished friend, and who became Ira's musical archivist. Michael did the discography for Rosie's *Girl Singer* biography in later years.

Bing Crosby coaxed Rosie out of retirement, and she joined him in a live concert tour that took them throughout the country and then to London, where they met the queen and her royal family. Another of my songs made it into Bing and Rosie's repertoire as a duet, "The Poor People of Paris." This French song had been written by Marguerite Monnot, who gave Edith Piaf so many wonderful hits. The American publisher who acquired the rights called me from California to ask me to write an English lyric and sent me an instrumental demo made by Les Baxter and his band. The publisher told me on the phone that the song's title was "Pauvres Gens de Paris," which my high-school French translated as "Poor People of Paris." I played the demo, fell in love with the lilting melody, and wrote a tongue-in-cheek lyric explaining what a terrible life all those poor Frenchmen had in their romantic, enchanting city of Paris. It wasn't until I got a copy of Ms. Monnot's French sheet music that I read the real title of the song: "Pauvre Jean de Paris." Poor JOHN! But *gens* and *Jean* are pronounced alike in French, so I like to think I made a natural mistake. Still, the American publisher liked my ironic lyric and kept it. Bing and Rosie made a chuckling, witty duet, which they performed in their tours.

Despite her increasing weight, Rosie became a brilliant solo performer in cabarets, theaters, and even Carnegie Hall, gaining in stature through her remaining years and attracting huge audiences. She won Grammys, accolades, and honors from the Society of Singers, which gave her its ELLA award. In New York, she played the Rainbow Room and Michael Feinstein's club at the Regency Hotel. She lived to see herself become a legend in her lifetime. Along the way, she helped her children to musical careers and her nephew, George Clooney, to his auspicious film career. And a few years before her death, she married Dante Di Paolo, an old, faithful flame who had once, long before, been her choreographer.

On the last occasion I talked with Rosie on the phone and asked her how she was doing, she replied, "Not too shabby for a fat old broad!"

Rest easy, Rosie. Your dues are all paid.

CHAPTER TWENTY-FOUR

The Real Thing

A truly eventful change in my life took place in late 1945.

Let me lead into it slowly.

The Astor Hotel on Broadway, which has since been torn down, had a very accessible oval bar right off the street surrounded by cocktail tables and chairs. During and after the war, that bar became a well-known rendezvous for the straight and gay military and civilians. It was a great cruising place. All the gay guys collected on the lobby side, and on the street side stood all the so-called straight men.

In the past, I had been there in uniform and afterward in mufti. It was a convenient meeting place for friends before and after dinner and theater. This particular night, I stood on the gay side in a solitary, pensive mood. A few months before, I had broken off my relationship with Bernice. I stood at the bar nursing my drink, and after a while, across from me on the "straight" side, I noticed an attractive man about my age drinking alone. Our glances crossed occasionally, but there was not the slightest indication that he was at all interested.

I decided to be bold. I not only moved to his side of the bar, but to the empty spot next to him. Inevitably, we began to chat. He was from California, a recently discharged captain in the army who had seen service in the Pacific. He had been an aide to General Eichelberger, who was assigned to rewrite Japan's economy and had been with him there for a considerable time. We introduced ourselves.

His name was Walter Myden, and he had come east to see publishers about a book he had written based on his experiences in the Pacific area. The book contained an unflattering portrait of General MacArthur, who at that time was considered a great war hero. Walter had some friends in New York and Washington who he hoped could help him get the book published.

I was tremendously intrigued. Not only was he masculine, he was bright, a great conversationalist—and most attractive. But I couldn't sense anything about his sexual proclivities—nothing in his voice, not a scintilla in his conversation.

We closed the bar at 2 A.M. He was staying nearby at the Edison Hotel, but I asked if he would like to come back to my apartment and continue our interesting conversation, which had ranged from politics to the war to Israel. I was taking a big chance since I really expected nothing to continue our talk—although I secretly hoped for more.

He surprised me when he told me that he was Jewish and that as a nineteen-year-old student, he had won a fellowship and trip to what was then Palestine to study ancient languages and mores. His return trip had taken him through Italy and France, and by the time he reached his home in Los Angeles, he was convinced that Germany and Hitler were becoming a world threat. At UCLA, his university, he made many speeches about coming war clouds and was often attacked as a communist.

Everything he told me made him more intriguing. He was not only intelligent, but had a wry sense of humor.

We took a cab back to my penthouse, sat in the living room, talked and drank, talked and drank, drank and talked—and there was still not the slightest indication that he was sexually interested in me. Toward morning, I suggested that he might enjoy seeing the dawn rise from one of my terraces that overlooked Washington Square. We took our drinks out, leaned against the terrace railing, and watched while the sky became streaked with dawn.

I was so strongly drawn to this man, I couldn't take much more ambiguity.

As we stood at the railing, my little finger touched his. He didn't draw away. I got bolder and put my hand on his. His palm met mine. There were no words spoken. We turned toward each other, and I kissed him. It took a moment for him to respond. I put my arms around him, and he returned my embrace. We went into the bedroom and fell on the bed. Not a word was spoken, but both our hearts were pulsing, beating hard. It was not only wonderful. It was mutual!

When we parted the next morning, we had done very little confessing. He told me that he was expected by his friends in Washington that evening, He took my phone number and promised to call, although he planned to be gone for about a week. We had not spoken at all about what had taken place between us. I didn't know what he felt, but I could not stop thinking about him.

He phoned two days later and said, "I've been doing a lot of thinking—mostly about you."

I said, "Same thing here!"

He said, "I'd like to come back to New York tomorrow—if you're free."

I assured him I was.

I decided to have a small dinner party the night of his return with two interesting women I thought he would enjoy meeting. I wanted him to see that I had women friends, since I was still uncertain about what had taken place between us. My dinner was most successful, Walter charmed my two gal friends, and I was completely enraptured. At the evening's end, I offered to drive everyone home. First I dropped off the two ladies at their different uptown addresses.

On the way back, I asked hesitantly, "Walter, would you like to come home with me?" There was a momentary pause. Then he answered yes, but said he would like to stop at his hotel to pick up some toiletries. When we got to the Edison, I blurted out,

"Look, why don't you just pack all your luggage and take it to my house?"

He thought about it for a moment and then said, "All right." I took him and his luggage home, he hung up his clothes—and stayed for thirty years!

Walter was a most unusual human being, bright, warm, tender, and understanding. In retrospect, I cannot recall any great disagreements we had in those thirty years. His parents and older sister were living in Los Angeles where he had grown up. Although they were Jewish, they were not religious. He had not even had any Hebrew training or a bar mitzvah. His visit to Palestine had awakened the dormant Jewishness within him. And I, despite my Orthodox upbringing, had never been instilled with any particular feeling about a Jewish homeland. It was Walter who imbued me with all that love for Israel and the need for a Jewish state.

Academically, he was far better educated than I was. He had a couple of college degrees and was currently attached to a clinic doing social work from which he had taken a leave of absence when he joined the army. His decision to remain with me in the East did create problems. Not with the clinic; that was easy. But explaining to his family was a lot more complicated. He had never lived away from home until his service years and had just recently returned. For an excuse to stay in New York, he used the manuscript he was trying to get published.

As I stated, this book was based on his observations in the Philippines and Japan where he had served. Fortunately, since he was an aide to generals, he never experienced close action and was always quartered with the top brass. His book recounted incidents of General MacArthur's exploits, the fact that he made certain that his Philippine-rich holdings inherited from his father were adequately safe and protected. In the book, Walter told how the general staged his landing on the island three times until the cameras got it to his satisfaction. Unfortunately, MacArthur's popularity was so high that no publisher was willing to print anything derogatory, so his opus never saw daylight.

Walter had intended to go back to school and work for a Ph.D. in psychology, and I encouraged him to enroll in NYU, whose psych department had a high rating. That became his more legitimate excuse for remaining in New York. Explaining me was a bit harder, but when we made our first trip back to his home and I met his family, I trotted out all my Jewish charm and won them over. Of course, they knew and suspected nothing of our true relationship. In their mind, we were just close friends.

That summer when we were well ensconced in our union and our home, still in my small penthouse, his sister, Ethel, came for a visit. She was not an attractive woman and a lonely, unbedded female. Since we had only one bedroom, we made up the couch in the living room for her to sleep on. Things went well until the second week of her stay when she tried to seduce me onto the couch one night. I managed to extricate myself without hurting her feelings. In later years, she put one and one together and realized that Walter and I were truly one, and she seemed able to cope with the situation.

Walter had a great interest in art, which bolstered my own burgeoning appreciation. He did a bit of daubing himself and created some charming montages, usually for my birthdays, objects I still have. Our art collection grew with our mutual choice of works, American art, pre-Columbian, African, Oriental, and Grecian artifacts, many of which we gathered on our subsequent worldwide trips. When he had been stationed in Tokyo, because of the importance of his position, he had been courted by high-ranking Japanese. He had made a study of Orientalia and expressed a desire to see and possibly make some purchases. So arrangements were made by Japanese businessmen he met for him to have private viewings of art that had been hidden during the war for safekeeping. Usually, when he visited these antiquarians, they would invite him into a small, rear chamber, lock the door, roll back a carpet, lift part of the wooden floor, and display priceless items. He told me quite a lot about his experiences in Japan, invitations to formal dinners by royal nabobs where wives were not allowed, but geishas were on hand; weekends at geisha resorts where he and fellow officers would be entertained both musically and sexually.

As a result, he told me, while most of the G.I.s were buying cheap export items, he was carefully acquiring exquisite Oriental art. Another great advantage Walter had during that time was the ability to ship all his purchases home via army transport because of his position. In that manner, he had acquired some priceless Japanese and Chinese bronzes, delicate prints and scrolls, and a set of screens consisting of twelve panels, fifty feet in length, depicting the founding of the Tokagawa Shogunate and painted with jewel-like colors on a gold-leaf background. In celebration of this acquisition, his influential Japanese friends tendered him a special dinner. He described sitting low on the floor with his feet in an unseen well while geishas, hidden under the table, would orally pleasure the guests.

Inevitably we brought each other up on our past lives. He confessed that growing up, he had suppressed whatever homosexual urges he'd had and indulged in a series of affairs with women at the university and in the army. He also confessed that on some few occasions, he had allowed gay men to service him, enjoyed it, but always felt guilty. He had surprised himself by his sudden reaction to me and his desire to give me mutual satisfaction. No guilt at all!

In 1946 we decided that we could use more space and bought the first of our many homes, a twenty-two-foot-wide brownstone on a most unusual street in Greenwich Village called St. Luke's Place. It was only one block long, running from Seventh Avenue South to Hudson Street (the extension of Eighth Avenue). On the south side of the block, there was a park and on the north side a row of similar Georgian-style, four-story homes set among a lush archway of old gingko trees on either sidewalk. Number 6, which we owned, was historic. It was the house that had belonged to a Dr. Walker, whose son Jimmy grew up to inherit it. When Jimmy Walker became the playboy mayor of New York during the twenties, there was no Gracie Mansion mayoral residence. Therefore each successive mayor's home became the official residence, and two stanchions capped by lamplight were installed on the street in front of the entrance.

It was obvious from the details we found in our newly purchased home that the city had spent a fortune converting No. 6 to Jimmy's taste as mayor. Two drawing rooms, each with an Adams fireplace mantle, had been converted into one long room with sliding doors leading into a twenty-two-foot-square dining room plus fireplace facing the garden. One entire wall of the basement was festooned with telephone connections that looked as though the entire city's phone system had run through the mayor's home. Also in the basement, we found an old-fashioned trunk which was chock full of Walker memorabilia, official photographs, old periodicals, and loads of old sheet music, including copies of a well-known song written by Jimmy Walker: "Will You Love Me in December as You Do in May?" What a prescient title that was. Jimmy's reign as mayor ended in disgrace after the Seabury investigation revealed fraudulent dealings in his administration. He had left his Catholic wife to live with his mistress, the musical comedy performer Betty Compton, and his deserted Catholic wife committed suicide in No. 6 St. Luke's Place.

A French family had purchased the house from the Walker estate, and then, with ten thousand dollars down, I became the next owner. I mention that low down payment because years later a good friend, Frank Campini, loved to tell everyone how that was the basis of my future real estate dealings that brought me great financial gain.

Walter couldn't contribute to the purchase. He was attending NYU on the G.I. Bill. We loved that house and did a lot of work on it ourselves. Most of the rooms still had the original shutters that had been painted over for years. We filled a big galvanized barrel with paint remover and soaked the shutters, then scraped them down to the raw wood. When we rehung them, they looked elegant.

Papa was still alive and loved to visit us to do small carpentry chores. The rear yard had been long neglected. We dug and spaded and arranged stones and plants, creating a garden of beauty with a small waterfall and goldfish pond. We both had a flair for décor, and the result won us four pages in *House Beautiful*.

In due time, Walter earned his Ph.D., became an assistant professor at NYU and a practicing Freudian psychologist. We had a full life and a wonderful circle of friends, both straight and gay. My three brothers were all married, running their successful fuel-oil company, and raising families.

To retrace a few years, my brother, Murray, who felt the loss of Mama most keenly because he was the youngest, had a childhood sweetheart. When he was about to be drafted in 1943, he said he wanted to marry the girl. My older brothers were adamantly against this, pointing out that he was going into the service and might not return. I insisted that it was all the more reason for his marriage, and I was happy to attend as his best man, give him away, and send them on a honeymoon.

Billie Holiday—"Lady Day" as she was fondly called—in an unusual photo. The pain and demons that eventually destroyed her are quite evident. Though she sang many of my songs, my favorite was her rendition of "Foolin' Myself."

Ella Fitzgerald—In 1934, at age sixteen she won the Harlem Apollo Theater amateur contest and became vocalist for Chick Webb's popular swing band. She was still sweet and shy when we became friends in '38. What a great talent!

Frank and Bing—the two greatest singing talents of popular songs in the 20th century. Each of these gifted troubadors created his own inimitable style. How fortunate I was to have them sing my songs.

The Andrews Sisters—They were by far the most successful sister trio with an unending parade of blockbuster records. In their first teaming with Bing Crosby, they gave me a big winner: "Ciribiribin."

To Jack
Sin—sationally yours
Mae West

Mae West—One of a kind. She was her own creation. She told stories about herself in the third person. This is the autographed picture she gave me in her bedroom.

Nat "King" Cole—He was the prince of singers, a mellow fellow who sang with perfect diction and invested every lyric with love. His phrasing was impeccable.

Starting from the left: Peter De Rose ("Deep Purple"), Jean Schwartz ("Chinatown, My Chinatown"), J. Fred Coots ("Santa Claus Is Coming to Town"), Charles Tobias ("Little Lady Make-Believe"), and the youngest one, me ("If I Didn't Care").

Here I am in 1941 in front of a mike as chief petty officer leading the Coast Guard band.

A quick promotion: Me as lieutenant on the far right, leading the Maritime Service Orchestra in its weekly CBS coast to coast broadcasts from the base in Manhattan Beach, Brooklyn. If you can find him, Nelson Riddle is seated in the trombone section.

My first Hollywood studio contract with Peter Tinturin at Republic Pictures in 1938. We wrote songs from "Manhattan Merry-Go-Round" through Gene Autry's "At the Old Barn Dance." (Photo by Otto Dyar.)

Here I am in 1941 performing on the Loew's State stage, just before I went into the service.

Me with my school chum, Sylvia Fine, at the Trocadero on the Sunset Strip in Hollywood. Sylvia married another Brooklyn friend, Danny Kaye.

Yes my darling
songwriter Jack
Love,
Dinah

Dinah Shore—We had a long and warm relationship, ever since my song, "Yes, My Darling Daughter," gave her instant stardom. She was a honey of a girl with a voice full of honey.

Richard, me, and Harold Wheeler, who conducted *Lena Horne, the Lady and her Music*, of which I was one of the producers.

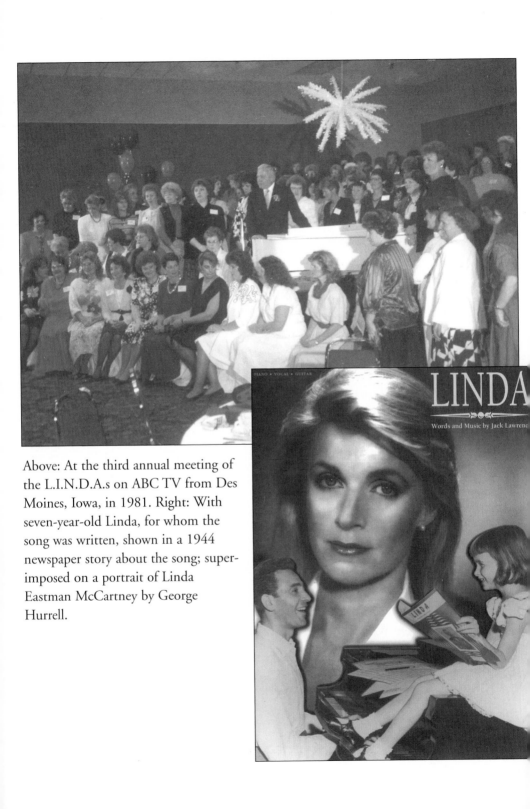

Above: At the third annual meeting of the L.I.N.D.A.s on ABC TV from Des Moines, Iowa, in 1981. Right: With seven-year-old Linda, for whom the song was written, shown in a 1944 newspaper story about the song; superimposed on a portrait of Linda Eastman McCartney by George Hurrell.

PIANO • VOCAL • GUITAR

LINDA

Words and Music by Jack Lawrence

Joan Crawford rehearsing for her singing/dancing star role in *Torch Song,* which featured my song, "Tenderly." It turned out that Joan's singing in the film was dubbed by India Adams, whom I later helped to obtain an RCA recording contract.

Quincy Jones—An incredible musician, composer, arranger, and conductor. An extraordi-nary human being. He has a great heart and is a superb friend.

Murray was fortunate. He became an air force instructor and was able to have his wife with him throughout the war years. After D-Day, when they returned with their new baby to New York, I loaned them my Washington Square penthouse until they could get settled. Murray soon went to work for my brothers in the oil business.

Papa was living alone in our old Van Siclen Avenue house, and I urged him to find a woman and live with her. But Papa was too old fashioned for that. He found a local widow and married her. My brothers were upset, but I was pleased that he had someone to keep house for him. It was an ill-fated union that lasted just a short couple of short years. Papa developed stomach cancer and went quickly, only seven years after Mama's demise. He was all of sixty-eight, but had lived a hard life. We all sat *shivah* in my home, and Walter was a bulwark of strength during this sad time. He endeared himself to the entire family as they got to know and appreciate this unusual man.

Today, as I write this on the computer in my office, each time I glance up, I am faced with two photos of Walter Myden, one younger and one older. Both pictures seem to gaze at me lovingly and warm my heart and sometimes bring tears to my eyes, which is why I like to keep them there near me.

From 1946 to 1958, while Walter and I lived on St. Luke's Place, we pursued our interest in art and became active on the political scene. The latter happened because of a close friendship we developed with Manya and Morris Novik, who lived nearby in Chelsea. Novik, as he preferred to be called, had been intimately associated with Fiorello La Guardia before and after La Guardia became the dynamic mayor of New York City, a position he held for three consecutive terms. La Guardia's administration came on the heels of Mayor Jimmy Walker's disgrace and resignation—and there we were, Walter and I, living in the previous mayor's residence.

We did get to meet Mr. and Mrs. La Guardia at the Novik's one night some months before La Guardia died of pancreatic cancer. Manya was a great cook, and I recall that happy, boisterous evening with the Little Flower (as Fiorello was fondly known) asking repeatedly for Manya to mix him another of her "shit and geese" gin martinis. That nomenclature came about when Manya was once asked to explain how she made such delicious martinis. Manya, who spoke English that got mixed up with idiosyncratic Yiddish, gave her recipe: "I don't measure—I just shit and geese [sift and pour]."

After La Guardia's death, our friendship with his widow, Marie, blossomed, and with the Noviks, we visited her often in her Riverdale home. The La Guardias had adopted a boy and girl whom Marie was raising. The daughter, Jean, was both a physical and mental problem and at Marie's request, went into analysis with my Walter. Jean was an extremely bright teenager who stayed in treatment with Walter for about ten years until her demise from physical complications.

Preelection times, Novik would always phone to alert me that my services would be required, either to entertain with special material at fund-raisers or to write jingles promoting forthcoming candidates. I wrote and worked on campaigns for Herbert Lehman, Averill Harriman, and John Lindsay, among others. Unfortunately, the ditty I wrote, "Make Morris Mayor," did not result in his victory. I had more success in publicizing my protest song about an unfair labor bill, "Have a Heart, Taft-Hartley, Have a Heart," which I recorded with a hillbilly band and with Novik's help, took to the heads of unions in Washington, who encouraged their members to buy the record. The ILGWU and the Liberal Party of New York were potent forces in the political arena, and I was happy to be of service. But my contributions were small compared to that of my composer friend, Harold Rome, who wrote the long-running revue *Pins and Needles.*

Mention must be made of another outrageous and shameful event that took place in our nation's capital during that same period: Sen. Eugene McCarthy's vituperative, out-of-hand, unsubstantiated attack on the "Red Menace" that had supposedly infiltrated Washington, the rest of the country, and primarily Hollywood. Although Walter and I followed the daily reports with horror, we remained, fortunately, unimplicated. It affected the Broadway theater world less than film and television, although Zero Mostel, whom I knew, was blacklisted and lost out on some productions.

To bolster his diatribes, McCarthy viciously attacked the film industry. The powerful heads of studios ran like scared rabbits, created an endless blacklist, and fired hundreds of workers: stars, directors, and technicians. They then set up their own censorship boards, checking and emasculating every script and film. This resulted in such a bland output for the next few years that audiences saved their money, stayed home, and watched the new miracle: television. Hello Uncle Milty!

When I moved up to Connecticut a few years ago, I became friendly with Ring and Frances Lardner Jr., two charming people. Ring, the Oscar-winning screenwriter of M*A*S*H*, was always reluctant to talk about his blacklisting and subsequent jail sentence, but shortly before he passed on, he wrote a powerful biography in which he detailed the McCarthy inquisitions and their devastating impact.

CHAPTER TWENTY-FIVE

It's a Crapshoot Business

I can look back fondly on my years at St. Luke's Place. Those were truly my halcyon days. First and foremost, I had Walter, and we were building a new home and a new life together. Both Walter and I were successful, and living was a joy as we traveled through the world, tasting its sights and pleasures. All my wildest dreams had come to fruition. My hit songs were piling up, my ASCAP ratings increased, and the royalties were rolling in.

I was even being paid to sing! An outfit called Langworth Transcriptions, the forerunner of Muzak, had heard me on my Maritime broadcasts and signed me to record whatever songs I chose. Naturally, all of mine were included along with numerous standards. I recorded approximately a hundred songs and still have many of those transcriptions.

The music business is far from an exact science. No one can predict what will be a hit or flop with the public. Strange events can always spell the difference. For example, I collaborated once again with my old friend, Arthur Altman, in 1939. Our song, "All or Nothing at All," was recorded by three big bands at that time: Jimmy Dorsey, Freddy Martin, and Harry James. They were all good recordings, but I had gone to Harry James's recording session because I wanted to hear his new vocalist, who was going to do the song. Since this was a sixty-four-bar song—twice the length of the ordinary song —with many emotional lifts, I wanted to make sure that Harry's new singer could do it justice.

There stood a skinny young man in front of the microphone waiting to sing.

Harry, trumpet in hand was conducting his orchestra. The opening bars of the arrangement came with a blasting fanfare, predicting a momentous melody. And that skinny youngster started to sing. The voice, the phrasing, the tone were unbelievable coming out of that reedlike frame.

In a recording session, after each take, the record engineer plays back what's just been recorded so that everyone can correct possible mistakes. Lou Levy, the publisher of that song, and I complimented Harry on a great arrangement and the promising new vocalist to whom we were introduced. Frank Sinatra was his name. I shook his hand and congratulated him.

He asked, "This your song?"

I nodded.

"So how'd you like my vocal?"

I told him that he was doing a wonderful job for a first take, but the song could use a little more emotion in the release when he sang:

> But please don't bring your lips so close to my
> cheek.
> Don't smile or I'll be lost beyond recall
> The touch of your hand, the kiss in your eyes
> make me weak
> And my heart may grow dizzy and fall.

Frank Sinatra squinted his eyes and looked at me. A few moments passed. Then, "You're gonna tell me how to sing?"

And he turned and walked away.

Keep in mind, this was his first big job with an important band, and he wasn't about to take advice from anyone. He must have been born with some innate knowledge that carried him through to the end. He stayed with Harry James for a while and recorded a few more of my songs, but we never became as close as he was with Sammy Cahn.

Sammy knew how to ingratiate himself. I never had that talent.

All three records of "All or Nothing at All" were released and disappeared quickly. Lou Levy, Arthur Altman, and I couldn't understand it. We were so certain we had a big hit.

Let's skip a few years. Sinatra had suddenly stepped out on his own and was breaking box-office records at the Broadway Paramount, his first solo appearance. Those old enough will remember the scenes of hysteria, the screaming bobby-soxers, teenage girls fainting in the aisles, and the police who couldn't control the crowds.

Columbia Records had signed Frank and was anxious to start recording him when suddenly the American Federation of Musicians called a strike because of a money dispute with all the record companies—who then tried recording a cappella groups, with vocals backed by kazoos, harmonicas, tissue paper over combs. The public wouldn't buy, and the big record companies were in a panic.

Then Lou Levy had a brainstorm. He reminded Columbia that it had a recording in which Frank was practically a solo performer because of the length of the song. The original record label read HARRY JAMES ORCHESTRA in large letters. Below, in much smaller print, was vocal by Frank Sinatra. Columbia gleefully made a new label and rushed out the same old record. Only now it read, in LARGE print FRANK SINATRA. And in small letters: accompanied by Harry James Orchestra.

Let Frank tell the story in his own words. There are pertinent reasons why he remembered the song so vividly in this interview in Hollywood with Louella Parsons.

"All or Nothing at All" was the song that gave
Harry James and me our walking papers out of

the old Victor Hugo Café, and, incidentally, out of Hollywood! The first night we played there, the manager came up and waved his hands for us to stop. He said Harry's trumpet was too loud for the joint and my singing was plain lousy. He said the two of us couldn't draw flies as an attraction. And I guess he was right. The room was as empty as a barn.

It's a funny thing about that song; the recording we made of it years ago is now in one of the top spots among the best-sellers. Most people think it's a new one—but it's the same old recording. It's also the song I used to audition for Tommy Dorsey, who signed me up on the strength of it. And now, it's my first big record!"

Over the years, Frank recorded many new versions of this song. One of his best is the one with Nelson Riddle's arrangement, and it's included in most of his retrospective albums. Glory be! That's the music business—completely unpredictable. Sure bets rarely happen, and surprises are wonderful. Anyway, I've always been proud of this particularly sophisticated lyric.

ALL OR NOTHING AT ALL
Half a love never appealed to me,

If your heart never could yield to me

Then I'd rather have nothing at all!

ALL OR NOTHING AT ALL

If it's love, there is no in-between,

Why begin then cry for something that might
have been.

No, I'd rather have nothing at all!

But please don't bring your lips so close to my
cheek,

Don't smile or I'll be lost beyond recall,

The kiss in your eyes, the touch of your hand
makes me weak

And my heart may grow dizzy and fall,

And if I fell under the spell of your call . . .

I would be caught in the undertow,

So you see, I've got to say No! No!

ALL OR NOTHING AT ALL!

Music by Arthur Altman

Strangely enough, Sinatra in his solo career never recorded any other of my hit songs, although he did perform them in personal appearances. I've always had the feeling that he harbored a grudge against me ever since that long-ago day when I made that suggestion. On those rare occasions when we would meet, he was barely cordial. I don't know what his reaction would have been had he ever discovered that his daughter, Tina, was in analysis with my lover, Walter.

Another unpredictable story concerns my song, "Linda." In the late thirties, when I became friendly with a prominent music-business attorney named Lee Eastman, I took him on to represent me. He was handling not only some big band leaders like Tommy Dorsey and Sammy Kaye, but also songwriters Carolyn Leigh, Sammy Fain, and others. I was a frequent visitor at the Eastman home in Scarsdale and quite fond of Lee's wife, a Shaker Heights girl he had met at Harvard. We developed a good friendship, and I shared delight with Lee and Louise as their family increased. I also introduced Lee and Louise to the world of art, for which I had developed a passion. They expressed great interest, so one Sunday, I drove up with a couple who owned a well-known gallery. As a result, Lee began to represent gallery owners and painters like de Kooning and Léger and instead of fees, took his remuneration in good works of art. In short order, he started an important collection of modern art.

On one of my visits to his home in Scarsdale, Lee requested a favor.

"Jack, you know that my wife has a name song—'Every little breeze seems to whisper Louise'—and my son has more than one—'Oh, Johnny, Oh Johnny, how you can love'—and our little Laura also has a name song. But our baby, Linda, doesn't have any. Would you write her a song?"

Why not? Baby Linda was a doll, and besides, I liked the name. When I started to create the words and music, I decided that it should tell a romantic tale that baby Linda would appreciate when she was grown up. So it became a lilting melody with the following story:

> When I go to sleep, I never count sheep
> I count all the charms about LINDA,
> And lately it seems in all of my dreams
> I walk with my arms about LINDA.
> But what good does it do me?
> For LINDA doesn't know I exist,
> Can't help feeling gloomy . . .
> Think of all the loving I have missed!
> We pass on the street, my heart skips a beat,
> I say to myself, "Hello, Linda!"
> If only she'd smile, I'd stop her a while
> And then I would get to know Linda
> But miracles still happen . . .
> And when my lucky star begins to shine,
> With one lucky break
> I'll make Linda mine!

By this time in my career, I had had a fair amount of hits, so publishers always listened attentively to whatever I wrote. You can imagine my chagrin when the first few publishers turned down this song. Since the title didn't have to rhyme, one man said, "Why don't you call it 'Ida?' That's my mother-in-law's name. Call it 'Ida,' and I'll publish it."

I said, "There already is a song with that name, 'Ida, sweet as apple cider.'"

Another maven suggested "Mandy." I pointed out that name had already been used in a song by Irving Berlin, no less.

Suddenly, it was 1941, and Pearl Harbor brought us into the war that was raging in Europe. I decided to enlist and put "Linda" away for the time being. Whenever I trotted that ditty out for my friends, they loved it and sang along. But publishers still didn't buy the title name.

Four years later, I was out of the service and spending a weekend with my fiancee, Bernice, at the Eastmans. Cute little Linda entertained us with her lisping version of my song. She was a precious little ham, singing my words, which I'm sure she didn't comprehend. She took a bow, we gave her a big hand, and she escaped with her brother, Johnny. Then her father told me that a new client, the bandleader Charlie Spivak, would record "Linda" if I gave him publishing rights for his new company.

I agreed, went into Spivak's new firm, and signed contracts. But before he could get around to recording it, Ray Noble had somehow gotten a copy, fallen in love with it, and made a toe-tapping arrangement with a vocal by wonderful Buddy Clark. Buddy, whose career was at an ebb, made an overnight comeback with the record. That title no publisher liked took the country by storm.

Such are the vagaries of the music business. A song that was rejected by so many publishers becomes a public favorite.

Lee and I were ecstatic. But this story has an ironic ending.

It seems that my good friend, Lee Eastman, my attorney and confidant, lied to me. He didn't tell me that he was the true owner of Spivak's music company and therefore owned the copyright to my creation. I was working in Hollywood a few years later when I discovered not only this ownership, but the fact that Eastman was trying to acquire another of my important copyrights, "Sunrise Serenade," because the publisher had been lax in making royalty payments. Further, I discovered that Lee had acquired copyrights of some of his other writer-clients. I wrote him a scathing letter telling him that he should be disbarred and ended our relationship.

Much later, when the first twenty-eight years of copyright ended, Lee tried to charm me into giving him renewal rights to "Linda." In those days, copyright law covered each work for fifty-six years with a renewal term for the creator at the end of the twenty-eighth year. Instead of making renewal deals as each of my songs came up, I stockpiled them in my own publishing firm. When Lee made his request, I had my attorney in California inform him that the song was part of my entire catalog, and I was not interested in making any deal with him. By that time, Lee had used his attorney connections to build up a substantial library of music.

To cap all this, his little Linda had grown into a lovely woman who married Paul McCartney. See what a hit song can do for you?

It's been rumored that Lee caused the breakup of the Beatles, but I can't vouch for that. In my case, I suppose Lee won in the end, since I was offered enough money and wound up making a renewal deal for my entire catalog with the firm owned by his son-in-law, Paul McCartney.

And who do you think was the attorney representing Paul for that deal?

Through the years, I had no contact with Johnny or Linda Eastman until sometime in the 1990s, when Lee had passed on. I wrote Linda to tell her about an organization of ladies in the Midwest, each and every one of them named Linda, they claimed, because of my song! These ladies were meeting annually in various cities and kept inviting me to attend their conventions. Finally I did go to Des Moines on their third annual anniversary, and it was strange to be among three hundred females, all named Linda and all singing my song along with me. My note to Linda McCartney was to tell her about their upcoming tenth annual meeting. (I have just been invited to their fifteenth anniversary, in Rockford, Illinois.)

Linda's reply was a short note. "It's so nice to hear from you after all these years, Jack. I've always been proud of the song you wrote for me and I'll bet you're the only writer who has a ladies' group named after one of his songs. Let's try to see each other the next time Paul and I are in town. With love—Linda."

We never did meet again. That sweet, lovely woman died of breast cancer in 1999, and Paul kindly invited me to her New

York memorial service, which ended with his playing a recently recorded version of "Linda" he had made for her last birthday.

It was a beautiful and touching service. The seating was all assigned and by invitation. The audience consisted of family and friends. My assigned seat was on the aisle. When Paul was exiting, he stopped at my seat, embraced me, and said a few loving words, "You're a sweet man!" and walked on.

I believe that the reason I can recall so many details involving many of my songs is because there were such close associations with either the artists or other principals. I hear some particular song I've written, and inevitably, unforgotten incidents and ghosts flood my mind and the circumstances replay themselves.

CHAPTER TWENTY-SIX

Beyond the French

The behavior of the French is often beyond comprehension, particularly when it comes to the English language. If they could pass a law making it illegal to use English expressions or phrases, they would not hesitate to do so. They are undoubtedly disgruntled that English has become the universal language.

I use the word "beyond" in the above because it relates to an English lyric I did for a French song way back in 1946 that seems to have become an international incident recently. The song I'm referring to is "Beyond the Sea," which was first published in France as "La Mer" with words and music by Charles Trenet.

Trenet had a long career as a popular and ebullient performer of hundreds of French songs that he wrote and sang with great style. Many of his songs came to our country, were given English lyrics, and achieved great success. One of his most-performed songs in English is the lovely ballad "I Wish You Love."

Charles made frequent trips to America, where he also performed. On one of these occasions, we met, and he asked me to write an English lyric for one of his hits titled "Vous qui passez sans me voir," literally "You Who Pass Without Seeing Me." I told him that I didn't like doing direct translations since that didn't call for much creativity on my part. He suggested that I let the melody dictate what I wrote.

As I became more familiar with his melody, it seemed to me that it had a toe-tapping lilt to it, that it was hardly a sad song. So I proceeded to write a gay English lyric titled "Passing By," which told of two people who fell in love while casually meeting.

Charles liked my lyric well enough to include it in his English-speaking appearances.

Through him, I also met his publisher, Raoul Breton, and over the years had many occasions to write English lyrics to Breton's French hits. One of the biggest of these, "Symphony," came right after World War II. It garnered a prestigious roster of recordings from Bing Crosby to Marlene Dietrich.

In 1946 Max Dreyfus of Chappell Music called me into his office to listen to a new French hit written by Charles Trenet and published by the Bretons. It was called "La Mer," and like Debussy's composition, was a tone poem both musically and lyrically. Trenet had outdone himself. I was intrigued by and loved the melody, but could not warm up to his lyric, in which he talked about the different moods of the sea and how they affected him. The Bretons came to my home on St. Luke's Place to talk about the song, and I explained my reaction.

"Charles trusts you!" they said. "Write the lyric as you feel it."

Which I then proceeded to do. I decided to make it a romantic story about a sailor out on the ocean knowing that his lover is waiting for his return, and I added one word to the title: beyond. It was a lovely, musical word that I could play with and use in different ways throughout the song.

Charles' French "La Mer" was achieving the status of a hymnal classic in his own country, and this resulted in a number of almost symphonic renditions by Mantovani, Percy Faith, and even Benny Goodman with strings, but it was far from being a big hit in America. Then one day around 1958 in a publisher's office, I was introduced to a brash young man named Bobby Darin who had made a few records. No writer would ever pass up the opportunity of pitching a song to a recording artist, and so I let him hear some of my current output. The one he liked most was "Beyond the Sea," but he said he did not agree with any of the interpretations he heard. He said it needed a beat.

Some months later, Darin sent me an album he had just recorded titled *That's All*. It contained a song he had written called "Splish Splash," plus that classic "Mack the Knife" and "Beyond the Sea." The entire album of novelty songs and ballads was done with finger-snapping arrangements that carried an irresistible beat. It was wonderful.

Did I say that the music business is a crapshoot? Who could have predicted what happened next? This same song, one which in twelve years had never achieved hit status in lush arrangements, took off into the stratosphere overnight because of a finger-snapping delivery by a fresh, young talent. And on a small (at the time) label like Atlantic Records. The song even catapulted Bobby Darin into a film career. How tragic that this great young talent died a few short years later.

Now the song gained many new recordings, all in the style Bobby had given it. His classic recording has since turned up in many major films such as *Apollo 13*, *Father of the Bride*, *Diner*, *Sea of Love*, and *Funny Bones*. Darin's version was also used in the Susan Stroman production, *Contact*, which played at Lincoln Center for almost three years.

After my friend, Raoul Breton, died, his publishing business was acquired by France Music, to me an unknown conglomerate. Suddenly, strange things began to happen. France Music complained to ASCAP that I, as the English lyric writer, was being awarded too high a percentage for performances. This, despite the fact that it was "Beyond the Sea" that was getting all those performances, not "La Mer." I had become a writer-member of the French performing rights society, SACEM, and when I received their quarterly reports, I noticed that there were no credits for performances of "Beyond the Sea." I wrote to SACEM, in English (all their communiqués were in French), and asked why I was not being given credit for "Beyond the Sea," which, I'm certain, was being performed in France. I received no answer. Then I learned that France Music had an American attorney, Michael Sukin, whom I knew, representing them and that he had been making deals with film and record companies and commercials for the use of "Beyond the Sea" without ever consulting me, despite the wording of my contract. I finally contacted Sukin and was told that France Music and SACEM claimed that they had all rights, did not have to check with me, and besides—"Beyond the Sea" was never performed in France, only "La Mer."

I said this was impossible. If not the English-language recordings, all the American films that had used the song played throughout the world and resulted in performance monies paid to me—that is, all over including France, who didn't pay me. When my current publisher and I threatened a suit, all the monies were suddenly put in escrow until the situation was settled, but they refused to disclose how much money there was.

All of this brouhaha resulted in an article by Will Friedwald in the November 2002 *Vanity Fair*. Friedwald has written many articles and books about the music business and its legends, and many times he would phone me to check on certain facts regarding Sinatra or the Big Bands. Graciously, he always gave me credit for whatever bits of information I was able to supply. Somewhere along the way, I must have given him a rundown of all the problems I was having with France Music.

Now I would like to quote from Will's *Vanity Fair* article.

> The careers of the two men who wrote La Mer
> and Beyond the Sea—Charles Trenet and Jack
> Lawrence—are likewise similarly disparate. Both
> men were long-distance runners with careers that

lasted from the depression to beyond the millennium. Each in his own way is a perfect representative of his country's musical culture. Trenet, who lived to be 87, was an archetypally flamboyant Frenchman—a singer-songwriter before that concept became popular in the states. Lawrence, still going strong at 90, was and is, in the best Tin Pan Alley tradition, a specialist who concentrates on lyrics.

When Charles Trenet passed away in 2001, France reacted almost as dramatically as America did following Frank Sinatra's death almost three years earlier. It was a time of national mourning . . . It was on a train that Trenet got the idea for the song La Mer, shortly after the defeat of the German army . . . and the song soon became a source of national pride for the newly liberated nation . . . which he recorded shortly thereafter with an orchestra and chorus conducted by Albert Lasry.

Note that name: Albert Lasry, who had conducted the recording session. Because when attorney Sukin, at the insistence of France Music, started making claims that I was not entitled to my share of performance money, they also came up with the news that Albert Lasry was a cowriter of "La Mer" and thus entitled to a full third of royalties.

My attorney, Bella Linden, did a comprehensive search of all existing copyrights of "La Mer," and there was only one name listed as lyricist/composer: Charles Trenet. Despite that, France Music put out a new version of "La Mer" crediting Trenet and Lasry.

Once again I would like to quote from the *Vanity Fair* article.

> Lawrence's words to Beyond the Sea constitute a lyric of the highest order. In the song's bridge (middle section), Lawrence goes beyond 'beyond' by using the word as a linchpin of a series of phrases, each with a slightly different meaning: 'Beyond a star' . . . 'Beyond the moon' . . . 'Beyond a doubt." The word 'star' arrives on an accidental C-sharp, which charges the phrase with unexpected oomph and gives the word an especially starry feeling. Changing the title, paradoxically, allowed Lawrence to remain phonetically faithful, at least, to Trenet's original: in Trenet's text, each eight-bar 'A' section begins with the words 'La mer'; in Lawrence's version, each of these sections commences with 'Somewhere' so that the English lyric has the same sonic feel as the original.
>
> Exactly whether the song is French, American or a product of world culture is an issue that the courts may soon decide . . . France Music's

method of asserting Gallic pride has been to deny Lawrence his share of the royalties . . . Fortunately, there's more than enough to go around . . . the accumulated royalties from the Darin version alone would be sufficient to support Lawrence's and Trenet's heirs for as many generations as the song remains under copyright. Lawrence certainly didn't seem bitter when, at a Carnegie Hall concert in June 2002, he was introduced by Michael Feinstein, who said: 'I hope I look that good when I'm 90.' (Amen to that.) 'Everybody was applauding, oohing and ahing,' says Lawrence. 'I guess I am a phenomenon.' He's almost as much a phenomenon as this most remarkable of his songs, a piece of music that has existed in two cultures at once, (for almost 50 years) and thereby can be said to express the universal aspirations of man.

Thank you, Will Friedwald, for those kind words. You'll be happy to know that at this time of writing, we are on the verge of a settlement.

CHAPTER TWENTY-SEVEN

Life with Walter

After several years together, Walter and I were truly happy in our relationship and had forged permanent bonds with no reservations. Everything seemed natural to both of us. We even shared a lady friend a few times. She had been having an affair with a married composer friend of mine and expressed a desire to go to bed with either of us. *Voilà!* A *ménage à trois!*

That reminds me of another threesome Walter and I were inadvertently involved in on our first trip together to Europe in 1948. A good friend of ours, Arnold Weissberger, a theatrical lawyer handling many international stars, was kind enough to give us introductions to people abroad. He also advised us to stay at his favorite hotel, the Savoy in London, which was close to all the theaters. Arnold had arranged that we would meet a client of his, Noel Coward, who was appearing with Margaret Leighton in a revival of Bernard Shaw's *The Apple Cart.*

It was my first trip to London, and I loved every day, every new sight, every adventure. We went to the theater practically every night, and after the performance of Shaw's play, we went back-stage. Noel was gracious, witty, and completely charming. Since none of us had had any dinner, we invited Noel to dine with us. However, London was still undergoing rationing, and there were no restaurants open after theater hours, so Noel suggested that the wisest place to dine that late would be the Savoy, our hotel. He explained that the Savoy had kitchen service on each floor, and we could order meals in our room and be comfortable.

After ordering, Noel suggested that we all get "cozy." He re-moved his jacket, tie, and shoes, urging us to follow suit. I still re-call the splendor of that room service, two waiters impeccably dressed, wheeling in a table and setting out the silver and linen napkins. Then came the crowning presentation, Noel's order of lamb chops. The waiter ceremoniously carried in an enormous silver platter covered by a humongous silver bell, which he care-fully raised to expose a single small chop on a bed of watercress. We laughed, and the waiter apologized with the whispered word, "Rationing."

While we were enjoying our small meal and two bottles of wine, Noel regaled us with hilarious gossip about the royal fam-ily and London society. It was getting rather late when Noel an-nounced, "Enough small talk . . . let's go to bed!"

What he meant, of course, was our big double bed—and he started to disrobe.

Walter and I looked at each other as Noel stripped down to his boxer shorts and bounced onto the bed saying, "Come, come, chaps—don't be bashful!"

He was charming, he was funny, and he was Noel Coward—so we shrugged, stripped, and joined him on the bed. Noel, in a jovial mood, continued telling stories, and we laughed so hard that we never got around to sex. We finally all dozed off, and an hour or so later, Noel, fully dressed, woke us, kissed us good-bye, and left. We went on to Paris the next day and stayed at a delightful hotel Noel had recommended.

During the time Walter was at NYU, teaching and treating patients, I was going back and forth to Hollywood on demand by various studios. On one of these trips, I ran into my old school chum, Sylvia Fine. The last time I had seen her was opening night of a show on Broadway called *The Straw Hat Revue*.

This entertainment had been born one summer at a resort, Camp Tamiment, in the Poconos. The creative staff was under the direction of Max Lieberman, and some of the members were Imogene Coca, James Shelton, Sid Caesar, and Danny Kaye. Sylvia and Danny never knew each other back in our Brooklyn neighborhood, but had met at Camp Tamiment.

My seat for *The Straw Hat Revue* was in the first row, and as I looked down into the orchestra pit, I was amazed to see Sylvia playing piano. Naturally, at intermission I said hello. She was equally surprised to see me. She asked if we could meet for a drink after the show.

We went to a nearby bar and caught up on all the years we'd been apart. She was well aware of all my success and couldn't understand how someone as musically untrained as I could have achieved it. She had written special material for the *Straw Hat Revue*, mostly in a Gilbert and Sullivan vein, and Danny Kaye had stopped the show with her tongue-twisting songs.

Sylvia felt that this was the start of her big career as a writer. She was madly in love with Danny and told me, "Danny doesn't know it yet, but I'm going to marry him!"

Then she asked for a big favor. Now that her future seemed to be assured, she had put down a deposit on her first mink coat. It was ready to be picked up, and all she needed was the final $1,000. Of course, I loaned her the money, which she paid back in dribs and drabs out of her weekly salary.

The revue closed, and Danny, with Sylvia accompanying him, was booked into a club on Fifty-seventh Street, the Martinique. Their act was dynamite. He was a wonderful mimic, and all New York was talking about him. Naturally, Walter and I went frequently and as friends of the star, had no difficulty in getting through the thick crowds.

In a short time, Moss Hart caught Danny's act and signed him up for *Lady in the Dark* starring Gertrude Lawrence. True to her word, the day they stopped performing at the Martinique, Sylvia whipped Danny down to Florida and married him. I always thought that Danny's performances, even in pictures, were just this side of gay camp and that he had what we referred to as "a touch of the brush." But throughout his career, he was linked with female stars—Gwen Verdon, for one. Then, after his death, a biography reported that he had had a homosexual affair with Laurence Olivier—which Joan Plowright, Olivier's last wife, denies. If it is true, I hope they enjoyed it.

Danny was soon signed to star in Hollywood films, and Sylvia was right there by his side, writing the songs. Everything she wrote sounded like special material; she had no knack for popular lyrics or melodies. Theirs was a strained marriage. They were living in Beverly Hills when Walter and I moved to Bel Air, California, and I resumed my friendship with Sylvia. We visited their home often, mostly when Danny was away on location or performing, and she would complain to me about how miserable she was. She admitted that he had asked for a divorce, but she said NEVER—in no uncertain terms. She felt she had made him a success and that he owed her. They had a quirky child Danny had named Deena after one of his parodies of the song "Dinah."

Sylvia was a lonely lady and a frequent dropper-in at our home without phoning, which irritated Walter. I tried to explain how needy she was, but he felt she was taking advantage of an old friendship. One of the snapshots I have shows me, Sylvia, another gal, and Nicholas Brodzky, with whom I was writing an MGM score for a Lana Turner film, at a Hollywood nightclub. Sylvia looks so forlorn!

When Danny was at home, they gave wonderful, fun parties to which Walter and I were always invited. Every comic in town and their wives were usually there—Red Skelton and his wife, Jack Benny and Mary Livingston, George Burns and Gracie Allen, Milton Berle. After dinner the ladies would always adjourn to the living room, and the guys would go to the library where they could be macho and light up their cigars. What was always amusing to Walter and me was the fact that, with all those comics in one room, there was only one wit who entertained and rolled them on the floor in paroxysms of laughter: George Burns.

He was a hilarious clown with his songs and stories. He would invent a verse that had nothing to do with the chorus of the song. Let me try to simulate a Burns invention.

> *Verse:*
> While traveling through Vladivostok one day,
> I met this Russian muzhak who played his balalaika,
> When he asked me did I like a balalaika, I replied,
> What's not to like-a? But I lied!
> Anyway this muzhak introduced me to Russian muzak,
> And more importantly a lady whose name couldn't have been Sadie,
> A Sadie I would never fall for,
> But this lady I wanted more and more and more . . .
> I would sing to her every night
> In the pale Vladivostok moonlight

Chorus:

It had to be you! It had to be you!

I wandered around and finally found

A somebody who—etc., etc.

As he continued with the rest of that old standard, George rolled them in the aisles.

Whenever Sylvia was working on a new score for one of Danny's films, she had no compunction about phoning me any time of the day or night for a reaction to her lyrics. I suppose she trusted my criticism. Walter would be annoyed when she woke us out of a sound sleep to pick my brain. She was alone most of the time and a night owl. He wanted me to tell her to stop, but I knew how insecure she was, so I put up with these late calls. Eventually, Sylvia discussed the fact that none of her film scores had resulted in hits and suggested that we collaborate. So we wrote five or six numbers and played them for Panama and Frank, Danny's writer/producers. They liked our songs, and when the next film was set to start, they suggested to Danny that it would be a good idea if Sylvia and I wrote the score. That might give them a winner.

After all that brain-picking, after using me to show Panama and Frank that she was capable of producing melodic songs, when faced with everyone's decision that she should work with a collaborator—she didn't choose me. She asked Sammy Cahn, who had a great track record in films. I was hurt, I was bitter, and it was the end of our friendship. Sylvia never had a hit song, never let go of Danny, never was a happy woman. To me, it's interesting how she perpetuated their names after his death. Danny died before she did, so she left enough money to Hunter College, where she had matriculated, to name its auditorium the Sylvia and Danny Kaye Playhouse. She made certain that they would be linked in perpetuity.

Since Walter had never liked Sylvia, he was relieved that I had ended that one-sided friendship. Strangely, I felt the loss. She and I went back in time so many years—to our neighborhood, our school days, our childish plans. She was a direct tie to my adolescence.

CHAPTER TWENTY-EIGHT

Edith Halpert and the Downtown Gallery

When I came out of the service in '45, I started to spend hours in museums educating myself, discovering old and new wonders to marvel at: Rubens, Velásquez, Fragonard, Lippi, Giotto, and all the Renaissance painters at the Metropolitan. Then the Museum of Modern Art, with Monet, Manet, Rouault, Braque, Picasso. And the Whitney Museum, with those exciting Americans: Grant Wood, John Marin, Childe Hassam, Charles Demuth, Georgia O'Keeffe. I became drunk with it all.

When I met Walter, who had studied art and was so much more knowledgeable than I, my interest increased. I introduced him to a gallery that dealt in American art, run by a formidable woman, Edith Gregor Halpert. As yet I couldn't afford the French impressionists, so, encouraged by Edith, I had made a couple of purchases from her gallery of young Americans.

She had started a downtown gallery in the early thirties on Twelfth Street in Greenwich Village. When I met her she was in her fifties, a remarkable creature who had come to America from Odessa as a sixteen-year-old with her mother and sister. Her first job after high school was at Macy's, but she had larger ambitions. She enrolled in the Art Institute on Fifty-seventh Street to study art. Quickly she realized that she really had no knack for painting and became a model for the young artists at the institute. One of the tutors was an older artist named Samuel Halpert who specialized in painting women, and Edith became one of his favorite models. This relationship blossomed, and in due time, she became his wife.

I doubt that love was the motivating force. Sam Halpert probably represented a father figure she had sorely missed. Sam decided that a stay in Paris might polish his technique and enhance his reputation, so he and Edith moved there for a couple of years. While that move did little for Sam, it was most fortuitous for Edith. She realized that her artistic talents were small and became more interested in the commercial aspects of the art world. She was a familiar figure at Paris art galleries, got to know the most enterprising dealers, and asked questions, quickly absorbing their business practices.

When the Halperts returned to New York, Edith knew exactly what she wanted to do with her life. First, she amicably divorced Sam. Then she opened her first Downtown Gallery in Greenwich Village. Quickly she attracted many of the young painters she had first met at the institute and gave them an art venue. Among these young painters were Ben Shahn and Stuart Davis.

In these early days, Edith was a dynamic art dealer. She knew how best to display her artists, how to attract attention, how to get them talked about. Alfred Stieglitz, a brilliant photographer who was married to Georgia O'Keeffe, had decided to close his gallery, A Private Place, where he had not only introduced American, but European artists to New York and the world. Young Edith made such an impact on the art scene that Alfred Stieglitz contacted her, asking her to take on the American artists he had been nurturing at A Private Place. John Marin, Max Weber, John Sloan, Charles Demuth, Marsden Hartley, and Georgia O'Keeffe thus became Edith's charges in one fell swoop. It was quite a coup for Edith, and her reputation soared. She soon became good friends with Mrs. Gertrude Vanderbilt, herself an amateur artist, who had started the Whitney Museum of American Art in a small building on Eighth Street in the Village.

Edith had bought an eighteenth-century farmhouse in Newtown, Connecticut, which had all its original fireplaces, creaky stairs and floors, and a working well with pump handle out front. Walter and I visited her there often, slept in the uncomfortable beds, and endured the rigors and discomforts of early-American life.

Edith had discovered hidden treasures in the attics, cellars, and barns of New England, and through extended expeditions into the countryside, she came back with untold marvels: ancient hand-sewn samplers and quilts; copper weather vanes of horses, roosters, angels; anonymous portraits painted by itinerant artists. Oddly enough, some of these portraits had been executed by Asian artists who had given the eyes a slight slant and the hands and feet a smaller, more delicate look than American features.

Among Edith's greatest discoveries were some remarkable surprises: paintings by two realist artists of the mid-1800s who had not only been prolific, but had sold their entire output quickly. They were not to be found in museums and had been overlooked and forgotten. Their names were William Harnett and John Peto. With enough of their paintings and other artifacts of the nineteenth century, Edith mounted "Early American Art," an exhibition that had a wide attendance and also attracted Mrs. Abby Rockefeller, mother of John Jr. and Nelson. Mrs. Rockefeller became a frequent visitor and developed an interest in Edith's stable of young artists, whose works she bought along with a great deal of the folk art Edith had unearthed.

Edith loved to tell us the story of the time when Abby Rockefeller asked her for a favor. Would Edith take her seventeen-year-old son, Nelson, in hand? He was too naïve and shy, and needed to be introduced to Greenwich Village life, to develop more worldly views. Edith didn't know exactly what was expected of her, but she took timid, pimply-faced Nelson to one of her favorite *boîtes* where all the bohemians congregated. One of the attractions at this bar was Romany Marie, a gypsy who read palms. Edith called her over to read Nelson's hand without introducing him. Romany Marie picked up his right palm and examined it. A puzzled expression crossed her face. She then picked up the left palm and gave it equal scrutiny. She put his hand down, clucked, and shook her head disbelievingly. "I see nothing but money, money, money!" she said.

Was this callow youth's hand so blank that the only thing to be seen was the great wealth surrounding him?

A positive result of Abby's friendship with Edith culminated in the establishment of the American Folk Art Museum in the restored town of Colonial Williamsburg many years later. Edith was invited to the opening by Nelson Rockefeller (by then governor of New York) as an honored guest and was gratefully thanked for her guidance and encouragement of his mother in the acquisition of American folk art.

Edith Halpert played an important role in Walter's and my appreciation of art. She taught us new ways to look at art and encouraged our acquisitions and collection. Although we didn't have that much money, she wisely allowed us to make purchases on a payment plan. We were never dunned, but paid at our own pace. And we were not the only young people being given such privileges. In like manner, Edith aided others in acquiring collections.

By this time her gallery was located on East Fifty-first off Madison, still known as the Downtown Gallery. We attended all the exhibitions of the many artists already well known and the younger ones yet to make their mark. Slowly, our art collection grew: Stuart Davis, Ben Shahn, Max Weber, Yasuo Kuniyoshi, Charles Sheeler, William Zorach, Georgia O'Keeffe—they all became our friends. Their successes and reputations are largely due to Edith's devotion and faith in American art and her insistence in placing their most important works in museums throughout the world. She was also responsible for getting the government to employ many of these artists during the World War II years. They were kept busy creating murals for public buildings. Other works I bought from Edith were those of deceased artists whom she had known intimately: Charles Demuth and Jules Pascin.

Another wonderful trait Edith had as a dealer: She never insisted that we buy art that didn't appeal to us. She was very keen on paintings of Arthur Dove, who had passed on. Although his abstractions were in demand by museums and collectors, they never appealed to Walter and me. Occasionally Edith would remark that Dove would appreciate in value and should be in our collection.

Walter once said to her, "Edith, we are buying the art we would like to live with. Not because it may appreciate in value." I felt exactly the same.

Walter and I had sold the St. Luke's Place house for a handsome profit, then bought and gutted a brownstone on East Fifty-second Street. The street-level floor was made into Walter's waiting room and office facing the garden; he had quite a busy practice by then. In due time, all the floors were overflowing with our eclectic collection of art and artifacts. Most of Edith's artists whose work we had bought came to visit us, particularly to see how prominently we had displayed them. One evening when Ben Shahn came to dinner, he was upset at seeing a handsomely framed drawing of his that had not been purchased from Edith.

Immediately he demanded, "Where did you get that?"

I smiled smugly. "We found it in a junk shop on a side street in Rome."

He fumed. "That bitch! I'll never again give anyone a gift of my work!"

Ben had been invited to the Spoleto Festival in Italy the year before to create sets for some of the ballets. He had given that drawing as a gift to a young girl in return for her assistance. At least, that was his explanation. Walter and I visited Italy annually and always poked around in antique shops. In the rear of a junk shop, we had spied this drawing, cheaply framed and hanging in a dark corner. We immediately recognized Shahn's style and questioned the kid who was in charge while his father had gone to lunch. Where did this picture come from? How much was it? Could we take it out of the frame to examine it to see if it was real or an etching?

The kid's English was minimal, but he got the gist of our questions and phoned his father at home. A rapid salvo of Italian ensued, and our questions were answered somewhat. A young lady had left it in the shop to be sold; the price translated to seventy-five dollars; and yes, we could take it out of the frame to examine it. We proved to ourselves that it was an unsigned drawing, took the shop's number, and explained that an Italian friend would phone the proprietor later. We got our friend to make the call, and after a furious conversation that sounded like an angry battle, our friend hung up triumphantly and said, "You can pick the picture up tomorrow! The price is fifty dollars." This story did not improve Ben Shahn's appetite that night.

Another visitor to our home was Georgia O'Keeffe, usually brought by Edith. Georgia was a tough bird; the New Mexico sun and desert had dried her face and I believe, her manner. She spoke a minimum of clipped, terse words and always fought with Edith because she felt Edith was not charging enough for her paintings. We owned two O'Keeffe's: a brilliant small oil, "Jack-in-the-Pulpit, No. 1" and a rather atypical painting titled "Front of Ranchos Church," a fairly large oil in pastel colors, depicting a lovely old New Mexican church and steeple.

One afternoon, Georgia marched in preceded by Edith, went directly to her "Front of Ranchos Church" painting, and announced, "You'll have to stop loaning this picture for exhibitions. It's been all over the world, and it'll be ruined!"

"Well, Georgia," I answered, "then you'll have to stop including it when you make up lists for your exhibitions. We usually get a letter stating 'Miss O'Keeffe specifically requested your picture for her exhibition.'"

She muttered something incomprehensible and left shortly afterward.

Two or three years later, Georgia's feuds with Edith ended their relationship. She withdrew all her work from the gallery and found another dealer to act as her personal representative. That arrangement didn't last too long and ended up with Georgia being sued for commissions.

However, before this rupture, we received a phone call from the dealer, who explained that Ms. O'Keeffe was concerned about pictures she had painted during certain years. She was afraid they were deteriorating rapidly because of a batch of bad paint. One of the pictures she was specifically concerned about was "Jack-in-the-Pulpit, No. 1." The dealer insisted on viewing the picture herself, even though we assured her there was nothing wrong with it. She walked into our living room and saw the small painting on a far wall at least fifteen feet away. From that distance, she spoke.

"Oh yes, that picture is in bad shape. Miss O'Keeffe will buy it back from you for what you paid."

Walter had bought it and said, "It's not for sale!"

"What do you mean it's not for sale? That's Miss O'Keeffe's picture."

"No, my dear! Miss O'Keeffe painted it. I bought it. It's mine!"

It was not until Georgia died many years later that I discovered why she had tried to reclaim that picture. In her will, she left the National Museum in Washington her entire series of "Jack-in-the-Pulpit" paintings. The series numbered two through ten. Ours was the number one.

Walter and I owe Edith Halpert a great debt for her patience, her wisdom, and her friendship. In the late sixties, Edith developed a brain tumor and deteriorated rapidly. We took her to New

York Hospital a few times for examinations by specialists who recommended surgery, but she would have none of it. She was too far gone to recognize her true condition. We watched this woman, who had always been so chic and smartly turned out, virtually become a bag lady with mismatched, torn stockings and stained dresses. She would phone to invite us out to dinner, but to avoid having people see her in public, we always insisted on eating at home. She would appear carrying her belongings in a Bloomingdale's shopping bag. Her speech was incoherent, and her talk was nonsense. For those friends who had known her over the years, this was heartbreaking, but there was little we could do. We were shocked to learn that some "friends" had actually taken advantage of her incompetence and bought important artworks at ridiculous low prices that she had quoted in error.

Walter had a heart attack when he was about forty-four years old and was cautioned to take care during the harsh winters. In 1969 we decided to move to the West Coast so that he could avoid inclement weather. We learned sadly that Edith had been placed in a nursing home by her niece and was *non compos mentis*. Friends who went to visit her reported that she did not recognize them and childishly showed a notebook in which she claimed she was writing her autobiography. The book held nothing but scribbled nonsense.

Edith died in 1970, and her only niece, claiming there was no will (we all knew better!), inherited everything. This was far from what Edith wanted. She had spoken frequently about her will and what she was leaving whom. Many important paintings from her own collection were to go to various museums. On many occasions, and in front of her niece, she told us that certain works were destined for certain museums and that her niece was to get money, but no art. Since no will was ever produced, once the estate was settled, her niece put all the art up for auction and took the proceeds. It seems a shame that the works Edith intended to give to various museums never got there because none of her wills were ever found.

Musing on Edith's life, it seems so incredible to me that this little Russian immigrant, with no particular education or training, should have been able to accomplish so much and leave so indelible a mark on the American art scene. She was truly the dean of American art dealers. My hope is that one day someone will pore through the archives that she gave to the Smithsonian and write her fascinating story.

CHAPTER TWENTY-NINE

Artists and Artifacts

Collecting art is a rare, incurable disease.

In the late forties on a trip to Mexico, Walter and I were passing a junk shop when we spied what seemed to be ancient stone bowls used for grinding meal. We asked the proprietor if he had any other old pieces, and he motioned to the back of his small store. We parted beaded string curtains and in the small back room came upon two large cardboard cartons bulging with dirt-encrusted objects. It was a veritable treasure-trove of pre-Columbian figures, still covered with the soil from which they had been excavated. Very few were intact; most of them were broken, with heads, legs, and arms scattered.

We explained in our halting Spanish that we would return later with a Mexican friend to discuss the purchase. Our Mexican friend was a painter living in a seedy, small village named Ajijic where there were also some American wannabe artists who had opted out of civilization. Mostly they lived in poverty, drank tequila, and smoked marijuana. One of these "artists," formerly a violinist with the New York Philharmonic, had amputated one of his fingers so that he could collect insurance and retire to Ajijic to paint.

When our friend engaged the junk-shop owner in conversation, we learned that all these pieces had been dug up by local farmers who sold their find for a pittance. We made a deal to buy it all, as is, sight unseen, for the munificent sum of fifty dollars. The proprietor refused to give us a sales receipt. Our Mexican friend explained that the country was passing laws against the sale of any artifacts and that we might have our hoard confiscated at the border.

He then made a bright suggestion. The nearby town of Tlaquepaque was known for its colorful ceramic ware. We loaded our two cartons on the backseat of our convertible, drove to Tlaquepaque, and bought lots of junk ceramics, which we piled on as a top layer to the two cartons. From the factories that made the ceramic ware, we got printed strips that read: MADE IN TLAQUEPAQUE, which we pasted on the cartons. Then we proceeded to the border into El Paso.

Yes, we were nervous as we approached the bridge across the sluggish Rio Grande. If the Mexican border guards did an inspection, we would surely lose our treasures. The car top was down, our two cartons sitting high on the backseat with their printed signs prominently displayed. We were halfway across the bridge when we heard a piercing whistle.

"Shit! They've got us," I said to Walter, who was driving.

He said, "The guard is waving for us to back up. I'd better do it."

Slowly, he backed the car on the bridge. We reached the guard who held out his hand and muttered some gibberish. We couldn't understand him. I pointed to the two cartons. He shook his head, NO! and just kept repeating words and thrusting his hand at us.

Finally, the driver of a car in back of us leaned out and yelled, "You forgot to pay the bridge toll. Give him five centavos."

We both heaved sighs of relief and hurried to the American side where the guards stopped us and made us open our trunk while they examined the inside of the car. They glanced into our cartons and dismissed the contents, but they did confiscate an open bottle of tequila from the trunk, then waved us on.

Not until we reached Los Angeles were we able to unpack and examine the contents of our cartons. We washed every piece carefully, then found the missing matching parts. With the advice and help of a local museum curator, we reassembled the broken figures and were assured we had made quite a coup. This was the start of an important assemblage of pre-Columbian art, which in the forties, was not as yet in demand. It led us to a new interest—African art, which we pursued assiduously on all our European trips. Our large home in Bel Air became a veritable museum of various cultures: early American, American Modern, European, pre-Columbian, African, Chinese and Japanese Dynastic, and Cycladic carvings acquired on trips to Greece.

We became actively involved with the Friends of the Whitney Museum of American Art and sponsored a few American and European exhibitions, with a special one of our own collection that we toured both in America and Israel. We loaned art to the Embassies Program initiated by Nancy Kefauver and to various museum shows. Then, because of our growing interest in the state of Israel due to frequent trips there, we joined Billy Rose and started the Friends of the Israel Museum, which funded the eventual construction of what is today the remarkable National Israel Museum in Jerusalem. All in all, it has been a most satisfactory and rewarding experience.

We even had the satisfaction of discovering and sponsoring a highly talented artist, Claudio Bravo. Walter and I made annual trips to all parts of the world, always looking, always learning. One summer, I remained behind in Madrid when Walter had to return to the States early. On a lunch visit to a fascinating American lady's Madrid apartment, while admiring her Picassos and Monets, I came across an arresting portrait of my hostess and her dog. I could not identify the artist. She was pleased to explain that he was a young Chilean living and working in Madrid and offered to introduce me.

The next afternoon, she took me to Claudio Bravo's apartment/studio. He was doing the portrait of a client who was sitting for him, so we browsed about the apartment waiting for him to be free. On a table, I spied a large photograph volume of portraits he had done of some prominent people on commission;

wonderful paintings in a glowing, realistic style that reminded me of Zubaran's work. Most of the portraits had an added bit of whimsy, for example, there was a regal dowager who I was told was a duchess. She was elegantly gowned, displaying all her jewels and pearls, and wore a gold-studded eye patch that gave her an air of comic mystery.

Bravo called us into his studio and introduced us to the lovely young matron he was painting. In a sand-colored evening gown, she reclined on a slanted platform, but in the painting she appeared to be lying on a beach. One arm was gracefully extended, and in her palm stood her five-year-old daughter, on her toes, in a tutu. The lady's husband sat by watching the process approvingly. Claudio invited us to look around some more and have a drink until he could join us.

In Claudio's bedroom, I saw an interesting self-portrait with some hand-written lines that mentioned future work the artist intended to do. There was also a small still life. Both pictures intrigued me. But in a back room, I came across a half-finished large oil that really excited me. When completed, it would be an enormous six-foot-by-eight-foot painting of a flat, electric-blue, paper-wrapped package tied with a string. Even in its unfinished stage, it was stunning, and I decided that I had to have it. When Claudio joined us, I asked if the self-portrait and still life were for sale. He explained that the self-portrait, with its work notes, was really personal, but after some hesitation, he decided to sell me both. Then I told him that I really wanted to buy his "Blue Package."

"But," he said, "it isn't finished! How do you know you'll like it? Besides, I get so little time to paint anything but portraits. I'd like to finish the package and enter it in the Sao Paulo Biennale."

"Sell it to me," I said with chutzpah. "I'll do you more good than the Biennale."

The lady who had brought me spoke up. "Believe him, Claudio. I've been to his house in New York, and I know it's true."

He looked at me quizzically. "Whose paintings do you own?"

I ran through my list. He nodded approvingly. Then I capped it all by telling him how closely associated I was with the Whitney and other museums and galleries. We agreed on prices for the three works, I took the smaller two with me, and we parted amicably.

When I returned home and showed Walter the two paintings, he was quite impressed. I refused to describe the large package painting that was to come one day, wanting it to be a surprise. Some months went by before I heard from Claudio that he had shipped the finished painting. It arrived in a huge, flat wooden crate—too large to take into our Fifty-second Street home to un-crate, so we opened it on the sidewalk. We pried off the top cover and revealed brown wrapping paper. Carefully, I unfolded the brown paper and exposed the "Blue Package." It was so magically realistic, the painted string binding it so palpable that Walter, looking down on it, said, "Open it. Let me see what's inside."

I laughed. "That's it!"

We hung it in our living room on a white-painted brick wall directly opposite the entrance door. When my friend, Lloyd

Goodrich, head curator of the Whitney Museum, came to dinner one night and I opened the door to welcome him, he stood in the doorway thunderstruck.

"Who did that?" he gasped.

"Too bad," I said. "He's *Latin* American."

On our next visit to Madrid, Walter and I sat down with Claudio and convinced him that he had to forego those commissioned portraits and devote himself to doing enough paintings for a one-man show in New York. We assured him that it would make his reputation. A year later, Claudio consigned and shipped to us about twenty-five paintings of various sizes, all on the wrapped paper-package theme. In some of the paintings, the wrapping paper showed torn areas through which floating clouds could be seen. Very Magritte! There were one or two paintings of different-colored paper grocery bags standing upright, in a row. All of the paintings were imbued with a sense of mystery. What could be in those packages and bags?

We had moved to California before Claudio's one-man exhibition at the Staempfli Gallery. Not only was every picture sold even before the official opening, but John Canaday, who was art editor of the *New York Times*, raved about the show in a full-page review captioned BRAVO! BRAVO! BRAVO! These days Claudio's work can be seen at the Marlborough in New York and other prestigious galleries and museums throughout the world.

Eventually, our art acquisitions in so many fields grew to such voluminous proportions that we required special help simply to keep track and collate all of them.

Upon request, we loaned various artworks to traveling exhibitions and even organized our own cataloged exhibition of American art that we toured with, both in this country and abroad.

Unfortunately, in my last move from a New York triplex to a country house in Connecticut, there was no wall that could accommodate the large size of the "Blue Package." Christie's took it for auction, reproduced it brilliantly on the cover of its catalog of Latin American art, and I was well compensated for parting with my treasure.

Because of space, I've had to dispose of many of my gems. But truthfully, I have no regrets. Walter and I took pride in owning them, we loved displaying them, we enjoyed daily viewing and living with them. But it's time for other art lovers to feel the pride of possession.

Don't think for a moment that I've denuded myself of all my art. There are certain possessions I still keep and cherish.

What's left now fits comfortably in my home—and in my heart.

CHAPTER THIRTY

Two Great Ladies— Bella and Tallulah

Yes, I still have that same Steinway that I bought on time payments many years ago. It has traveled many miles with me, from apartments to houses I've owned on the East and West coasts. It has been child, wife, friend, and enemy. But on the whole, it's treated me well. In return, I have coddled and treasured it, cursed and blessed it. But I confess after these many years of partnership, I haven't learned to play it that much better than my old upright. Oh, musically speaking, I have absorbed a lot. That's inevitable when one spends a lifetime in the same career.

With the help of the songs that came out of that instrument, I became in 1934 the youngest active member of ASCAP, the

American Society of Composers, Authors and Publishers. Next came admittance to the American Guild of Authors and Composers, in which I as vice president and Burton Lane as president fought writers' battles in the Washington political arena and instituted a royalty-collection plan that has kept publishers on guard and honest.

It was during my active period in the guild nearly a half-century ago that I met another incredible lady who was the attorney for our organization then and has remained my attorney, friend, adviser, and spiritual sister lo! these many years. She is a most unusual lady, and the saga of her life deserves a separate book. You know the old saying:

"You can't choose your relatives, but you *can* choose your friends!" I chose Bella Linden a long time ago, and she is closer to me than a relative.

When we first met, she had recently passed her bar exam and joined the firm of John Shulman, a copyright expert who was the Songwriter Guild's attorney. Bella had grown up in Montreal and had married the first violinist of the New York Philharmonic, with whom she had two sons. When he died in a tragic train accident—practically before her eyes—she shipped her two young sons to her mother in Montreal, went to day and night classes at NYU Law, and within two years had passed the bar.

We became friends when we sat next to each other at guild meetings, but we never socialized. I was keeping my private life with Walter quite separate from my professional life. A year or so later, Bella married Leonard Linden, an attorney she had known who was also a widower. They were on their honeymoon in London when Walter and I ran into them at the Royal Court Theater. Of course, I introduced Walter, and we arranged to meet after the show for a bite. The play, by Arnold Wesker, had been about an English Jewish left-wing family and its politics. Bella came from a similar kind of family and also spoke and wrote perfect Yiddish. She had assumed that Walter was not Jewish and questioned his reaction to the play.

She was completely surprised when Walter not only identified with the play's Jewish family, but expressed his sympathy for their left-wing discourses. From that moment on, Bella and her new husband practically adopted Walter and me. Back in the States, we introduced them to Edith Halpert, whom they came up to Newtown to visit, and they wound up buying a summer home in that area.

Leonard Linden had a successful insurance-law practice, but as a hobby, loved all phases of construction. Walter and I became frequent visitors in Newtown and made many suggestions as to how their cottage could be improved. Nothing fazed Leonard. He put in new heating and plumbing systems, built a larger, more comfortable bathroom next to the master bedroom, removed and raised ceilings, and fulfilled one of Bella's desires by building her a glassed-in garden room.

When Bella opened her first law office, Walter and I helped Leonard put up the bookshelves, arrange the furniture, and hang the pictures. We also became her first clients and brought her others. Bella and Leonard had a good marriage until about fifteen years ago when he was operated on for a brain tumor. Over the years, he had deteriorated mentally to the point where he required twenty-four-hour supervision. Bella sold their Newtown home and had moved him into a small apartment on a lower floor in her apartment building. It was a sad situation, but Bella refused to "warehouse" him. "He worked hard all his life," she said. "He deserves to be taken care of as long as the money holds out." Unfortunately, Leonard's condition became so bad that he had to be sent to a nursing home where he finally passed away.

Meanwhile, Bella still keeps at her law practice, taking care of my affairs and those of many of her prestigious clients: Isaac Stern (who died recently), Midori, Eugene Istomin, Loren Maazel, and many others. To add to all that, she is also active on the boards of Carnegie Hall and NYU Law. A remarkable woman and a good friend for more than fifty years.

With my film scores, I became a member of the American Motion Picture Academy of Arts and Sciences; with my Broadway scores, I joined the Dramatists' League; and my catalog of songs got me elected to the Songwriters Hall of Fame when Johnny Mercer first created it. On that good workhorse, my Steinway, I wrote political commentaries that I performed actively in campaigns for mayors, governors, and presidents.

In 1948 Tallulah Bankhead and I were among the few show-business people who believed in and worked for Harry Truman's reelection. (There was also another Democrat who worked for

Truman at the time—in Hollywood. Ronald Reagan.) The rest of the country and many of Truman's own Democratic party had prematurely assumed he would be defeated by New York's Thomas E. Dewey when the ILGWU put me on the air for about thirteen weeks singing my parody of an old song, "Mr. Gallagher and Mr. Sheen." I concocted a mock musical one-upmanship battle between Truman and Dewey in which Harry, of course, always won. Tallulah duetted with me, she as Truman, I as Dewey. Consequently, I remember vividly that election night when headlines screamed DEWEY ELECTED!

The following morning, they ate crow when the final vote gave it to Truman, and we were invited to the inauguration of our thirty-third president. Tallulah and I had invitations to sit in the president's box. Tallulah and the Truman family had already become warm friends, and she was a frequent visitor at the White House. Of course, that was hardly a new experience for her. She had known Washington intimately. Her grandfather, uncle, and father had all served in the House and Senate. "As proud Democrats," Tallulah would remind you.

That Washington inauguration day was cold and bitter, the Pennsylvania Avenue sidewalks were packed with half-frozen crowds exuding steamy breath, stamping their feet, and swinging their arms as they waited for the parade. Our inaugural party decided to warm up with a few drinks in the window of a hotel facing the avenue. When we sat down at the table, a distinguished, older black waiter approached Tallulah.

"Miss Bankhead," he said with a smile, "I had the privilege of serving your daddy when he was Speaker of the House. And I would take great delight in serving you today!"

Tallulah was touched. "Thank you, suh!" she said. "You've made my day. And I would enjoy a bourbon, if you please."

He beamed. "With branch water!"

"Naturally," she answered. "With branch water."

We were on our third drink when we noticed a definite commotion on the sidewalk and heard the faint sounds of a marching band. Tallulah jumped up and grabbed her mink coat.

"Oh, my God—they're starting! Come on, Jack! We've got to get to the president's box!" She tore out of the hotel with me in her wake. The crowd was packed in a solid mass, but that didn't deter our girl.

"Let me through!" she yelled. "I've got to get through!"

People turned to look at this small, shoving figure, hair and mink flying in the wind. Miraculously, they parted to let her through. But not for me! I was trapped in a wall of bodies while Tallulah inched her way into the middle of the avenue with the parade bearing down on her. Police guards tried to stop her, but she barreled ahead.

"I'm Tallulah Bankhead," she proclaimed, "and I'm sitting in the president's box!"

I watched her being escorted to the royal box, I saw her being greeted by the Trumans. And I, with eyes streaming and feet freezing, clutching my invitation in my coat pocket, saw the parade with the rest of the uninvited.

During the Truman presidency, Tallulah became the MC of a very popular radio program, "The Big Show." Designed to compete with television's newborn popularity, it boasted guest stars like Ethel Barrymore, Edgar Bergen and his dummies, George Burns and his Gracie, and other famous people. One of my songs, a favorite of Tallulah's, was her closing theme, "A Handful of Stars." One Sunday, Tallulah had Truman's daughter Margaret on the show. Margaret had been studying voice, so she sang a couple of songs. Truthfully, she was only a fair singer. At least she sang on key. A critic on one of the papers criticized both Tallulah for her Democratic partisanship and Margaret for her inadequate performance. President Truman was irate! He publicly chastised that critic and warned that if they ever met, he would punch his nose. And in defiance, Tallulah invited Margaret back on her program to sing once more.

I missed all these political shenanigans when we moved to California. We tried to get involved with various campaigns, donated funds, attended rallies. But somehow, it wasn't the same. We seemed to be living in an alien land. We tried, but we couldn't relate to or be part of the local political scene. We lived through the Reagan governorship, which left the state of California in financial difficulties—the same difficulties that befell our entire country after the Reagan presidency. To this day, I fail to understand people who claim that Ronald Reagan was one of our great presidents.

CHAPTER THIRTY-ONE

The Last Good-bye

I mentioned that I had parlayed my real estate holdings from that first brownstone purchase. Allow me to explain. We sold the St. Luke's Place residence because I was spending more time in Hollywood at the studios. We bought our next New York property on Fifty-second Street for $40,000 with the profit from St. Luke's Place. After gutting and rebuilding Fifty-second Street into a beautiful home, we occupied it for almost twelve years. When Walter's cardiac condition became a serious problem, we put the house on the market with the intention of buying a house with an elevator.

That was early in 1963, and New York real estate prices were quite high, beyond our range for the locations we wanted. We had our house on the market for $175,000, but were finding no bidders. As a final resort, we decided to stay put and install a small elevator so that Walter could avoid the stairways. The rehab on our building started during a severe winter, and at his doctor's order, Walter had canceled his practice temporarily and gone to Florida. Much of the house had been torn apart when one day a real estate broker appeared to tell me that he had a buyer for the property at our price.

I advised him that we had taken the house off the market; it was no longer for sale. He kept coming back day after day with the story that his client (whose name he refused to divulge) was hung up on our house, wanting it so badly that he would increase his offer. I told the broker I was not interested, having already laid out considerable advances on the work being done. His client could buy the brownstone two doors away that was empty. No! the broker insisted. His client wanted our house because he liked all the changes we had made. The offer was increased to $200,000, and the client would reimburse me all the money I had advanced for the rehab.

I called Walter in Florida and talked it over. He said, "Maybe if they've gone this high and want it so much, they might go even higher. Let's do it!"

Yes, they did go higher to $225,000, with an agreement that we had a full year in which to purchase another property that they would pay for so that we wouldn't get stuck for taxes on our profitable sale. We were still in the dark as to who the buyer was, but arrangements were made for me and my attorney to meet at his lawyer's office where we would sign the sale contract and receive a cashier's check for the full amount.

Thinking it all over, I came to the conclusion there was something not kosher about this deal. The price being paid was much higher than the market called for in similar properties. I did a bit of sleuthing and discovered that an apartment building on Fifty-third Street facing our rear had recently been sold. Further inquiry revealed that other buildings surrounding us on Fifty-second and Fifty-third had also been sold. My attorney was a young man, Dave, who had joined Bella Linden's much-expanded law firm, and I told him that I was convinced we were being hustled by a conglomerate with big assemblage plans.

That Friday, when we went to the closing, we had added one simple stipulation to the contract: If we were selling to a conglomerate, the price was $450,000. We were enthusiastically greeted, and things went pleasantly until the attorney got to that last added clause. He exploded, cursing and screaming, "You're thieves! Your attorney is misleading you. He's just lost you a check for $225,000. You're a shyster lawyer. A crook!"

I said coolly, "Don't call people names. Calm down. All you have to do is say this is not an assemblage, and we'll sign."

"That's not the point," he screamed. "You added something to the contract that shouldn't be there. You've just lost yourself the sale," he said, waving the check.

I said good-bye and left with my attorney, who was very upset. He thought I was taking a wild chance, that I could possibly lose the sale. I was more sanguine and assured him that even if I lost, it didn't matter. I had not stopped the work on the house, and we would be content to remain there.

I said, "Don't worry, Dave. They'll call back."

Dave called me Saturday. "Have they called?"

Sunday. "Did you hear anything?"

Monday at 9:30 A.M. "Any word?"

"Relax!" I told him. "They won't call this early."

At 10:30, my phone rang. It was hard to hear clearly because the workmen were hammering away. I told the caller to hold on while I went to a different phone. It was the buyer's broker.

"Jack," he said, "Can I call you Jack?"

"It depends what you're calling me for," I replied.

"Sonofabitch. You know you've got a deal."

What a sweet deal it was. So with almost half a million dollars (they had to pay for the contracts we had initiated), we began looking for a new residence. Walter would have willingly remained in New York, but I was concerned about the condition of his heart and suggested that we look in California. This had little to do with my future songwriting since the music scene all over the world had changed radically. No longer were the Harold Arlens, the Sammy Cahns, the Jimmy Van Huesens being hired to write scores for great musicals. As a matter of fact, they had stopped making musicals. Rock was taking over, groups were being brought in to supply scores that didn't need to have intelligent lyrics or be written out in black notes.

But nothing at this time was more important to me than Walter's health. He was under constant medical supervision, and I monitored the doctor's orders. I was conscious of the edge on which he teetered, and I didn't want to lose him.

I phoned a dear friend in Beverly Hills, Harriet Parsons, Louella's daughter, who had been a film producer and marking time, had become a real estate broker. Many a Hollywood personality dabbled in real estate between films.

My relationship with Harriet and her lady friend had started in the fifties when I was working for the studios and renting residences. At that time, Harriet had been given an okay by recluse Howard Hughes to proceed with a screenplay for his RKO company. She had fallen in love with a song I had written with Richard Myers, the Broadway producing partner of Gertrude Lawrence's husband, Richard Aldrich. Harriet was determined to use this song in her film.

Despite the fact that Hughes was allowing a small budget for the production, to her credit, Harriet persisted and finally put all the elements together. She had a fun-filled screenplay by Alex Gottlieb and a fine director of comedy, Frank Tashlin, and had lined up Dick Powell and Debbie Reynolds to star. The film was titled *Susan Slept Here* and concerned a mature bachelor and a teenager—hardly an original idea, but cute and funny in its execution.

Our biggest problem was how to insert my romantic song, "Hold My Hand," into the plot naturally. Both Dick and Debbie were singers, but the story line didn't call for either of them to burst into song and certainly not with a tender love ballad. I did write a lilting title song for the film and got a popular group, the Merry Macs, to record it for use over the title credits. But it was not that simple to invent a solution for using "Hold My Hand."

To solve the problem, I came up with the idea that teenaged Debbie would fall in love with a recording she had heard and kept tuning it in constantly on the radio. In that manner, the song would get lots of play in the film.

I made a special trip to New York recording companies to see if I could get a big-name singer to record my song for use in the film. It was discouraging. I was having zilch luck because no one I approached thought it was worth risking a star singer on what was perceived as a B picture. I was scraping the barrel when I went to the head of Coral Records. He was interested, but only if I would slip him a few hundred dollars for his trouble. I had little choice; I paid him out of my own pocket. In return, he gave me one of his lesser singers who hadn't had a top seller in a long time: Don Cornell. Don was a capable singer who came from Noo Joisey and had indigenous accents to certain words. Part of my lyric sounded like Don's hometown.

> So this is duh kingdom of Heaven,
> So this is duh sweet promised land,
> While angels tell of love
> Don't break the spell of love . . .
> HOLD MY HAND.
> So this is the Garden of Eden,
> In dreams it was never so grand,
> Let's never leave again
> Adam and Eve again,

HOLD MY HAND;

This is the meaning of what bliss is,

For bliss is what your kiss is,

At last I understand . . .

So this is the kingdom of Heaven

And here on the threshold we stand,

Pass through duh pertal now

We'll be immertal now . . .

HOLD MY HAND . . .

Surprisingly, the film wasn't badly received when it was released in 1954. It was called a light, comic frolic and went into general release. Then a strange thing happened. The more cities the film played, the more business it started doing, and suddenly all the D.J.s were getting requests for "Hold My Hand." Don Cornell's career zoomed with lots of club dates. At the end of the year, the song no one had wanted received an Academy Award nomination. (In the final count, we lost to "Three Coins in the Fountain.")

Now in the sixties when I made the decision to relocate in Los Angeles, it was only natural that I phone my good friend, Harriet, whom I knew I could trust. I told her what I had in mind and asked her to line up the best $450,000 houses available, and I would fly out to check them one weekend.

Harriet met me, and we did the tour. There were some promising properties for viewing, but at the conclusion, there was only one great house that had captured my imagination: a property on a sizable acreage in the older section of Bel Air, a most exclusive enclave. It had been built by a husband who was in the insurance business and his wife who had inherited money as a Cherokee Oil heiress. Recently widowed, she had taken off on a round-the-world cruise, leaving power of attorney with an alcoholic daughter in Santa Barbara. I returned to New York, and the following weekend, Walter flew out to view the properties I had seen and made the same conclusion. There was only one of interest, that great house in Bel Air. But at $650,000, it was beyond our price range.

Fate has strange twists! Mama oil heiress, on her world tour, was romanced by a much younger gentleman who had been the general manager at the Huntington Hartford Theater and had decided that he wanted to marry a rich, old widow. When the Santa Barbara daughter heard about her mother's marriage on the high seas, she was livid. The property's asking price was far above what I was offering ($450,000 that I was getting for East Fifty-second Street), and Harriet was nervous about it. I told her that an all-cash offering like mine was not to be disregarded. As a broker, she felt she had to make that offer even though it might be turned down.

A miracle! Santa Barbara daughter was so angry at Mama's unscheduled marriage that she pounced on our low offer. To top it, she didn't want her mother to get the full $450,000 cash and gave us a two-year payout clause. I must have been doing something right. Harriet was in complete shock!

It was a superb house that went from Nimes Road (where Ronald Reagan and Nancy live now and Johnny Carson, Jerry Lewis, and Sonny Bono used to live) to the street below, St. Pierre. It was a wonderful Tudor-style property that had been designed by a most talented man who did most of the great houses in Beverly Hills and Bel Air, a black architect named Paul Williams. He had a marvelous sense of form and space. All the rooms in his houses were designed taking in the height and square footage of each area, and the ceilings were adjusted to those measurements.

Certainly there was more than enough space for the two of us in that twenty-room mansion. The grounds were like a private park with every type of fruit tree, a prize rose garden, and an enclosed English garden with a charming fish pond and fountain. The wood-paneled library had an unusual feature, a Presbyterian bar. In case you're wondering what that is, it's a complete wall that slides open to reveal a fully-stocked bar. Entertaining in this glorious environment would be sheer joy. Once we knew the house was ours, we haunted every auction in New York City, stocking up on furnishings.

When we finally got settled in Bel Air, Walter resumed friendships with many old acquaintances and professional people he had known and in no time, had built up a rewarding practice in his field. He opened offices in Beverly Hills, which was convenient to where we lived. Aside from his private practice, he was also associated with a children's clinic to which he gave free time.

He had started writing a book to be called *The Psychology of Money*, which would trace the reasons why people begged, borrowed, stole, or killed to acquire riches. Day Publishing had read his outline and contracted for publication.

I was relaxed and happy, swimming every day, trimming the rose garden, planting vegetables and orchids, and getting an occasional writing job for films. Healthwise, Walter was being cautious, following doctors' orders, and seemed to be doing well. We were happy to have made the move to an improved climate and felt this would prolong his life. All the males in Walter's family history had suffered at early ages similar cardiac problems that had shortened their lives.

Walter finished the first draft of his book and got a congratulatory letter from his publisher. They were excited about its prospects and hoped he would entertain the idea of a tour around the country to promote sales. This letter reached him at his office one May afternoon, and he was so euphoric that he called me immediately and read it to me. When he came home, we celebrated with a drink. I offered to take him out for a fine dinner, but he said he would prefer a quiet evening, just the two of us, alone.

Our help prepared a nice dinner; we were relaxed and happy. We spoke about the book tour suggested by the publisher, and I said I would love to go with him. It was an early bed night for both of us, about ten, I believe.

I was awakened from a deep sleep by Walter's moans. He said he was in great distress, had already taken his medication, and asked me to phone Jim Blake, our doctor and close friend. I woke Jim and explained what was happening. He said he would order an ambulance and be at our house within minutes.

It was suddenly a nightmare. I tried to put Walter at ease, but could do little. True to his word, Jim was there quickly; so was the ambulance. They carried Walter out. Jim wouldn't let me get into the ambulance with him and told me to follow to the hospital. I was right at their heels and rushed in to be greeted by Jim.

Walter was gone.

Today, over a quarter of a century later, as I write those words, my heart feels a clamp, and my tears fall.

I had just passed my sixty-third birthday, and he would have been sixty years old that July 10.

My three brothers and their wives came from New York to Walter's funeral, and that brought home to me how much they had thought of him and of our thirty-year union.

I realized that after all these years, they must have been aware of what our relationship was. But not one uncomfortable word was ever spoken.

I never loved my family more.

All our friends, gay and straight, everyone Walter had been associated with professionally, even his patients, attended the funeral. His book was never published.

I thought my life was over. As finished as Walter's.

CHAPTER THIRTY-TWO

I Have a Son

Death is so final . . . but not for the living.

The living have to go on, have to find ways of assuaging the grief.

It's a cliché, but time does heal. I had wonderful friends who rallied around me. Oddly enough, a married couple with whom we had developed a close attachment turned out to be my Rock of Gibraltar. Walter and I had met Larry Worchell through a business venture in which we invested, and he became one of our warmest friends. He and his wife, Karen, were going through marital problems, which concerned us because we liked them both.

Eventually they split up after about twenty years of marriage, but our friendship remained strong. As a matter of fact, a few years later, my friend, Richard, and I took Karen with us on a tour of all the Iron Curtain countries. The following year, we took Larry on a tour of southern France, at which time he met the young girl who became his present wife. I was best man at their wedding, and our friendship thrives. I still can't believe that their marriage of fifteen happy years has produced a son whose bar mitzvah we attended last March.

Walter's will had specified that all of his estate was to go to the Israel National Museum, to which we had both devoted so much effort and money. As executor, it was up to me to carry out his wishes, to find the proper allocation for his estate. The year after his death, I made a special trip to Israel and met with our friends at the museum. We decided to use Walter's fund to set up an area within the museum where handicapped children could be made comfortable and learn about the treasures gathered there. Today there is a plaque in that assigned children's area acknowledging the contribution by Walter Myden, and I get annual reports telling me how successful this program has been.

I know that would have pleased him. Someday, I hope to have an adjoining plaque or my name added to his.

I returned from Israel to my lonely home in Bel Air on July 4, and among my piled-up mail, I found an invitation to a party that very afternoon at a lady acquaintance's home. I did not really know this lady well, but rather than face a solitary holiday—so close to Walter's birth date, July 10—I decided to go to this party.

While there, I was introduced to a number of her friends and a smattering of men. One was an attractive man by the name of Richard Debnam. He was from New York, and during our conversation, he reminded me that he had once met me and Walter through a mutual friend. He seemed to have perfect recall of that meeting down to the details of what Walter and I were wearing.

Naturally I was flattered that he recalled an impact at a short meeting years ago, so we spent the afternoon chatting. Richard had been sent to Los Angeles by a New York agency that handled theater advertising for shows. He was there to establish an L.A. office, furnish it, staff it, and supervise its operation.

The day was growing late, and I said that I had to go home to feed my dog and hoped we'd meet again. We exchanged phone numbers.

The next weekend, I invited him for an afternoon swim. Richard was attractive, twenty years younger than I, and lonesome. I don't believe that I was his type, but he was going through an extremely stressful period, and I think I was a bulwark he could cling to. Undoubtedly, the truth was that each of us, in our own desperate way, needed the other.

Richard hated California, hated his job, hated the advertising business in which he had already spent more than twenty years. This was quite an achievement for an unschooled, untrained young man who had left his Philadelphia home—and an abusive father—at age sixteen in 1948 and made his way to New York with little money in his pocket and no friends. But he did have some fortunate assets: a cute, turned-up nose, a shock of blond forelock, and a fresh, boy-next-door look. With such attributes, he was quickly taken up by the gay New York scene, particularly by such legends as Leonard Bernstein and Jerome Robbins. Soon he was in demand as a model for the fashion industry. But he was astute enough to realize he needed something more substantial.

Friends helped him to a job in the Doyle, Dane, Bernbach advertising agency as a gofer where, in a miraculously short time, he had worked his way up to an executive position representing such advertisers as Orbach's, Nieman Marcus, US Shoes, and Bartons Candy. From there, he switched to a more lucrative job with Wamsutta Mills, working with such talented designers as Marc Rohan of Dior, Cecil Beaton, and Donald Brooks designing floral and linear patterns for bed sheets.

After a few hard years of intensive work, he had come to a definite crossroads and had been out of work for more than a year before this present job. He was in such a miserable state of mind that he had been in Los Angeles for three or so months and had yet to unpack his belongings. He loved music—symphonies, operas, shows, and pop—and had a collection of a few thousand records sitting in their packing boxes on the floor of his apartment. Putting it mildly, he was at the lowest ebb possible.

Although he did not want to get involved, I felt he was a drowning man holding up a hand to be saved. And I wanted to rescue him. Truthfully, he fought me. He did not want any commitments. It wasn't as though we were having great sex. Either his libido was low, or I was not the partner to stimulate him. But day by day, I became more aware of his wonderful qualities, and I persisted.

As I said, we had met on July 4, and about a week later, as we sat smoking a cigarette in an upstairs sitting room, I suddenly began to cry. Richard was concerned and asked what was wrong.

"Today would have been Walter's birthday."

He came over and put his arms about me and said, "It's all right to cry, Jack. You loved him, and you miss him. Don't ever feel sorry for your tears about Walter. He was the love of your life, and I will never replace him. Nobody will."

That drew me even closer to Richard. I practically forced him to give up his apartment and move into my big house with all his baggage. He was still trying to fulfill his advertising job and hating it more each day. The situation solved itself when New York decided to close that L.A. office after a year or more because there was not enough business to make it worthwhile. I had a long talk with Richard. What did he want to do with the rest of his life? He said that he had always had a desire to work in the design field, doing houses, offices, whatever. He was certain that's where his talents lay. He had demonstrated a real aptitude for that field in many of his previous jobs.

I offered to back him until he established himself. He suggested that he would like to do over some of the rooms in my home, and I agreed. Richard tackled the work with great enthusiasm and proved that he had the ability to create something lovely.

I bought an inexpensive, run-down property in Brentwood and gave him another project to work on. The result was exceptional, and we sold the house profitably.

Based on all this, he got small and then bigger jobs. He really had a flair for this kind of work and loved what he was doing. Even his personality underwent a change. He was more relaxed and happier. He had a wicked sense of humor, a bit on the camp side, and all my friends took to him. My brothers were a bit upset, perhaps because I was involved with someone else, so much younger and not Jewish, a year and two months after Walter's death. But it was my life.

Yes, there were many differences between Richard and me. He had been raised as a Catholic, although he wasn't at all observant. He came from a rather dysfunctional family. His father had run away from home to be a sailor and was a rough, macho character who had married a well-brought-up Irish belle and produced four children, two girls, two boys. From a very early age, Richard was aware of his homosexual desires and acted on them with older neighborhood men and as a cute altar boy with priests. His father sensed this and was very rough and abusive.

His mother was a sweet woman, a widow by the time Richard and I met, and she visited us often wherever we lived. Richard always paid for her trips to California and with my help, took care of her mortgage and other expenses. She adored him, and he was a devoted son, unlike his other sisters and brother, who did nothing to help. On one of her visits to Bel Air, Richard opened up to his mother and confessed his sexuality. She told him she had always suspected it. Then she put her arms around him and said, "I couldn't have a more loving son and love him more. There's only one thing I want to tell you—be good to Jack. He's a good man!"

A few years later, when she passed on, we gave her a proper funeral and paid for everything including hotel accommodations for some relatives. Not only did his siblings not contribute, but the youngest, Judy, who had been vituperative about Richard's sexuality and hadn't talked to him in years, appeared at the funeral with her doctor husband and two bodyguards, in case Richard should attack her.

I can't say exactly how it started, but as time went on, our relationship became more like father and son than lovers. He gave me love and devotion and looked after my well-being and comfort, and in return, I gave him all the love and support I could— just as though he was my natural child. Those twenty years between us were a wide gap. I did not have the parity, the brotherly intimacy, the sexual love that I had enjoyed with Walter, but it had been replaced with a different kind of love with someone who put himself out to take care of me. Perhaps he was the child I'd never had. Perhaps I was the father he had always wanted. But we shared whatever we had, and it was good.

Richard never got used to Los Angeles despite the fact that we were living in great luxury. Continually, he kept talking about getting back to New York. I finally capitulated. There was no film or music business keeping me there. I felt it was time for a change. We put the house on the market, real estate prices were escalating, and we had a quick, anxious buyer, the country-music star Kenny Rogers, who was just then at the height of his career. He wanted the house so badly that he flew us to New York in his private plane so that we could find a place to move to without delay. Since prices for homes in Los Angeles were climbing so rapidly, people advised me to wait, that I could get much more. Based on what I had paid for the property, I wasn't greedy. Kenny paid a high price, even bought some of the furnishings, and we were all happy.

That December when Kenny jetted us to New York in his private plane to find a place, again my lucky star must have been in ascendance. We settled on a triplex maisonette on Sutton Place that was an estate sale, priced low because it was in such terrible condition. But the moment we looked at it, Richard and I realized its potential for our furniture and our art. We made our deal and moved in March 1979.

I had the furniture and the art (though we did have to scale down because this 5,000-square-foot apartment was so much smaller than the Bel Air home), but it was Richard's vision and design sense that turned the apartment into a showplace featured in *Architectural Digest*. The credit Richard received started him on a successful design career, which made both of us very happy.

Right about this time, I came to another realization. If Richard and I were to be father and son, I would make it legal. I adopted him. I wanted him never to have any financial worries or difficulties and knew that this legality would accomplish that. He had the choice of keeping his own family name, but instead chose to take mine. What is interesting about this adoption is that both our straight and gay friends were high with praise for the legal ramifications of what I had done. Yes, it was an unusual act—a sixty-five-year-old man adopting a forty-five-year-old man. Bella

Linden handled the proceedings personally, and the lady judge before whom we appeared couldn't have been more understanding. She asked us very few questions, and the process was accomplished in minutes. Richard and I have never regretted the commitment we made that day.

When my younger brother, Murray, heard about this adoption, he was upset and hesitantly questioned me about it. I explained to him that Richard was like a devoted son in the way he took care of me and worried about me.

Murray said, "But you have family! If anything happened to you, we would take care of you."

I answered, "Murray, you have children and grandchildren. You're a family who will take care of each other. Richard is my family."

That's the last we ever spoke of this matter. And through all the years since, I truly have come to believe that my family—what's left of them—have come to appreciate Richard for who and what he is and his devotion to me. Murray never talked to me by phone without inquiring about Richard and asking to be remembered to him. The year of Murray's eightieth birthday celebration, he made special mention of Richard while thanking everyone.

My little brother, Murray, the youngest and last of my immediate family, had a fatal heart attack in October 2001. He was proud of me, and I was equally proud of all he achieved. Murray was a successful businessman. He was also elected senator of New

York State for two terms and was defeated because of his pro-choice stand on the abortion issue. I will miss his frequent phone calls, his inquiries about my health, his concern. Murray was a good man, good of heart, but he gave too much of himself to everyone, and I'm convinced that's what killed him. Every Jewish holiday, he would call me to wish me well. He knew I was not religiously observant, so every Yom Kippur, he would call to tell me that he was fasting for both of us, attending his synagogue, and praying for atonement—not only for his sins, but for mine, too. We always laughed about this exchange, and I thanked him.

It pains me to know that I will never receive that phone call again.

CHAPTER THIRTY-THREE

There's No Biz Like Show Biz

Richard and I both had a passionate interest in the theater. So it is not surprising that, shortly after moving to New York, we became actively involved. I was contacted by two young producers, Fred Walker and Michael Frazier, who asked if I would be interested in investing in a one-woman show starring Lena Horne.

It had been some time since I'd last seen Lena in performance, and like any prospective investor, I wanted to get a feeling for the style and concept of her new show before deciding to back it, Therefore, I suggested that they invite me to a rehearsal so that I could make an evaluation of the show's potential. Lena didn't take to that idea kindly, but grudgingly agreed to let me watch. Richard and I went to the rehearsal studio one afternoon and were coolly received by the star. But we came away impressed with the lady's talent, and I decided to make the investment in return for a credit as associate producer. It turned out to be a great move. The reviews were ecstatic, and *Lena Horne: The Lady and Her Music* was a sellout for almost two years.

Lena and I never developed a friendship. When I went to congratulate her on the great reviews, she looked at me coldly and said, "Now are you satisfied that your money was well invested?"

She still resented my appearance at her rehearsal and during her long, successful stay at the Nederlander Theater, never allowed me to get closer to her. Oh well—she gave superb performances and had an incredibly long run. What was interesting was watching her gradual change as success made her more secure. Suddenly she was more militant and blacker than she had ever been in public. But this was not surprising to anyone who had followed her career over the years. Just imagine the frustrations and heartaches she endured as an extraordinarily beautiful light-skinned woman living in a world that constantly reminded her she was black. Signed by MGM for their musicals, she was never given a chance to play a leading role. She was used in cameos in many films and then was cut out of them when they played the bigoted South. Even in the film version of *Show Boat*, which had a great role for a woman of mixed race, that role was given to Ava Gardner using dark makeup.

But by the time Lena did her show, the world had changed considerably. Sidney Poitier had won an Oscar, and black stars were being featured in important films. And Lena Horne, after all those unhappy years and pushing sixty, had come into her own with the kind of unanimous reviews that must have warmed her heart. Her one-woman show was truly a soul's confessional, in which she talked about her life and its disappointments. It was time for her to be militant, to be blacker, to refer to her "sistahs and brothas."

One night I was standing at the head of the aisle when Sylvia Fine and Dorothy Rodgers walked up at intermission. I hadn't seen Sylvia for years and decided to be friendly, so I asked her what she thought of Lena's performance.

The bitch in Sylvia came to the surface. She said, "I knew her when she spoke English!" A funny one-liner, but undeserved.

Lena, too, could be a bitch. In an interview with David Frost, which I watched, he asked her about her marriage to Lenny Hayton, a fine arranger working for MGM, to which she was also signed.

Lena answered, "The truth is I married Lenny because we were both from minorities. He was white and Jewish, and I was black. But that didn't help me much at MGM. They still cut my scenes out of pictures that played down South."

She went on the road under our producing auspices, and we all made money, but Lena came to resent our participation. After a year, she decided she wanted the whole pie. So she went forth under her own auspices, but her tour promptly died.

The next production I became involved in was *Come Back to the Five and Dime, Jimmy Dean, Jimmy Dean*. A guy with a dubious reputation and a name that sounded like a venereal disease, Joe Clapsaddle, came to me with this production he was putting together, seeking a final investment. I couldn't help but be impressed with the talents he had corralled for this play. First, as director, he had snared Robert Altman, who had alienated so many people in Hollywood that he was at liberty. To Altman's credit, he cast the production brilliantly with Sandy Dennis, Karen Black, Sudie Bond, Kathy Bates, and Cher in her first Broadway appearance.

With all those stars, it was fairly easy to attract investors, and I came into the picture as a producer with substantial financing. Practically the day before we opened at the Martin Beck on Broadway, I discovered that my partner had raised very little of his share. In order to proceed with the opening, I had to bring in more money, and I took over control of the production.

We did not get great reviews, but they were good enough to survive. Then we were surprised to learn that our biggest draw was Cher. She was the main attraction and in constant demand for interviews. That was good for the box office, but after a couple of weeks, Cher began calling in sick. Nights when she didn't perform, people asked for refunds. Hirschfeld had made one of his clever caricatures of Cher, and wanting to bolster her spirits, I bought it, had it nicely framed, and sent it to her with a cheerful note.

She had missed almost a week of performances when Liz Smith wrote in her daily column that "Cher, who's been playing sick, has been seen nights at the discos around town." The show had been running at a loss because of her absence, so I decided to put up the closing notice. Altman screamed and raved. He was going to keep the show open. He was going to get more money. He was going to sue me. The closing notice remained.

Our last performance was on a Sunday afternoon. All the ladies in our cast (all except Cher) contributed to have a small farewell party on stage for all the theater personnel and stagehands. All concerned in the production joined in this farewell. All except Cher. She had a single dressing room offstage. In order to exit the theater, she would have to cross the stage or do what she did—she went below the stage to the other side and exited without saying good-bye to anyone.

Lots of luck, Cher. Here's hoping you enjoy the Hirschfeld drawing for which you never thanked me.

The one continuing joy that came out of that production was watching the phenomenal success of Kathy Bates in films. Not only is she a most talented lady, but a warm and loving one. May her success go on forever.

Through the grapevine, I discovered that a theater in a converted church on West Forty-eighth Street was for sale. Richard and I inspected the place and found it was in terrible shape, but we realized the possibilities. On the street level, it had a 199-seat house and on the upper level, 499 seats. It was considered a Broadway middle house that would be eligible for Tony consideration. Richard was very excited, visualizing immediately what magic he could produce in designing both theaters. My friend, Larry Worchell, joined me as a partner, and we bought the property. We spent about a million dollars in redoing the theaters, and Richard truly produced two jewel boxes.

We decided to name the larger house the Tennessee Williams and the downstairs theater the Audrey Wood. Audrey had been Tennessee's agent and discoverer, but they had had a falling out. She was in a nursing home, practically a vegetable, and he had recently died. All Broadway applauded our teaming—putting Audrey back together again with Tennessee. But a monster surfaced. An English lady (a dubious term for her) who had pimped for Tennessee and in his last drunken days, been left executrix of his estate. She brought an action in court to stop us from using his name for our theater. Not only was his name already up on the marquee, but we had commissioned a large oil portrait of him that we had hung prominently in the theater.

Our first show was being advertised when the court ordered us to desist from using the Williams name. We had to act immediately, so I announced that I would substitute my own name since nobody could sue me for that. Richard quickly arranged to have the theatre sign changed to read JACK LAWRENCE. *The New York Times* thought it was newsworthy enough to take pictures of me under the sign and run a story on the front page. Later, Tennessee's lady friend went to all the Broadway theater owners requesting that they name one of their properties after Williams. They all told her the same thing. "You turned down his name on a lovely new theater. Good-bye!"

The first production that opened the Jack Lawrence was a play by A. R. ("Pete") Gurney, *The Golden Age*, with Irene Worth, Stockard Channing, and Jeff Daniels, with sets by Oliver Smith and direction by John Tillinger. Unfortunately, even with that lineup, the play got lukewarm reviews and had a short run. We were equally unlucky with a small show we had booked into the Audrey Wood, a musical based on Murray Schisgal's successful play, *Luv*. This three-character show had Judy Kaye and Nathan Lane in it, but the critics turned thumbs down. The best thing that came out of that association is that I made friends with Haila Stoddard, who was one of the producers. We have since become very close and now live a short distance from each other in Connecticut.

Richard and I quickly discovered that we had a problem booking the large theater. Despite the fact that it was considered a Tony house, all productions were under union auspices. As a consequence, off-Broadway houses that had almost as many seats had much lower production costs. Our big mistake had been putting in 499 new plush seats. If we had kept it to 450, we would have qualified as an off-Broadway house. However, now it was too late. The unions would not allow a reduction in seats.

We made good friends with a charming man, Willard Swire, who was president-emeritus of Actor's Equity. To aid us, he agreed that actors in productions we were able to book could have an off-Broadway status. He even went with me to meet with heads of the various unions, trying to enlist their help in lowering our costs, but they wouldn't budge. We managed a few more bookings, but it was rough going.

Our little off-Broadway house did a lot better. One of the shows we coproduced, a charming musical with the odd title *Kuni Leml*, had a very long run and won an Obie award for best musical. We were involved in producing this same show in Miami and Los Angeles, and Richard did both sets and costumes.

Except for Equity, the unions were most uncooperative. I tried to defy them with a musical being managed by Liz McCann, a successful manager/producer who agreed to book my theater if I would designate it as off-Broadway. The unions put their goons out in front of the street to picket us and to yell at the audiences, "Don't go into that theater that's owned by two fags!" When that didn't deter people, they warned Equity there would be trouble if they didn't pull out their actors.

The show closed. I went to the unions one last time and told them that unless they would give us financial breaks, I was going to sell the property as real estate. They pooh-poohed my threat and said I would never do that. I said, "Watch me!"

Within two months, I had sold the entire property at a nice profit to a real estate empire that turned it all into a handsome six-story apartment building. Good-bye theaters!

My one regret is not having those two theaters today when there seems to be a shortage of off- and on-Broadway houses. Now, practically any available space that can accommodate seating is being turned turned into a "theater." Our houses would be in constant demand and use if they were still around.

These days my involvement in theater productions is relegated to investing in shows that I feel might be successful, and to date, I have a fairly good track record. As a matter of fact, except when I've been an investor, the theater has not been very kind to me. The two musicals I wrote that made it to Broadway left me with little but unhappy memories.

CHAPTER THIRTY-FOUR

Show Biz is No Biz for Me

would like to tell about my two musical failures, if only to il-
lustrate what a demanding mistress the stage is.

Creativity is an ephemeral process. Ideas sometimes flit
through your brain on butterfly wings and light for an instant,
leaving gossamer threads that you can weave into whole cloth. Or
you can spend endless hours and days perfecting the structure of
a sentence, seeking that one choice word that will give life to your
thoughts. No dramatist, no novelist, no songsmith sits down to
create something bad. However, failure is a human trait. How
would we measure success if we had not known failure?

In 1953 Don Walker and I were approached by two young producers who had heard some of our work and asked us to do the
score for a musical. Don was one of the top arrangers of Broadway
musicals at the time, and we had formed a good working relationship thanks to an introduction by Max Dreyfus. The two produc-

ers, Michael Ellis and Jimmy Russo, had acquired rights to a popular English comedy, *The Farmer's Wife*, by Eden Phillpotts. It had an amusing premise. A farmer who's a widower has a marriageable daughter raised by a housekeeper who's been with him for years, and suddenly he decides it's time for him to seek a wife. The housekeeper is delighted until he asks her to get paper and pencil and help him make a list of the eligible ladies in the neighborhood. She's livid, having to wash and press his clothes and watch him go courting, crossing each lady off the list as he repeatedly gets turned down. Of course, he realizes almost too late that the housekeeper is the right wife for him and manages to get her at the end.

We teamed up with book writer William Roos, who changed the title to *Courtin' Time* and the locale from Sussex to a farm in Maine. The name of that state led us to a specific period when Remember the Maine! and Teddy Roosevelt were popular subjects. Everything began to fall in place. As director, we got brilliant musical comedy star Alfred Drake (*Kiss Me Kate*) and as choreographer, the legendary George Balanchine.

With a large singing chorus, a separate dance group and twelve principals, we were budgeted at the enormous sum (in '54) of $350,000. While gathering our cast, we did endless backers' auditions. It became easier when we enticed a well-known film actor, Lloyd Nolan, to play the farmer. Although Lloyd was not a trained singer, he had a pleasant voice and charisma.

In our cast, we had Rosemary Kuhlmann and Theodor Uppman, both went on to sing with the Metropolitan Opera

Company. Lloyd managed to master most of the score, but his solo number, which ran about four minutes, scared him. It was a retrospective song in which he gets angrier and more furious as he sings about the ladies who have turned him down. Not having a trained voice, he kept pushing when he reached this solo and consequently strained his vocal cords badly. By opening night in Boston, he was practically hoarse. Nevertheless we got fantastic reviews. They dubbed us another *Oklahoma* and predicted a big new hit as soon as Lloyd's voice cleared up.

His voice didn't clear up. By the time our sold-out, two-week run was over, a throat specialist warned that if Nolan continued to strain his vocal cords, he might lose his voice entirely. We were booked into the Forrest Theater in Philadelphia, two more sold-out weeks. We decided that Lloyd should rest his voice, our director Alfred Drake should take over, and if we were lucky, the strained voice would heal.

Alfred was a fabulous musical performer who had starred in blockbusters, his most flamboyant performance having been in *Kiss Me Kate* five years before. Naturally, everyone was looking forward to his interpretation of that Maine farmer.

He was all wrong.

Alfred could play a dilettante, a pirate, a sophisticated lover—any bravura character. But a smug, pompous farmer? No. At the close of the Philadelphia run, our producers, creators, and cast were desolate. From the critics, we knew that we had a possible hit, but Lloyd was taking a long rest to save his voice. He went back to California, and we went looking for a replacement. That's when our smart young producers made the dumbest mistake of their careers.

In their desperate attempt not to close the show, our young producers made a fatal error. They replaced Lloyd with Joe E. Brown, a baggy-pants clown with a mouth like a tunnel and not a scintilla of romanticism. It was not only believable that every woman would turn down his proposal of marriage, but incredible that any woman would accept him at the end. All of us—writers, director, choreographer—fought against it, but our producers gave us an ultimatum: Joe E. Brown or close the show. We had no alternative.

Back in rehearsals in New York, we acquired an associate producer, Alex Cohen, who was a press agent for Bulova Watches, but wanted to be in show business. The additional money Alex supplied gave us two more weeks to rehearse. Joe E. was on his best behavior, never gave us the cavernous mouth once, really seemed to be trying to play the part. We began to have hopes. The producers decided to reopen in Pittsburgh because it was Joe E.'s hometown, and we'd be assured of a sellout.

Some sellout. It seemed that nobody wanted to see Joe E. Brown, not even for free. Opening night was a disaster. Mr. Brown unleashed every shtick he had been suppressing, the broad double takes, the yawning mouth, the hat gags. But the worst offense was just before the last curtain call. Mr. Brown stopped the orchestra, took the stage solo, and told the audience what a great patriot he was, how he had entertained the troops during the war. That night, as is usual, Alfred gathered the cast on stage to give directorial criticisms. He concluded by telling Joe E. that there would be no more curtain speeches to the audience, once the last scene was played, the show was over.

The next night, to preclude a recurrence, Alfred had ordered an earlier closing of the curtain. That happened on cue, but as the curtain descended, Joe E. Brown crawled under it and once again delivered his wartime speech. Alfred was so furious, he threw his hands up and went back to New York.

From then on the show turned into a shambles. Carmen Mathews, a wonderful actress who played the spinster who turns down the farmer's proposal, came off stage each night in tears. We had written a mock-operetta ballad called "This Is My Golden Moment" in which she rhapsodizes upon first hearing the proposal, then refuses him. Her number always got a big hand—that is, until Joe E. took over. While she was twittering, singing her solo, he did everything short of opening his zipper. He didn't get any great laughs, but he *did* manage to kill her performance.

I went to Carmen's dressing room to console her. Tearfully, she complained that she had never worked with anyone so unprofessional. I told her, "Carmen, you can destroy him. While you're doing your solo, you're wearing a long chiffon scarf around your neck. Take it off, throw it around his body, and draw him close to you. He can't do anything—he's a dead duck."

"Oh, Jack," she said, "I couldn't do that! I'm a good Christian."

However, opening night on Broadway—yes, we did come in—Carmen did exactly what I had suggested. She immobilized him. He was so shocked, he stood still, and Carmen brought down the house. It didn't help much. The coup de grâce was what some of the critics wrote. "Too bad the writers didn't deliver material as funny as Joe E. Brown could be." So there went all that talent, all that money, and a year out of my life.

My second musical fared even worse. In 1964, I had been collaborating with Stan Freeman, a brilliant pianist, and we were asked by the producer, Joe Kipness, to do the score for a libretto written by Jerome Chodorov. Joe Kipness was a true Damon Runyon character who valued his Mafia friends and investors. Our show, *I Had a Ball*, took place in Coney Island amid a microcosm of colorful boardwalk concessionaires. The leading part was a two-bit con man, just out of jail, trying out a new swindle by telling futures with a crystal ball. He surprises even himself when he actually starts to see coming events in his crystal ball.

Once again we assembled a great professional group: Lloyd Richards (*A Raisin in the Sun*) to direct, Onna White as choreographer, Ralph Alswang on sets, and a star cast, Richard Kiley, who had headed many a hit production, Karen Morrow, a real belter, and Rosetta Le Noire, a fine black actress. For the screwball con man, we had a comic who was riding the crest, Buddy Hackett. Buddy was a loudmouth, stand-up noisemaker whose specialty was foul language. But he was funny. He was currently a big hit in television appearances and Las Vegas, but the Broadway stage was a new venue to him. He had never worked in a play or musical where a certain discipline is required.

Those were the days when productions could still go out of town and try out before hitting Broadway. We opened in a Nederlander theater, the Fisher, in Detroit, with a newspaper strike in full force. But Hackett and Kiley were strong enough names to fill the house, and the audience loved us. We had had great problems casting Kiley's role, that of a con man and close pal of Hackett's character. We had auditioned any number of men, but were not happy with any of them. Finally, Kipness asked, "If you had your druthers, who would you want?"

We said, "Richard Kiley! But you'll never get him to play second banana."

Nothing deterred Joe Kipness. He got Kiley and his manager to listen to our score. Kiley told us that his wife had had a dream that he would play a con man—a role he had never played. He liked our score, but said he would do the show if we gave him a song intended for another character, "I'm an All-American Boy." We explained that it was written for an arm-breaking usurer with all the qualities of a thug who felt he was practicing business in the all-American manner. We assured Kiley that we would give him a new song guaranteed to stop the show.

Kipness didn't tell any of us that in order to persuade Hackett to sign, he had promised him that no other name but his would appear above the title and only his face would be used in advertising the show. When we told Hackett that we'd managed to get a big star, Richard Kiley, he began to show his true colors.

"I'm a big star!" he sneered. "When I walk down the street people recognize ME! Do they recognize Richard Kiley?"

We were in for a two-week run at the Detroit theater to be followed by two weeks in Philadelphia. Business was so strong that Jimmy Nederlander persuaded Kipness to part with some of his producer's percentage and allow him to buy into the show. Before our first week was up, Hackett started to complain. He didn't need any more rehearsals, he didn't want any more suggestions or criticisms as to how to play the role, he was ready to go to Broadway—and fuck all the rest of the time on the road.

He kept ignoring the book, throwing ad libs, and confusing the actors. Oddly enough, the only actor he didn't take liberties with was Richard Kiley, the man he didn't consider as big a star as himself. No one could reason with him. He had to steal every scene no matter what the cost to the book. Karen Morrow, a seasoned pro, complained to me that he was ruining one of her big songs. In that scene, he sat on a couch while she was singing in front of him, facing the audience. During her performance, he picked his nose, he made faces, he fiddled with his zipper.

I was reminded of Joe E. Brown and Carmen Mathews and told Karen that story and my solution. This time I suggested that instead of coming down front, she stay behind the couch, lean over while singing her song and embrace Hackett so that he couldn't move. She loved the idea, but like Carmen, decided to wait until the Broadway opening. That way she would surprise him, and he wouldn't have figured out a counterattack. Opening night on Broadway, it did work perfectly, and she got her deserved hand.

But meanwhile, we still had to play Philadelphia. Hackett's and Kiley's names were bringing sold-out business. I had a warm relationship with Kipness, who came to me with a big problem. His dilemma had to do with the billing concessions he had given Hackett, and now he confessed that he had promised Kiley above the title billing, too. What should he do? It was a couple of days before Christmas, so I took Joe to a smart men's store where we bought some expensive gifts for Kiley and invited him to a late breakfast.

I had and still have an enormous respect for Richard Kiley. The theater lost a consummate professional, a fabulous performer, and an unflappable gentleman when he died a few years ago. At our breakfast with Kiley, after a few minutes' chitchat over coffee, Joe handed Kiley all the wrapped gifts. Kiley had sensed Joe's nervousness. He smiled and said, "What's up, Joe? Come clean."

Joe turned to me and said, "You tell him, Jack!"

So I explained Joe's dilemma. I will never forget Kiley's response.

"Joe, a long time ago, I discovered that it doesn't matter a damn in what position your name appears. If you're good, they'll find it. Give Hackett what you promised him. Don't worry about my billing." What a lovely man!

By the time we hit Broadway, only the skeleton of our book remained. The actors never got the proper cue lines from Hackett, and consequently they had to ad lib to cover the gaps. The critics! Once again, they failed to recognize what had happened and faulted the writers for not delivering material commensurate with Hackett's comic talents.

Hackett was pleased at the critics' recognition, but disappointed in the general reception of the show. He decided to take revenge. Every night after that, at the final curtain call with the entire cast lined up on stage, Buddy would come down front and deliver his diatribe. (Shades of Joe E. Brown!) His opening line was "These New York critics have their taste up their ass. What the fuck do they know?"

That was the nicest part. He went scatologically on from there, each night his speech growing longer until finally he was practically doing his entire Vegas routine. Of course, the audiences loved it, and I must admit, it was bringing in business. Hackett was positive that he would be nominated and win a Tony for his great performance. When the nominations were announced, he wasn't mentioned, but Luba Lisa, a darling, talented youngster who played a delightful tart, received a nomination as Best Featured Actress in a musical. That night, with the entire cast on stage as usual, Buddy went into his spiel and announced, "To show you how fucked up this Tony committee is . . . they picked the least talented member of the cast to be nominated."

Poor Luba Lisa ran off the stage crying hysterically. About a year later, this sweet young girl was killed in a private jet accident.

Despite good business, despite the salary and percentage Buddy was earning, he kept complaining how tired he was doing eight shows a week and how much more money he could make playing Vegas. Another Kipness secret we now learned was that Hackett had refused to allow any understudy, and foolishly, Kipness had agreed. With Easter week coming up, when business is traditionally bad, Kipness decided to close and give Buddy a week's vacation. He hoped that this would negate a clause in Buddy's contract allowing him two weeks' vacation any time of his choice. So when we closed for Easter week, that tired, worn-out comic went to Miami and played the Fountainbleu Hotel.

We were in our fifth month, approaching summer, with out-of-town mail orders coming in regularly, when Hackett announced to Kipness that he would like to take his two weeks starting the following week. Joe argued that his timing was wrong, business was building, and he suggested that he could bring in Phil Silvers as a replacement for those two weeks. Oh no, said Hackett. *Nobody would replace him!* The show would close for his two weeks off. This argument was taking place in Hackett's dressing room one night after the show ended. I was sitting outside with Buddy's wife, Sherri, a sweet young woman, and we could hear the argument escalating.

Suddenly Kipness brought up my name, quoting something I had said about the danger of shutting down the show for two weeks at this time. Hackett went ballistic. "Who gives a fuck what that faggot cocksucker has to say!" he screamed. His wife looked at me and went pale.

"Don't pay any attention to Buddy," she said. "He's just angry."

"Your husband's crazy," I said. "He and his mouth should be committed!"

Inside the dressing room, Joe tried to defend me. One word led to another, and Joe finally did what all of us had wanted to do for months. He punched Hackett and knocked him to the floor. Whereupon Hackett announced, "Fuck you and the show! I quit!"

The next night, Kipness posted the closing notice, and that evening, Hackett assembled the cast before the performance and told them, "My wife is giving me a birthday party this Sunday. I'm inviting you all. Depending on how many of you Gypsies show up, I'll decide whether or not I want this show to continue."

Not one member of the cast went to Buddy's birthday party. We closed.

Too bad. *I Had a Ball* had a good, swinging score with great arrangements by my old Maritime Service friend, Phil Lang. The original cast album produced by Quincy Jones has been a collector's item, and recordings by Sarah Vaughan, Louis Armstrong, Bobby Darin, and others still get performed. My hope is that one day, this will be one of the concert versions that lead to a revival. Just the other day, I learned that Broadway Decca will be rereleasing the original cast recording shortly. May the *Encore* come next!

At this point, I would like to add some of the lyrics that Stan and I wrote for *I Had a Ball* because they demonstrate the difference between pop songs and show lyrics. Herein is a brief rundown of the plot: Coney Island in its heyday; the exciting rides, the freak shows, the food stands, the odors, the blaring music, the grifters, and even the con men. And a character self-named Garside the Great, newly sprung from prison and already involved in a new racket: telling your future by reading bumps on your head while making you comfortable on his couch under a large portrait of Sigmund Freud. To cap all this décor, he interprets pictures he claims to see in his crystal ball. Buddy Hackett, of course, played Garside.

His best pal, Stan the Shpieler (Kiley), shows up, also newly out of jail, and Garside offers him a free analysis. Though Stan scoffs at all this nonsense, he admits reluctantly that his life does lack focus, and he expresses himself in the following song.

Somewhere there has to be
THE OTHER HALF OF ME, THE OTHER HALF OF ME
I've yet to meet;
Some special someone whose heart has a similar leaning.
If she were right for me, day and night for me would have
    meaning;
THE OTHER HALF OF ME . . .

That unknown quantity, that unseen destiny
Could make me complete . . .
Is there a chart for the heart or a graph?
Will we meet on the street with a welcome laugh?
Will we know one another if I ever meet my other half?
THE OTHER HALF OF ME.

Richard Kiley had a great lyric voice that delivered all the longing those words expressed. Incidentally, Bobby Darin's recording of this song was recently featured in a film called *Sweet September*.

Writing songs for Hackett was a chore. He was not at all musical, and we had to teach him to count silently before delivering each line. We also had to discard most of the songs we had written for him and by rote, finally got him to deliver in song-speak fashion the following comedy song. This comes at a moment when he's convinced that he has really seen the future in his crystal ball. He panics:

Doctor Freud, Doctor Freud, Doctor please don't be annoyed
But I really saw a vision, yes, I did!
Doctor Freud, Doctor Freud, with your teachings I have
   toyed,
Now I've got a funny feeling in my id;
Does it mean that I'm repressing or perhaps I'm retrogressing,
Do I sound an itsy bitsy idiotic?
How does one dispel a vision when it isn't television?

Does it mean I'm going "skitzy" or psychotic?

So all right, so okay, I know just what you will say,

That my psyche has been playing a trick.

My psyche, Doctor Freud, my "shmikey," Doctor Freud,

Leave us face it, Doctor Freud, I'm sick!

For after what occurred tonight I'm not so sure about you,
    Doctor,

Even if you are a name of great renown;

In your methods, Doctor Freud, my faith is practic'lly
    destroyed

And I don't intend to take it lying down!

Now you wrote reams of explanations on all types of
    aberrations,

Not a word on super-nat'ral hocus-pocus;

Well, take a good look at my face and hold that ball up to
    your face

And give those eyes of yours a big, fat focus.

Aha, so I'm right maybe . . . Oh ho, Sigmund baby!

How do you explain a thing like that?

After spending all my life believing all you said was truth

Now I find you're just a no-good, lying rat!

When in the jug your fuzzy face was hanging up there on the
    wall,

No, I wouldn't dream of having any others,

But tomorrow I erase you, tomorrow I replace you,

And I hang up Doctor Joyce Brothers!

Who's afraid of Sigmund Freud, Sigmund Freud?

You're a fraud, Freud, yes, a fraud, Freud!

But I'm not afraid, Freud, not afraid, Freud,

'Cause now I've been freed, Freud,

Yes, Freud and I'm not even fried, Freud!

You're a frid frod and I'm not a fred fried,

You're a frad frode and I'm not a food fair!

Doctor Freud, your diagnosis is absurd

And for you I got one final word . . . HA-A-A-ALP!

Zany Hackett got lots of laughs with this manic song. Our romantic lead, Karen Morrow, lovely to look at and with a big, belting voice, played the "shlumpy" owner of a Ferris wheel who had somehow let romance pass her by. When Garside tries to psych her out and tell her what she lacks, she sings this number defensively.

I'm not rich, I'm not poor

Still I'm healthy and secure,

For a time I was love-sick

But in time I took the cure,

I'm alone, on my own, but I'm happy . . .

'Cause I got EVERYTHING I WANT!

Got a one-bedroom flat,

Got a self-sufficient cat,

I don't know where I'm going

But I sure know where I'm at,

On the shelf by myself, I'm so happy

'Cause I got EVERYTHING I WANT!

I've had love! It's out of the question . . .

I'm older, I'm wiser, I'm smart!

But with love I got indigestion

Plus a swift kick in the heart!

Now I'm well and that's that,

I go home and feed my cat,

Lock my door, heat my TV dinner,

Place my single mat,

Single fork, single knife,

It's a life free of strife

And I'm happy, I'm happy, I'm happy,

So happy I could cry . . .

So . . . pardon the tear in my eye . . . got . . .

EVERYTHING I WANT!

Please indulge me while I brag about another unusual number in this same show. Two young male characters who have been very successful meet in the second act and indulge in an exchange of one-upmanship. Stan and I racked our brains trying to decide what sort of duet we could write for this situation. What we finally came up with was not a song, per se, but more like two guys indulging in a rap session, interspersed with bursts of music. Here it is.

Stan:	Glad to have you aboard, sir!
Brooks:	Welcome to the club!
Stan:	Join the team!
Brooks:	Lunch some day? My treat!
Stan:	How sweet! See you at the nineteenth hole!
Both:	Lookee, lookee, lookee, two self-made guys
	Riding high . . . high finance wise!
Stan:	Read about me in the Kiplinger report!
Brooks:	Call me a Dow Jones av'rage sport
Both:	Affable members of the AFFLUENT SOCIETY
	What a comf'table stage in the age of anxiety
	Status symbols, go-getters, taste makers, pacesetters,
	With credit cards and credit letters,
	Awfully affable influential members of the affluent society.
Stan:	Got a big estate in Darien on a Swedish modern slant . . .
	One tennis court, two swimming pools, and a fluoridation plant.
Brooks:	Do tell! No sauna bath?
Stan:	No sauna bath!
Brooks:	*House Beautiful* recommends a sauna bath!
Stan:	*House Beautiful?*
Brooks:	*House Beautiful!*
Stan:	No sauna bath!

Brooks: Next month we fly to Europe.

Stan: Oh really!

Brooks: Lots of time, no rush, no strain . . .

Stan: How nice.

Brooks: One day in Italy, one day in Germany, two whole days in Spain!!

Stan: Two whole days?

Brooks: *Holiday* magazine says two whole days!

Stan: Hmm! Two whole days?

Brooks: No sauna bath?

Stan: Got a new cell phone in every room, got a TV in the car!

Brooks: In the car?

Stan: In the car! Not only that, got a fully stocked bar!

Brooks: In the car?

Stan: And the yacht!

Brooks: Mercy do, how very yar! Got a suite at the Waldorf Towers.

            Downstairs a pied-à-terre!

Stan: Pied-à-terre?

Brooks: Pied-à-terre! Yeah, I breed my beagles there! And incident'lly, I drive a Bentley! That's how well I've scored!

Stan: Well, I'm so well off, I can afford to be seen driving a Ford!

(Musical interlude while it's all digested.)

Brooks:	Welcome to the club, pal! Join the team!
Stan:	Glad to have you aboard!
Brooks:	My treat!
Stan:	How sweet!
Both:	See you at the nineteenth hole!

I hope these few lyrics give you some idea of the wide range this musical had. I still believe today that Stan Freeman and I, as a words and music team, could have left our mark on the theater world. Stan played a brilliant piano and was a true offbeat wit. Chain cigarette smoking did him in a couple of years ago.

Summing up I suppose that I've been lucky in my lifetime not to have experienced barrages of homosexual slurs. In retrospect, I've mentioned the only two I can recall: one from the Irish stage-hand Mafia picketing my theater and the other from foul-mouthed Buddy Hackett. I would like to go on record that in my long experience in Broadway and Hollywood, I have found that color, gender, and religion matter very little. All that really matters is talent.

Now that I've unloaded my chest of all those bad theater experiences, let me go forward in time. Richard and I were still living in luxury in our Sutton Place triplex, which he had designed in exquisite taste, and enjoying our sybaritic lives. We decided it would be nice to look for a weekend country house.

CHAPTER THIRTY-FIVE

Call Me Country Squire

After moving back to the East Coast, we had spent a considerable number of weekends in the Hamptons. But after a few summers, it got to be a bore, the same round of parties with the same old faces. Old, that is, except for new plastic surgery. Everyone was evaluating everyone else's bank account, striving to climb one step higher up the social rung. And that trip out and back to the city became worse, and longer, each summer. We decided to house hunt in areas no farther than an hour from the city.

We started our search in Westchester's Bedford Hills, then moved on to Pound Ridge, North Salem, and finally into Connecticut. After viewing roughly sixty properties, we found the ideal place in Redding, Connecticut. It was not the small house that intrigued us, but the geography of the property—six private wooded acres, its own secluded lake. Immediately, we visualized what we could create and achieve. The main part of the house had started out as a barn in the eighteenth century, and over the years, subsequent owners had added on to it. What had once been the barn now had a two-story living room with a stairway to a balcony leading to two charming bedrooms and bathroom.

The master bedroom and study were on the ground floor, plus an inadequate kitchen and a sunny, glassed-in dining room facing the gardens, which we dubbed the pond room. Richard's talents came to the fore as we made decisions. He created a huge, incredible kitchen with a spectacular design. Utilizing space properly is one of Richard's fortes. The kitchen he designed in Sutton Place was featured in many books and magazines. We also added an additional wing to the far end of the Connecticut house consisting of a luxurious bath, steam and shower room, and an incredible indoor forty-five-foot swimming pool with sauna and works of African and Greek art advantageously displayed. That pool has been our constant joy. We swim every morning of the year. It, too, has been well photographed and documented in many publications. Under Richard's supervision, the landscaping and gardens are picture-book material. Anyone who views the property understands how aptly it has been named after one of my songs, "Sleepy Lagoon."

I live a gracious, comfortable life surrounded by warm and loving friends, many of them still in or retired from the theater and films. We entertain and are invited out frequently. Although we sold our Sutton Street maisonette (at a handsome profit), we have not given up New York City. We manage to see each season's new productions, including those we choose to invest in. We are also faithful supporters of many innovative off-Broadway theater groups and attend their performances.

A few years ago, I was invited by Lucille Lortel to do a one-man performance of all my songs at her White Barn Theater in Westport, Connecticut. Richard enthusiastically went to work designing the look of the show. He used many of the old title pages of my sheet music to create a handsome framework around the proscenium and turned the stage into a summer bower with trees and branches. He not only dressed the stage, but dressed me, as well. I sang fifty or more of my songs accompanied by a fabulous trio: piano, bass, and reeds. We were a great success and ran for three sold-out performances. This led to more such performances, which I was delighted to do as fund-raisers for an AIDS hospice nearby which Richard and I supported wholeheartedly. Truth to tell, I loved performing—the latent ham in me emerged.

These days I read about and watch with interest the changes taking place on Broadway, in regional theaters, and in Hollywood. Gone are those golden days of movie musicals, the Fred Astaire/Ginger Rogers gems, the Gene Kelly, Judy Garland, Jane Powell extravaganzas, those legendary scores by the Gershwins, Irving Berlin, Cole Porter, and Kern, the unforgettable Van Heusen, Carmichael, Arlen, and Mercer songs that Bing and

Frank gloried in. Today what has replaced all that bonanza are the films meant for a younger generation, usually with rock scores.

Now that I've brought up legendary stars, I should mention that my neighbors are a few whom I love and adore: Jane Powell, who is as fresh and beautiful today as in her ingenue years, her husband Dick Moore, whom I remember as Dickie Moore, the child star, and Sally Ann Howes, that incredible musical talent whose voice is still as silvery as of yore. Those are our closest friends, but we're surrounded by a world of talented neighbors like that indomitable lady, June Havoc, and my lovable pal, Haila Stoddard. Living close by are Tony Award winner Debbie Gravitte, who appeared with me in one of my fund-raisers; also Harvey Fierstein; Lucie Arnaz and husband Laurence Luckenbill; Colleen Zenk and husband Mark Pinter; Maureen Anderman and her Frank Converse; George Grizzard; James Naughton; Joanne Woodward, who now runs the Westport Playhouse, and let's not forget Paul Newman; A. R. "Pete" Gurney; and Arthur Miller. Dinner parties are always a surprise and joy with the possibility of meeting any of these gifted neighbors.

I should mention an interesting phenomenon that has been surfacing these past few years in Hollywood. Important films have followed the advantageous practice of inserting old standards from the thirties and forties into their soundtracks, for which I will be ever thankful. At least thirty movies, including such blockbusters as *Apollo 13, The Shawshank Redemption,*

Diner, The End of the Affair, Father of the Bride, and several Woody Allen films, have used a good many of my old songs. I'm also pleased to note that there are new vocalists constantly recording standard material. Somebody must be buying those albums. Unfortunately, there are not too many of us old-timers still around. But our songs, it seems, still live on.

That brings to mind a funny conversation I had a short time ago with my old friend, Karen Worchell, in Los Angeles. Her son, whom I knew as an infant, is now an assistant district attorney living on his own. Suddenly, in his early thirties, he has discovered the music of my era. The other day he came by to visit his mother and brought a recording.

"Mom," he said, "I want you to listen to this song. Listen especially to the lyrics. They're so true—so wonderful." And he proceeded to play her Frank Sinatra's version of "All or Nothing at All."

Karen couldn't stop laughing. "Don't you know who wrote that song?" she asked. "You remember Jack Lawrence."

I was immensely pleased when Karen reported this occurrence. It seems that her son is one of many young people today who are suddenly discovering Gershwin, Kern, Porter—all that fabulous treasure-trove of evergreens, with many of mine included. My Website brings me many fan letters. I'd like to quote from a recent one.

Dear Mr. Lawrence,

I read an article in my mom's *Vanity Fair* about your classic song *Beyond The Sea* and I looked up your interesting website. I'm 22 but even though I'm sure I'm younger than your average fan, I love the songs of yours that I recognized.

If I Didn't Care, Tenderly, All Or Nothing At All, Linda and *What Will I Tell My Heart?* are all great songs and it was wonderful reading about you.

There was a lot more and it was signed:

Your friend,
Mark Eggers
Fenton, MO.

And another phenomenon that seems to be taking place is one that pop-classics D.J. Jonathan Schwartz keeps calling attention to in his weekly radio broadcasts. He refers to the "new wave" of singers who are recording and reinterpreting the old standards: Diana Krall, (included in one of her recent albums is a lovely rendition of "All or Nothing at All") and Jane Monheit, whose album of standards I enjoy listening to, and a best-selling new album of Louis Armstrong standards as interpreted by Tony Bennett and k.d. lang. I would gladly open my trunk to all these artists.

Life has been surprisingly generous to me. I have been most fortunate in my friendships, surrounded by people I admire and love, whom I respect, and who return the same affection to me. They make my life enjoyable and pleasant. Further, I have been blessed with lovers who enriched my life through their warmth, devotion, and understanding.

With the help of medical science and its continual new discoveries, I am not doing too badly healthwise. I'm amused on the frequent occasions when I go in for physical examinations and the nurse asks for a catalog of my past medical history, I do what I call "my organ recital," the numerous ailments and surgeries, the various parts removed and replaced, and conclude by saying that with a few more replacements, I could be called a bionic man. My darling friend, Haila Stoddard, calls me Lazarus. As Stephen Sondheim's clever song puts it, *I'm Still Here!* I must point out that I owe much of my state of health to my faithful Richard who watches me diligently, cares for me lovingly, and makes certain I take my medications as prescribed. He also ferries me back and forth to all my medical appointments.

I swim every morning in my indoor lap pool, I have a trainer three times a week who bends, twists, and works me out with weights in a small gym that Richard designed. My Richard is an incredible caregiver, and his devotion, attention, and love are to what I accredit my long life.

People constantly remark on how well I look. As compared to what? Every day when I see myself in the mirror, I can't help saying, "Who IS that old man?" In my mind's eye, I still see myself as that handsome youngster—and I have pictures to prove it!

Strangely enough, my greatest fear is one of living—not dying. I'm not content living in this world of daily terrorism, with a government that seems intent on scrapping whatever environmental progress we've made, of depleting Social Security, of doing little to curb the escalating medical costs. I can't help but worry about what will become of the fast-increasing geriatric population And worse than that, what sort of dark future lies in store for all babies being born today?

When I am asked what religion I am, I don't hesitate to answer. I don't believe in religion. Consider the Jewish religion that prides itself on having been designated by an unseen God as "the Chosen People." Chosen for what? Five thousand years of persecution, diaspora, holocaust, and anti-Semitism? I cannot condone Hassidic bigots who claim to have the power to decide who is or is not a Jew. Nor can I respect a Southern Baptist religion that teaches hate—hate of homosexuals and the murder of doctors who perform abortions. And the Catholic religion with an elected pope who assures us he knows exactly what God wants, who offers indulgences and promises that non-Catholics will surely go to hell. Let us not omit the Islamic religion that encourages mere boys to become suicide bombers and thus gain their heavenly delights, which treats women as second-class citizens, stoning them to death if they commit adultery, while the men who may have raped them go free. Religion through the centuries has always been divisive, has always resulted in bloody wars, has always pitted sects against each other.

So what do I believe in?

My faith has always resided in my lovers and my friends. I believe in being part of my little world, my community, of giving back some of what the world has blessed me with. In such sense, it gives me great satisfaction to have helped in rebuilding our local Mark Twain Library, expanding our Danbury Hospital, and acquiring more open acreage for our Land Trust. I believe all of that is my religion.

Undoubtedly all this is what keeps me active and functional. My greatest dread is the fear that I may become incapacitated and bed bound and/or mentally dysfunctional. I refuse to be a burden to anyone and would sooner be put out of my misery. I sincerely believe in euthanasia when someone is suffering a fatal illness. I only hope that if it happens to me, I will have enough wits about me to take the necessary action myself.

Summing up: I feel that I have lived a remarkable life. I'm content. I wouldn't really wish to have been born earlier or later; my time was the best time. The music, the bands, the singers, the writers—that was truly the Golden Age. I listen to the music of today. It seems to appear and disappear in the sea of our existence leaving no discernible ripples. And yet, ages after their birth, the songs of Gershwin, Kern, Rodgers, Porter, Arlen, and a host of others of that era are still being played and sung. Thank my lucky stars, my songs are among them and continue to be requested and performed.

Am I still writing words and music? Certainly. I have two finished scores waiting for some producer to fall in love and offer me a production.

Meanwhile, I sit and dream here beside my Sleepy Lagoon, coddled and cared for by my wonderful Richard. To quote one of Ira Gershwin's oft-repeated lines:

"Who could ask for anything more?"

Index

A & P Gypsies, 99
Abie's Irish Rose, 24
Aldrich, Richard, 303
"Alexander's Ragtime Band," 43
Allen, Gracie, 187, 270, 298
Allen, Woody, 10
Alley, Ben, 93
"All or Nothing at All," 10, 246, 249, 250, 352, 353
Allyson, June, 227
Alswang, Ralph, 333
Altman, Arthur, 73, 76, 77, 78, 81, 82, 83, 84, 86, 88, 91, 93, 94, 95, 99, 100, 102, 103, 246, 247, 250
Altman, Matilda "Tillie," 88, 94, 95
Altman, Robert, 323
Anderman, Maureen, 351
Andrews, Laverne, 149, 150
Andrews, Maxene, 149, 150
Andrews, Patty, 149, 150
Andrews Sisters, the, 123, 149, 160
Annenberg, Walter, 117
Apollo 13, 10, 260, 351
Apple Cart, The, 265
"April Showers," 25
Arbuckle, Fatty, 25
Arlen, Harold, 83, 98, 142, 162, 179, 302, 350, 356
Armetta, Henry, 127

Armstrong, Louis, 142, 339, 353
Arnaz, Lucie, 351
Arnstein, Ira, 98, 99, 100, 101, 102
Arus, George, 185
Astaire, Fred, 350
"At the Old Barn Dance," 134
Auer, Mischa, 128
Auntie Mame, 40
Autry, Gene, 126, 127, 131, 134, 135

Babes in Arms, 157
Bacharach, Burt, 152
Bachelor's Daughters, The, 200
Balanchine, George, 329
Bankhead, Tallulah, 209, 292, 295, 296, 297, 298
Barnett, Charlie, 185
Barry, Paul, 222
Barrymore, Ethel, 298
Barrymore, John, 99
Barrymore, Lionel, 44
Baruch, Andre, 202
Bates, Kathy, 323, 324
Baxter, Les, 229
Beatles, the, 83, 255
Beaton, Cecil, 313
Beery, Wallace, 99
"Bells of St. Mary's, The," 85
Bennett, Tony, 139, 353

Benny, Jack, 187, 270
Bergen, Edgar, 298
Berle, Milton, 76, 244, 270
Berlin, Irving, 26, 43, 61, 98, 154, 162, 170, 178, 179, 253, 350
Bernhardt, Sarah, 44
Bernie, Ben, 104
Bernstein, Leonard, 312
"Betty Coed," 117
"Beyond the Blue Horizon," 227
"Beyond the Sea," 10, 257, 259, 260, 261, 263, 353
Big Broadcasts of 1938, 127
Big Broadcasts of 1937, 127
Bigley, Isabel, 209
"Big Show, The," 298
Billingsley, Sherman, 116
Black, Karen, 323
Black, Phil, 70
Blake, Jim, 309
"Blame It on My Youth," 206
Bleyer, Archie, 137, 138
Blondie, 127
"Blue Package," 288, 289, 291
"Body and Soul," 202, 205
Bond, Sudie, 323
Bono, Sonny, 307
Boswell, Connee, 145, 146, 150
Boswell, Martha, 145
Boswell, Vet, 145
Boswell Sisters, the, 145
"Boy Scout in Switzerland," 153
Boys from Syracuse, The, 154
Braque, Georges, 273
Bravo, Claudio, 287, 288, 289, 290
"Breezin' Along With the Breeze," 227
Breton, Raoul, 258, 260
Brice, Fanny, 25, 104
Brisson, Carl, 111
Brisson, Fred, 111, 112
Broadway Melodies, 127
Brodzky, Nicholas, 269
Brooks, Donald, 313
Brothers, Joyce, 342
Brown, Joe E., 331, 332, 333, 335, 337
Buldrini, Freddy, 185
Burns, George, 187, 270, 271, 298
Butterflies and Ballots, 131
Byrd, Ralph, 131
"By the Bend of the River," 146
"By the Sleepy Lagoon," 148

Cabin in the Sky, 179
Caesar, Sid, 267
Cagney, James, 79
Cahn, Sammy, 162, 247, 271, 302
Calloway, Cab, 127
"Camel Hop," 145
Campini, Frank, 239
Canaday, John, 290
"Candy," 152
Cantor, Eddie, 117, 128, 175, 176
Carillo, Leo, 127
Carle, Frankie, 150, 151
Carmichael, Hoagy, 13, 198, 350
"Carolina in the Morning," 25
Carroll, Madeleine, 187
Carson, Johnny, 307
Channing, Stockard, 325
Chaplin, Charlie, 24
Cher, 323, 324
"Chicago," 25
"Chinatown, My Chinatown," 178
Chodorov, Jerome, 333
Churchill, Frank, 218, 219
"Ciribiribin," 10, 149, 159, 162
Clapsaddle, Joe, 322
Clark, Buddy, 253
Clooney, Betty, 224, 225
Clooney, George, 230
Clooney, Rosemary "Rosie," 10, 186, 223, 224-230
"C'mon-a My House," 225, 226
Coates, Eric, 148, 149
Coca, Imogene, 267
Cohen, Alex, 331
Cole, Nat King, 162, 172, 173
Coleridge, Samuel Taylor, 63
Collins, Judy, 83
Columbo, Russ, 107
Come Back to the Five and Dime, Jimmy Dean, Jimmy Dean, 322
Come On Up, 210
"Come Rain or Come Shine," 228
Compson, Betty, 239
Comstock, Frank, 228
Contact, 260
Converse, Frank, 351
Coogan, Jackie, 24
Cook, Barbara, 183
Coolidge, Calvin, 55, 80
Coots, Fred J., 178
Cornell, Don, 304, 305
Courtin' Time, 329

Coward, Noel, 265, 266, 267
Crosby, Bing, 104, 106, 107, 108, 109, 110, 125, 145, 149, 160, 162, 226, 228, 229, 230, 258, 350
Crosman, Henrietta, 113

Damone, Vic, 139
Daniels, Eliot, 115, 116, 137, 138
Daniels, Jeff, 325
Daniels, Jimmy, 70
Darin, Bobby, 10, 259, 260, 264, 339, 341
David, Hal, 152
David, Mack, 152
Davis, Stuart, 275, 278
Day, Doris, 79
Debnam, Richard, 311, 312, 313, 314, 315, 316, 317, 318, 320, 324, 325, 326, 347, 349, 350, 354, 357
Debussy, Claude, 13, 258
"Deep Night," 117
"Deep Purple," 178
De Haven, Gloria, 227
de Kooning, Willem, 251
Demuth, Charles, 273, 275, 278
Dennis, Sandy, 323
De Rose, Peter, 178
Deutsch, Emery, 85, 86, 87, 88, 91, 92, 93, 94, 99, 100, 101, 102, 103
Dewey, Thomas E., 296
Dietrich, Marlene, 136, 258
Dietz, Howard, 104
Di Maggio, Joe, 127
"Dinah," 269
Diner, 260, 352
Dinner at Eight, 10, 99
Di Paolo, Dante, 230
Disney, Walt, 218, 219
Dolly Sisters, the, 178
"Do Me a Favor," 121
Dorsey, Jimmy, 139, 172, 185, 246
Dorsey, Tommy, 139, 185, 249, 251
Dove, Arthur, 278
Downey, Morton, 83, 104
Drake, Alfred, 329, 330, 332
Dreiser, Theodore, 44
Dressler, Marie, 99
Dreyfus, Louis, 163
Dreyfus, Max, 124, 140, 148, 163, 164, 165, 167, 168, 170, 171, 174, 176, 206, 207, 258, 328
Drutman, Irving, 198
Duchamp, Marcel, 44

"Dust Over the West," 134
Dvorak, Ann, 127
Dylan, Bob, 83

Eastman, Johnny, 251, 253, 255
Eastman, Laura, 251
Eastman, Lee, 11, 251, 253, 254, 255
Eastman, Linda, 11, 253, 254, 255
Eastman, Louise, 251, 253
"Easy Goin' Woman," 78, 79
Eberly Brothers, the, 139
Edwards, Clara, 146, 147, 148
Edwards, Cliff, 128
Eichelberger, Robert L., 232
Einzig, Dora, 110, 111
Einzig, Lou, 111
Ellington, Duke, 104, 139, 144
Ellis, Michael, 329
End of the Affair, The, 352
Etting, Ruth, 78, 79
"Everybody's Doin' It," 43
"Everything I Want," 343, 344
Eythe, William, 194

Fain, Sammy, 13, 217, 218, 251
Fairbanks, Douglas, 24
Faith, Percy, 226, 259
Farmer's Wife, The, 329
Farrell, Charles, 71
Farrell, Glenda, 130
Father of the Bride, 260, 352
Faye, Alice, 115
Feinstein, Michael, 9, 11, 15, 229, 230, 264
Ferber, Edna, 208
Ferrer, José, 228, 229
Feuer, Cy, 131
Fierstein, Harvey, 351
Fine, Sylvia, 60, 61, 62, 187, 267, 269, 271, 272, 322
Finegan, Bill, 185
Finnell, Carrie, 213
Fitzgerald, Ella, 124, 125, 139, 140, 141, 142, 162, 167, 186
Flame and the Flesh, The, 203
Flanagan, Ralph, 185, 188, 224
Fleniken, Ralph. *See* Ralph Flanagan.
"Fleurette," 59
Fonda, Henry, 147
"Foolin' Myself," 162
Foore, Diana, 146
"For All We Know," 178
4 Girls 4, 227

Fragonard, Jean-Honoré, 273
Francis, Kay, 136
"Frasquita's Serenade," 85
Frazier, Michael, 320
Freeman, Stan, 187, 225, 333, 340, 344, 347
Freeman, Ticker, 173, 174, 175
Freud, Sigmund, 340, 341, 342, 343
Friedwald, Will, 261, 264
Friml, Rudolph, 93
"Front of Ranchos Church," 280
Frost, David, 322
Funny Bones, 260
Furness, Betty, 202

Ganz, Norman, 142
Garbo, Greta, 66
Gardner, Ava, 321
Garland, Judy, 112, 173, 175, 227, 350
Gaxton, William, 163
Gaynor, Janet, 71
Gershwin, George, 98, 162, 163, 199, 206,
     207, 350
Gershwin, Ira, 76, 77, 83, 104, 142, 162, 163,
     198, 199, 207, 229, 350, 352, 356, 357
Gershwin, Leonora, 198, 229
Geva, Tamara, 127
Gibson, Hoot, 50
Gilbert and Sullivan, 61, 268
Giles, Bill, 19
Giotto, 273
Girl Singer, 229
Gish, Dorothy, 24
Gish, Lillian, 24
Gleason, Jimmy, 127
"Glow Worm, The," 85
Going My Way, 107
Gold, M.D., Arthur, 81
Goldberg, Doc, 185
Gold Diggers, 127
Golden Age, The, 325
Goldwater, Barry, 205, 206
Gone with the Wind, 154
Goodman, Benny, 144, 162, 259
Goodrich, Lloyd, 289, 290
Gordon, Bert, 128
Gordon, Irving, 124, 125
Gottlieb, Alex, 303
Gould, Morton, 185
Grant, Cary, 66
Gravitte, Debbie, 351
Grayson, Kathryn, 227
Green, Johnny, 198, 202, 203, 204, 205

Green, John W. See Johnny Green.
Green, Mitzi, 157, 158
Grey, Zane, 44
Griffith, D. W., 44
Grizzard, George, 351
Gross, Walter, 205, 220, 221, 222, 223
Guare, John, 224, 226
Gurney, A. R. ("Pete"), 325, 351
Gusman, Meyer, 80
Guys and Dolls, 209

Hackett, Buddy, 333, 334, 335, 336, 337, 338,
     339, 340, 341, 343, 347
Hackett, Sherri, 338, 339
Hall, Radclyffe, 67
Halpert, Edith Gregor, 273, 274, 275, 276,
     277, 278, 279, 280, 281, 282, 283, 294
Halpert, Samuel, 274
Hammerstein, Oscar, 83, 163, 205
"Handful of Stars, A," 171, 172, 298
Handy, W. C., 44
"Happy Days Are Here Again," 90
"Happy Farmer, The," 23
Harburg, Yip, 104
Harding, Warren G., 24, 55, 80
Harlow, Jean, 81, 99
Harnett, William, 276
Harriman, Averill, 243
Harris, Maurice Coleman, 155, 156, 157, 158,
     160, 161, 177, 179, 194
Hart, Larry, 76
Hart, Moss, 268
Hart, William S., 50
Hartley, Marsden, 275
Hassam, Childe, 273
"Have A Heart, Taft-Hartley, Have a Heart,"
     243
Havoc, June, 351
Hayes, Peter Lind, 128
Hayton, Lenny, 322
"Heave Ho, My Lads, Heave Ho (It's a Long,
     Long Way to Go)," 187
Herbert, Victor, 98
Hines, Earl, 144
Hirschfeld, Al, 323, 324
"Hold My Hand," 303, 304, 305
Holiday, Billie, 70, 162
"Home," 91
"Hooray for Hollywood," 227
Hoover, Herbert, 55, 81
Horlick, Harry, 99
Hornblow, Jr., Arthur, 161

Horne, Lena, 203, 320, 321, 322
Howes, Sally Ann, 19, 351
"Huckleberry Duck," 153
Hughes, Howard, 303
Hunger, 59
Hupfeld, Herman, 104
Hurok, Sol, 73
Hyams, Barry, 73
Hyams, Peter, 73

"I Can Dream, Can't I?," 217
"I Cover the Waterfront," 202
"I Don't Stand a Ghost of a Chance," 108
"If I Didn't Care," 10, 138, 139, 140, 162,
    163, 167, 353
I Had a Ball, 10, 187, 225, 333, 339, 340
"I'll Be Seeing You," 217
"I Love You Madly," 100, 101
"I'm an All-American Boy," 334
"I'm Just a Prisoner of Love," 107
"I'm Just a Vagabond Lover," 106, 117
"I'm Still Here," 354
"In an Eighteenth-Century Drawing Room,"
    153
Inherit the Wind, 40
Inkspots, the, 10, 138, 139, 140, 151, 167
"In Praise of Older Women," 11
"In the Land of Oo-Bla-Dee," 145
Istomin, Eugene, 295
"It's Funny to Everyone But Me," 151
"I Wish I Could Shimmy Like My Sister Kate,"
    25
"I Wish You Love," 257

"Jack-in-the-Pulpit, No. 1," 280, 281
James, Harry, 10, 13, 148, 149, 152, 159, 160,
    246, 247, 248
Jolson, Al, 25, 104, 109
Jones, Quincy, 339

Kapp, Dave, 108, 122, 123, 124, 125, 137,
    144, 151
Kapp, Jack, 108, 110, 145
Kaye, Danny, 60, 74, 187, 228, 267, 268, 269,
    271, 272
Kaye, Deena, 269
Kaye, Judy, 326
Kaye, Sammy, 139, 185, 224, 251
Kefauver, Nancy, 287
Kelly, Gene, 350
Kennedy, King, 131
Kern, Jerome, 83, 98, 142, 162, 163, 350, 352,

356
Kid, The, 24
Kiley, Richard, 333, 334, 335, 336, 340, 341
Kipness, Joe, 333, 334, 335, 336, 338, 339
Kirk, Andy, 123, 124, 143
Kiss Me Kate, 329, 330
Kostelanetz, Andre, 185
Krall, Diana, 353
Kreisler, Fritz, 93
Kuhlmann, Rosemary, 329
Kuni Leml, 326
Kuniyoshi, Yasuo, 278

La Centra, Peg, 200
Lady Eve, The, 147
Lady in the Dark, 268
"Lady, Play Your Mandolin," 206
"Lady Who Walks Alone, The," 202
La Guardia, Fiorello, 242
La Guardia, Jean, 242
La Guardia, Marie, 242
"La Mer," 13, 257, 258, 259, 260, 261, 262,
    263
Lamour, Dorothy, 111
Landis, Carole, 187
Lane, Burton, 205, 206, 293
Lane, Nathan, 326
lang, k.d., 353
Lang, Philip, 185, 186, 187, 188, 339
Lansbury, Angela, 200
Lanza, Mario, 203
Lardner, Jr., Frances, 244
Lardner, Jr., Ring, 244
Lasry, Albert, 262, 263
Lastfogel, Abe, 210, 214, 215
Latouche, John, 179, 194
"La Vie en Rose," 152
Lawlor, Andy, 136, 137
Lawrence, Gertrude, 268, 303
Lawrence, Jerome, 40
Leave It to Me, 163
Lecuona, Ernest, 93
Léger, Fernand, 251
Lehman, Herbert, 243
Leigh, Carolyn, 251
Leighton, Margaret, 265
Lena Horne: The Lady and Her Music, 321
Le Noire, Rosetta, 333
"Le Pauvre Jean de Paris," 13
Levant, Oscar, 198, 206, 207, 208, 209
Levinson, Peter, 180
Levy, Lou, 123, 149, 150, 246, 247, 248

Lewin, Albert, 199, 200
Lewis, Jerry, 307
Lewis, Ted, 127
Lieberman, Max, 267
Life with Father, 154
"Lili Marlene," 152
Lincoln, Elmo, 50
"Linda," 11, 222, 251, 252, 253, 254, 256, 353
Linden, Bella, 19, 263, 292, 293, 294, 295, 301, 317, 318
Linden, Leonard, 294, 295
Lindsay, John, 243
Link, Harry, 173, 174, 175, 176
Lippi, Filippo, 273
Lisa, Luba, 337
"Little Lady Make Believe," 178
Livingston, Mary, 187, 270
Lloyd, Harold, 24
Loesser, Frank, 209
Lombardo, Guy, 106, 185
London, Jack, 44
Loos, Anita, 44
Lortel, Lucille, 350
"Love Is A Many-Splendored Thing," 217
"Love Me or Leave Me," 78
Luckenbill, Laurence, 351
Lunceford, Jimmy, 143, 144
Lute Song, 152
Luv, 326
Lyons, Leonard, 214

Maazel, Loren, 295
MacArthur, Douglas, 232, 236
"Ma! He's Makin' Eyes at Me," 68
"Mack the Knife," 259
"Make Morris Mayor," 243
Mancini, Ginny, 142
Mancini, Henry, 204, 205
"Mandy," 253
Manet, Edouard, 273
"Man From Music Mountain, The," 134
Manhattan Merry-Go-Round, 127
Mantovani, 259
Man Who Came to Dinner, The, 154
"Manya," 26
Marie, Romany, 276, 277
Marie, Rose, 227
"Marie from Sunny Italy," 43
Marin, John, 273, 275
Marks, Edward B., 93, 100, 101, 102, 103, 107
Marlo, George, 91

Martin, Freddy, 115, 246
Martin, Mary, 152, 164
Mathews, Carmen, 332, 333, 335
Mathis, Johnny, 172
May, Billy, 139
McCann, Liz, 327
McCarthy, Eugene, 243, 244
McCartney, Linda. *See* Linda Eastman.
McCartney, Paul, 11, 254, 255, 256
McDonald, Audra, 207
McGuire Sisters, the, 137
McNulty, Dorothy. *See* Penny Singleton.
Meet the People, 192
"Melancholy Baby," 44
"Memphis Blues," 44
Menjou, Adolphe, 200
Mercer, Ginger, 227
Mercer, Johnny, 83, 162, 223, 227, 295
Mercer, Mabel, 182, 183, 350
Merman, Ethel, 209
Mexican Hayride, 169
Midori, 295
Milland, Ray, 111
Miller, Arthur, 351
Miller, Glenn, 139, 144, 172, 185
Miller, Mitch, 225, 226
Mills, Irving, 104
Mills Brothers, the, 124, 142, 162
Mix, Tom, 50
Monet, Claude, 273, 287
Monheit, Jane, 353
Monnot, Marguerite, 229, 230
"Moonlight Masquerade," 35
Moore, Dick, 350
Moore, Victor, 163
Morris, Buddy, 222
Morris, E. H., 222
Morris, Leonora, 161
Morris, Wayne, 161
Morris, William, 196, 214
Morrow, Karen, 333, 335, 343
Mostel, Zero, 243
Mozart, Wolfgang Amadeus, 13, 153
"Mr. Gallagher and Mr. Sheen," 296
"My Bel-Ami," 199, 200
Myden, Ethel, 236
Myden, Walter, 232, 234, 235, 236, 237, 240, 241, 242, 243, 245, 250, 265, 267, 268, 269, 270, 271, 272, 273, 275, 277, 278, 279, 281, 282, 284, 286, 287, 289, 290, 291, 293, 294, 299, 300, 301, 306, 307, 308, 309, 310, 311, 312, 313, 314, 315,

316
"My Heart Belongs to Daddy," 164, 167, 168, 169, 170
"My Ideal," 227
Myers, Eric, 19
Myers, Richard, 303
"My Yiddishe Mama," 75

Naughton, James, 351
Navarro, Ramon, 66, 135
Nazimova, Alla, 50
Neal of the Navy, 50
Nederlander, Jimmy, 335
"Never Smile at a Crocodile," 219
"Never Took a Lesson in My Life (But I Still Know How to Make Love)," 145
Newman, Paul, 351
"New York Hat, The," 44
Noble, Ray, 253
Nolan, Lloyd, 329, 330, 331
Novik, Manya, 241, 242
Novik, Morris, 241, 242, 243

O'Connell, Helen, 139, 142, 227
O'Day, Anita, 139
O'Keeffe, Georgia, 273, 275, 278, 280, 281
Oklahoma, 330
Olivier, Laurence, 269
"Once Upon a Dream," 218
"On Moonlight Bay," 44
"On the Isle of May," 152
"Other Half of Me, The," 340, 341
"Out of Nowhere," 202
Outside of Paradise, 127, 128

Parks, Bernice, 191, 192, 193, 194, 195, 196, 197, 198, 231, 253
Parsons, Harriet, 131, 303, 305, 306
Parsons, Louella, 131, 248, 303
Pascin, Jules, 278
"Passing By," 258
Pastor, Tony, 224, 225
"Pauvre Jean de Paris," 230
"Pauvres Gens de Paris," 229
"Peggy O'Neill," 22
Perils of Pauline, The, 50
Pestalozza, Alberto, 159
Peter Pan, 219
Peto, John, 276
Phillpotts, Eden, 329
Piaf, Edith, 229
Picasso, Pablo, 273, 287

Pickford, Mary, 44
Picture of Dorian Gray, The, 199
Pins and Needles, 157, 243
Pinter, Mark, 351
"Play, Fiddle, Play," 10, 87, 88, 93, 95, 99, 101, 103, 107, 114, 162
Plowright, Joan, 269
Poitier, Sidney, 321
Polen, Nat, 185
"Poor People of Paris, The," 229
Porter, Cole, 76, 83, 142, 162, 163, 164, 165, 166, 167, 168, 169, 170, 171, 174, 176, 350, 352, 356
Powell, Dick, 303
Powell, Jane, 350, 351
Power, Tyrone, 161
"Pretending," 26
Private Affairs of Bel-Ami, The, 199
Psychology of Money, The, 308

Queen Elizabeth, 44

Rae, Douglas, 19
Raisin in the Sun, A, 333
Raye, Martha, 111
Reagan, Nancy, 307
Reagan, Ronald, 296, 298, 307
Regan, Phil, 127, 128
Reynolds, Debbie, 227, 303, 304
"Rhapsody in Blue," 10
Richards, Lloyd, 333
Riddle, Nelson, 180, 185, 186, 188, 228, 249
Robbins, Jack, 112
Robbins, Jerome, 312
Rockefeller, Abby, 276, 277
Rockefeller, Jr., John, 276
Rockefeller, Nelson, 276, 277
Rodgers, Dorothy, 322
Rodgers, Richard, 76, 163, 356
Rodgers and Hart, 83, 98, 157
Rogers, Dale, 134
Rogers, Ginger, 350
Rogers, Kenny, 316, 317
Rogers, Roy, 134
Rohan, Marc, 313
"Roll 'Em, Trumpets No End," 145
Roman, Bernice, 191
Roman, Ken, 191
Romang, Fred, 19
Romberg, Sigmund, 98
Rome, Florence, 157, 158
Rome, Harold, 157, 158, 243

Rooney, Mickey, 227
Roos, William, 329
Roosevelt, Franklin D., 48, 90, 154
Roosevelt, Teddy, 44, 329
Rose, Billy, 104, 105, 287
Rose, Fanny. *See* Dinah Shore.
Rouault, Georges, 273
Rubens, Peter Paul, 273
Rubinoff, Dave, 99
Russell, Rosalind, 112
"Russian Lullaby," 26
Russo, Jimmy, 329

Sacco and Vanzetti, 24
Sachs, Manny, 225
"Sadie Salome, Go Home," 43
Sanders, George, 199
"Santa Claus Is Coming to Town," 178
Schinasi, Ruby, 160, 161
Schinasi family, the, 160
Schisgal, Murray, 326
Schubert, Franz, 58
Schwartz, Arthur, 104, 205, 206
Schwartz, Barney, 40
Schwartz, Fanny, 40
Schwartz, Jean, 178
Schwartz, Jonathan, 353
Schwartz, Willie, 185
Scott, Raymond, 13, 152, 153
Sea of Love, 260
"Second Hand Rose," 25
Seigel, Moe, 131
Seigel, Sol, 131
Sennett, Mack, 44, 107
September in the Rain, 180
Service, Robert W., 59
Seventh Heaven, 71
Seymore, Joe. *See* Nelson Riddle.
Shahn, Ben, 275, 278, 279, 280
Shanaphy, Ed, 11, 18
Shapiro, Ted, 171, 172
Shaw, Artie, 185
Shaw, George Bernard, 265, 266
Shawshank Redemption, 10, 351
Sheeler, Charles, 278
Sheet Music Magazine, 11, 18
Sheik, The, 24
Shelton, James, 267
"Shenanigans," 128
Sherman, Jackie, 227
Shore, Dinah, 10, 162, 174, 175, 176
Short, Bobby, 182

Show Boat, 208, 321
"Shtane, Shtane, Tiyurah Shtane," 75
Shuberts, the, 212, 215
Shulman, Alan, 185
Shulman, John, 293
Silvers, Phil, 74, 338
Simon, Carly, 83
Simon, Paul, 83
Sinatra, Frank, 10, 152, 182, 186, 246, 247, 248, 249, 250, 261, 262, 351, 352
Sinatra, Tina, 250
Singleton, Penny, 127, 128
Six Degrees of Separation, 224
"Skater's Waltz, The," 85
Skelton, Red, 270
Sleeping Beauty, 217, 218
"Sleepy Lagoon," 10, 349
"Sleepytime Gal," 227
Sloan, Joan, 275
Slye, Len. *See* Roy Rogers.
Smirnoff, Zelly, 185
Smith, Liz, 323
Smith, Oliver, 325
Snow White and the Seven Dwarfs, 218, 219
Snyder, Colonel, 78, 79
"Somebody Loves You," 178
Sondheim, Stephen, 83, 354
"Song of Sorrow," 26
"Songwriters on Parade," 178
Sons of the Pioneers, the, 134
Sousa, John Philip, 181
Spitalny, Phil, 99
Spivak, Charlie, 185, 253, 254
"Splish Splash," 259
Stafford, Jo, 139
Stanwyck, Barbara, 147
"Star-Spangled Banner, The," 181
Stein, Gertrude, 110
Stern, Issac, 295
Stieglitz, Alfred, 275
Stoddard, Haila, 326, 351, 354
Stokowski, Leopold, 44
"Stone, Stone, Memorial Stone (Once You Used to Be My Mother)," 75
"Stormy Breezes," 84
Straw Hat Revue, The, 267, 268
"Street of Dreams," 108
Stroman, Susan, 260
Styne, Jule, 162
Sukin, Michael, 260, 261, 262
Sullivan, Ed, 183
"Sunflower," 152

"Sunrise Serenade," 150, 162, 254
Susan Slept Here, 303
Sweet September, 341
"Sweet Sue," 108
Swire, Williard, 326
Symes, J. Foster, 101
"Symphonie," 13
"Symphony," 10, 258

Taft, William Howard, 44
Tarzan, 50
Tashlin, Frank, 303
Tchaikovsky, 13, 58, 218
"Tea for Two," 206
"Ten Cents a Dance," 78
"Tenderly," 10, 14, 204, 220, 221, 222, 223,
   226, 353
Terrell, Pha, 123, 143
Terry, Dave, 185, 186
"That Old Feeling," 217
That's All, 259
"That Sweet Irish Sweetheart of Mine," 128
Thief of Bagdad, The, 24
"This Is My Golden Moment," 332
Thomas, Michael Tilson, 207
Thompson, Kay, 127
Thornhill, Claude, 139
"Three Coins in the Fountain," 305
Tillinger, John, 325
Tinturin, Peter, 120, 121, 122, 124, 125, 127,
   134, 135
Tobias, Charley, 178
"Tomorrow," 169, 171
"Toot, Toot Tootsie," 25
Torch Song, 10
Tormé, Mel, 227
"Trembling of a Leaf, The," 203, 204
Trenet, Charles, 13, 257, 258, 259, 261, 262,
   263, 264
Trevor, Claire, 200
Trigger, 134
Truman, Bess, 297
Truman, Harry S., 295, 296, 297, 298
Truman, Margaret, 298
Tucker, Sophie, 163, 168, 171, 172
Turner, Lana, 203, 269
Turner, Ted, 203
"Twilight Song," 200
"Two Tickets to Georgia," 178

Ukelele Ike. *See* Cliff Edwards.

"Underneath the Russian Moon," 80
Uppman, Theodor, 329

Valentino, Rudolph, 24
Vallee, Rudy, 83, 104, 106, 107, 115-119, 137
Vanderbilt, Gertrude, 275
Van Heusen, Jimmy, 162, 302, 350
Vaughan, Sarah, 222, 339
Velásquez, Diego, 273
Velez, Lupe, 169
Ventura, Diane, 19
Vera-Ellen, 228
Verdon, Gwen, 269
"Viyet Viyetri," 84
Von Stade, Frederica, 207
"Vous qui passez sans me voir," 13, 258
Vunk, Lyman, 185

"Wagon Wheels," 178
Wain, Bea, 139, 142, 202
"Waitin' for the Robert E. Lee," 44
Walker, Don, 328
Walker, Fred, 320
Walker, Jimmy, 238, 239, 242
Waller, Fats, 120, 162
Walter, Cy, 182, 183
War Brides, 50, 51
Warhol, Andy, 83, 139
Warnow, Harry. *See* Raymond Scott.
Warnow, Mark, 152, 181
Warren, Harry, 98
Waters, Ethel, 179
Wauchope, Captain, 183, 184, 188
Webb, Chick, 124, 140, 141
Webb, Jimmy, 83
Weber, Max, 275, 278
Webster, Paul, 144
Weissberger, Arnold, 265
Well of Loneliness, The, 67
Wesker, Arnold, 294
West, Mae, 209, 210-216
"What Can I Do?," 86
"What's Your Story, Morning Glory?," 143
"What Will I Tell My Heart?," 64, 122, 123,
   125, 162, 353
"When I Take My Sugar to Tea," 68
"When the Blue of the Night Meets the Gold
   of the Day," 107
"When Your Hair Has Turned to Silver," 178
"Whispering," 68
White, Onna, 333

White, Pearl, 50
White Christmas, 228
Whiteman, Paul, 83, 106
Whiting, Margaret, 219, 220, 227
Whiting, Richard, 227
Wicker, Irene, 93
Wiley, Lee, 108, 109, 110
Williams, John, 143
Williams, Mary Lou, 123, 143, 144
Williams, Paul, 307
Williams, Tennessee, 325
"Will You Love Me in December as You Do in May?," 239
Wilson, Julie, 183
Wilson, Woodrow, 24, 44, 51
Winchell, Walter, 90, 140, 167, 168
"With the Wind and the Rain in Your Hair," 146
Wizard of Oz, The, 154

Wolpin, Eddie, 171, 173, 174
Wood, Audrey, 325
Wood, Grant, 273
Woodward, Joanne, 351
Worchell, Karen, 310, 352
Worchell, Larry, 310, 324
Worth, Irene, 325
Wuthering Heights, 154

Yablokoff, Herman, 95
Yates, Herb, 127, 128, 134, 135
"Yes, My Darling Daughter," 10, 169, 170, 173, 176, 178
"You Go to My Head," 178
Young, Victor, 13, 108, 109, 110, 111, 112
"You Who Pass Without Seeing Me," 258

Zenk, Colleen, 351
Zorach, William, 278